1987

ALEXANDRIA:
A HISTORY AND A GUIDE

"Surely the best guide-book ever written."
– Bonamy Dobrée

This annotated edition of Forster's classic History and Guide is of practical use to anyone exploring Alexandria and her environs, whether by local transport or by armchair.

Vue d'Alexandrie extraite du

IOVRNAL

DES VOYAGES

DE MONSIEVR

DE MONCONYS

LYON MDCLXV

See p. 90.

ALEXANDRIA:

A HISTORY AND A GUIDE

BY

E. M. FORSTER

WITH AN INTRODUCTION
BY LAWRENCE DURRELL

*If a man make a pilgrimage round Alexandria
in the morning, God will make for him a golden
crown, set with pearls, perfumed with musk and
camphor, and shining from the East to the West.*
                                          Ibn Dukmak.

*To any vision must be brought an eye adapted
to what is to be seen.*   Plotinus.

OXFORD UNIVERSITY PRESS
New York

Opposite: title page of the first edition

First edition published in Alexandria, 1922
Second edition published in Alexandria, 1938
First American edition (reprinting the first Alexandrian edition),
with a new Introduction by E M Forster, published in New York,
1961
First British edition (reprinting the first Alexandrian edition and
including E M Forster's Introduction to the 1961 edition), with a
new Introduction by Lawrence Durrell and Afterword and Notes
by Michael Haag, published in London, 1982

Published in Great Britain by Michael Haag Limited, PO Box 369,
London NW3 4ER, England
UK ISBN 0 902743 48 1 (paperback)
UK ISBN 0 902743 59 7 (hardback)
Published in the United States in 1986 by Oxford University Press,
Inc., 200 Madison Avenue, New York, New York 10016, by arrange-
ment with Doubleday & Company, Inc.
US ISBN 0–19–504066–X (paperback)

Printed, bound and additional typesetting in Great Britain at the
Bath Press, Lower Bristol Road, Bath BA2 3BL

ALEXANDRIA:

A HISTORY AND A GUIDE

By

E. M. FORSTER, M.A. CANTAB.

If a man make a pilgrimage round Alexandria in the morning, God will make for him a golden crown, set with pearls, perfumed with musk and camphor, and shining from the East to the West.   *Ibn Dukmak.*

To any vision must be brought an eye adapted to what is to be seen.   *Plotinus.*

ALEXANDRIA :
WHITEHEAD MORRIS LIMITED

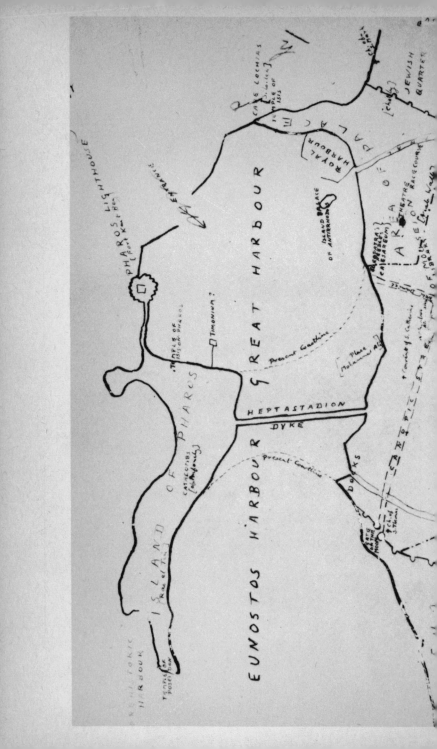

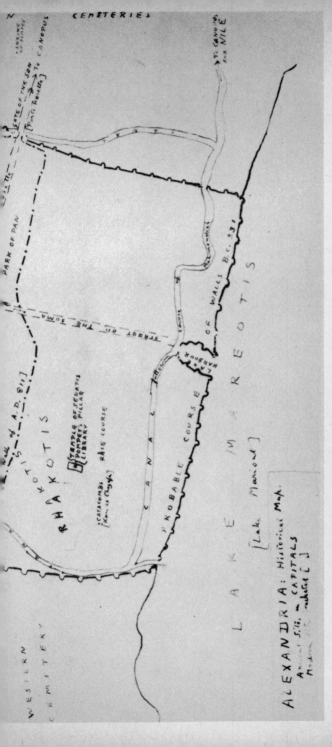

Forster's hand-drawn map of Alexandria. The obscured landmark at the centre is the Church of St Athanasius.
courtesy of a private collector

CONTENTS

SECTION VI: FROM THE SQUARE TO MEX

SECTION VII: ABOUKIR AND ROSETTA

SECTION VIII: THE LIBYAN DESERT

INTRODUCTION TO THE NEW EDITION
BY LAWRENCE DURRELL

This guide is something more than just a work of
literary piety devoted to that strange and evocative city
called Alexandria: in its way it succeeds in being a small
work of art, for it contains some of Forster's best prose,
as well as felicities of touch such as only a novelist of
major talent could command. The author who was
marooned here during the First World War must (one
feels it) have been deeply happy, perhaps deeply in
love, for his *joie de vivre* rings out in every affectionate
line, and there is hardly an aspect of the city's many
moods and nuances of colour which his meticulous eye
and fastidious pen have not captured and fixed for us.
Paradoxically, if that is the word, the book is also
saturated with the feeling of loneliness, that of a cultivated man talking to himself, walking by himself. ("The
best way to see the city is to walk about quite aimlessly,"
he advises, a perfectly true finding.) Once the first sense
of estrangement is over, the mind finds its surcease in
the discovery of the dream-city Alexandria which
underpins, underlays the rather commonplace little
Mediterranean seaport which it seems, to the un-
initiated, to be. It plays even today a somewhat unwill-
ing role as a second capital for Egypt, the only relief
offered a resident of Cairo – that burning-glass of a city,
wedged between its deserts. It opens upon a dreaming

sea and its Homeric waves are rolled and unrolled by the fresh breezes from Rhodes and the Aegean. Going ashore in Alexandria is like walking the plank for instantly you feel, not only the plangently Greek city rising before you, but its backcloth of deserts stretching away into the heart of Africa. It is a place for dramatic partings, irrevocable decisions, last thoughts; everyone feels pushed to the extreme, to the end of his bent. People become monks or nuns or voluptuaries or solitaries without a word of warning. As many people simply disappear as overtly die here. The city does nothing. You hear nothing but the noise of the sea and the echoes of an extraordinary history.

We used to think of Forster and his peers as 'silver age' stylists. The line of descent from Swift was easy to plot. It spelt lucidity, limpidity and urbanity. Though effortlessly graceful, it had bite. One thinks of Strachey, of Norman Douglas – particularly the latter who performed the same service for Capri as Forster did for Alexandria by writing a guide – though *that* begins with a geological survey of the very earth! Heaven knows what such a survey would yield in Alexandria, in an earth so stuffed with precious historical relics.

I arrived in 1941, twenty-three years after this book was written and eight years after the death of the great poet-friend of Forster, Constantine Cavafy. Magically, nothing had changed that I could discern. For two years I was able to walk about in the pages of this guide-book, using it as piously as it deserves to be used, and borrowing many of its gleams of wisdom to swell the notes for the book I myself hoped one day to write. The only real change, as far as I could judge, was the empty chair in the favourite café of the poet; but the circle of friends remained unbroken, men like Malanos and Petrides, who would later write books about their singular friend. They too had all glimpsed the phantom city which underlay the quotidian one. But for the majority of people Alexandria was a dull hole with only good bathing and many French restaurants to commend it. "There is nothing to *see!*" they repeated endlessly, and this too was true. Pompey's pillar was an aesthetic calamity, the site of the Pharos was out of bounds, and Alexander's tomb had disappeared under a thousand conjectures. Yet to many of our sailors it was still Eunostos, 'port of safe return', as it had been in Homer's time.

The author has supplied an account of the somewhat complicated publishing history of the book; it was published by a printer who did not have the orthodox channels of distribution at his disposal. In consequence it was hard to get and even the second edition which appeared in 1938 could not be got through the book-shops. By a series of maneuvres verging on sharp practice I managed nevertheless to secure my own copy which I carried about for years and annotated heavily on the spot. It was an invaluable companion, just as Lane's *Modern Egyptians* proved to be in Cairo. While packing them to send to an American university I noticed that they were slightly sweat-stained – a mark no doubt of the ardour with which I read and re-read them.

But of course the classical Alexandria is never in question save as a historical echo – how could it be? With the arrival of Amr and his Arab cavalry the famous resplendent city nosedived into oblivion; the sand dunes encroached and covered it. Between Amr and Napoleon stretch nearly a thousand years of silence and neglect. It had been something of an artefact, born of a whim of the boy Alexander who had not stayed to see it actually built, but whose body had been brought back to be buried in the centre of it, thus to become its tutelary god. The despatch that Amr sent back to the

Caliph of Arabia mentions his conquest of the city with a beautiful succinctness. "I have taken a city of which I can only say that it contains 4000 palaces, 4000 baths, 400 theatres, 1200 greengrocers and 40,000 Jews." No trace of this elaborate beauty remained to greet Forster when he stepped ashore in 1915; but the little town which shared its favours between Greek, French, Italian, British and other mercantile nations compared very favourably to a small French watering place like St Tropez, or a Levantine one like Beirut. There were good schools apart from the Greek Gymnasium – even a British public school which had much to do with the excellent English spoken in the city.

It is a dispiriting exercise to bring the story up to 1977, the date of my last visit to the city, for much of what was left has vanished with the foreign population of business folk – five languages was considered quite normal for an Alexandrian *commercant*! They have vanished and the harbour is a mere cemetery – no life, no movement animates it. The long flirtation of Nasser with Communism had produced the inevitable deadening effect. The blue Chinese get-up of the female students of the University is rather fetching at first but soon palls. Listless, spiritless, the modern business man goes about his tasks without much enthusiasm today. The cafés still have their immortal names – Pastroudis, Baudrot, but no trade to set them twinkling with light and music. All foreign posters and advertisements have vanished, everything is in Arabic; in our time film posters were billed in several languages with Arabic subtitles, so to speak. Now a leaden uniformity rules. It is particularly exasperating to find that all the medicaments in the chemists are now known by Arabic names. Try and obtain some aspirin or throat tablets and see what happens!

I spent a week there in the old familiar room at the

Cecil, now stripped of all its finery and echoing like a barn with the seawind sweeping under the doors and through the windows; I reflected on exile in general and my own in particular. When I came here there was no reason to suppose that the war would ever end, that I should ever leave Egypt. It was lucky that I was rootless by background and inheritance – a colonial. It is remarkable that Forster, who had good English roots, should have responded to his own exile in such a positive fashion, putting down new roots in this unfamiliar soil. We are the gainers.

The old apartment which Cavafy once occupied is now a small pension of the kind described in many Middle Eastern novels, modest and somewhat seedy. But his books and his furniture have been rescued and most suitably housed in a little museum created for it on the top floor of the Greek Consulate, to visit which one still takes the little bucking, clicking tram of yore with its festoon of hangers-on who disappear when an inspector shows his face. It is marvellous, the little room of Cavafy recreated in the airy consular building; here you can sit at the desk upon which his hand traced those famous poems, 'Ithaca', 'The Barbarians', 'The God Abandons Antony', or best of all, 'The City', which is his real monument to modern Alexandria. You can browse among his books – one has the feeling that he did not own a great number; and seated all the while on the rather uncomfortable chairs and settees – neo-Byzantine in style – which were fashionable at that period in middle class households. It is unlucky that the only bust of the poet is insipid. But in general this is a worthily contrived tribute to the great Alexandrian.

So once again Alexandria has sunk into oblivion, and I must be forgiven for finding that the present town is depressing beyond endurance – especially when one thinks of the treasures of Cairo, or the tremendous outburst of vegetation and ancient monuments which gives Upper Egypt its resonance. Perhaps some happy accident will in the course of time once more renew the secret spring and make it evocative for a new generation of poets. Appolonius, Theocritos, Cavafy inspire one to believe in such a future despite the evidence of today.

E M FORSTER'S INTRODUCTION TO THE 1961 EDITION

There have already been two editions of this little book. Here is the third, and here is my opportunity of unfolding a slight but complicated tale.

The text of the first edition (the one here reproduced) was written by me during the First World War when I was stationed in Alexandria as the result of volunteering for the Red Cross. I arrived there in the autumn of 1915 in a slightly heroic mood. A Turkish invasion was threatened, and although a civilian I might find myself in the battle line. The threat passed and my mood changed. What had begun as an outpost turned into something suspiciously like a funk-hole, and I stuck in it for over three years, visiting hospitals, collecting information, and writing reports. "You are such a wonderful *sticker*," a detestable Red Cross colonel once said to me scathingly. I was; and I dared not retort that it takes both stickers and climbers to make a world.

I was dressed like a sort of officer myself, but allowed to take the things off between whiles, and it was thus that I apprehended the magic and the antiquity and the complexity of the city, and determined to write about her. A guidebook suggested itself. I have always respected guidebooks—particularly the earlier Baedekers and Murrays—and I tried to work in some history as well, by a technique explained on p. xix. My

friends encouraged me—English, Greek, American,
French, Italian, Norwegian, Syrian, Egyptian were
then among them, for I had inserted myself a little into
Levantine life. And visions kept coming as I went about
in trams or on foot or bathed in the delicious sea. For
instance, I would multiply the height of the Fort of Kait
Bey by four and so envisage the Pharos which had once
stood on the same site. At the crossing of the two main
streets I would erect the tomb of Alexander the Great.
I would follow Alexander in imagination to Siwa, the
oasis of Jupiter Amnon, where he was saluted as the
Son of God. And I would follow the monks too, to the
desolate Wady Natrun whence they burst to murder
Hypatia.

Which was all very well; but how was one to get
published?

Here a piece of amazing good fortune befell me.

There is, or rather was, in the Rue Chérif Pacha (if
it is still called that)† an unobtrusive-looking shop. It
sold stationery. But it was actually the Alexandria
branch of an important London printing firm—Messrs.
Whitehead Morris of Tower Hill. The local manager,
Mr. Mann, heard of my project and was interested in
it, though it lay outside his normal work. There were
many delays and some differences of opinion, but it
duly came out after the war and after my return to
England, in 1922.

Shortly after publication a disaster occurred. As the
result of a fire in the storerooms nearly the whole of
the edition was destroyed. That is why copies of it are
so rare.‡

It was a sad setback, and a few years later as I was
passing through Alexandria, on my way back from
South Africa, I actually lost my way as I came out of
its new Railway Station. What a humiliating experience for the writer of a Guide! I could not even find

my way about my own city! It seemed to me that a
new edition was called for, although there was not
then any audible call, and although I could not under-
take the work of revision. But in one respect Alexandria
had not changed; she was still the city of friends who
were willing unselfishly to set aside their own work
and to work for others. They brought the "guide" part
of the book up to date by visiting all the sites and objects mentioned, and they corrected my worst blunders
in the "history" part. This edition came out in 1938,
again under the auspices of the Alexandria branch of
Messrs. Whitehead Morris. It did not sell well, perhaps
because the Second World War started next year.
Copies of it are rare. The friends in question once suggested a new (local) edition, and pointed out that certain alterations must be made, or the book would
offend Egyptian national suceptibilities. I bet it would.
There are scarcely any national susceptibilities it does
not offend. The only locality it shouldn't offend is
Alexandria herself, who in the 2,000 years of her life
has never taken national susceptibilities too seriously.

And this brings me to Cavafy. One of the joys of
those years was my friendship with the great Greek
poet who so poignantly conveys the civilisation of his
chosen city. C. P. Cavafy was not then widely known
and the translation of "The God Abandons Antony"
(p. 104) by our friend George Valassopoulo represents
his first appearance in English. He has been fully
translated since, and widely eulogised—for instance by
a later lover of Alexandria, Mr. Lawrence Durrell. I
dedicated the second edition of this book to Cavafy
after his death.

The first edition was dedicated to G. H. Ludolf, another of the many who helped me.

The present edition appears through the courtesy of

Messrs. Walter & Whitehead, Ltd., the representatives of Messrs. Whitehead Morris.

Finally: this is not my only tribute to Alexandria. There is also *Pharos and Pharillon,* a volume of essays, published in 1923 by Messrs. A. Knopf in the United States and by the Hogarth Press in England.

E. M. Forster
Cambridge, England. 1960

PREFACE

This book consists of two parts: a History and a Guide.

The "History" attempts (after the fashion of a pageant) to marshal the activities of Alexandria during the two thousand two hundred and fifty years of her existence. Starting with the heroic figure of Alexander the Great, it inspects the dynasty of the Ptolemies, and in particular the career of the last of them, Cleopatra; an account of Ptolemaic literature and science follows, and closes this splendid period, to which I have given the title of "Greco-Egyptian." The second period, called "Christian," begins with the rule of Rome, and traces the fortunes of Christianity, first as a persecuted and then as a persecuting power: all is lost in 641, when the Patriarch Cyrus betrays Alexandria to the Arabs. An interlude comes next—"The Spiritual City"—which meditates upon Alexandrian philosophy and religion, both Pagan and Christian: it seemed better to segregate these subjects, partly because they interrupt the main historical procession, partly because many readers are not interested in them. History is resumed in the "Arab Period," which is of no importance though it lasts over 1,000 years—from Amr to Napoleon. With Napoleon begins the "Modern Period," the main feature of which is the building of the city we now see under the auspices of Mohammed Ali: and the pageant concludes, as well as it may, with an account of the

events of 1882, and with surmises as to future municipal developments.†

The "History" is written in short sections, and at the
end of each section are references to the second part—
the "Guide." *On these references the chief utility of the
book depends,* so the reader is begged to take special
note of them: they may help him to link the present
and the past. Suppose, for instance, he has read in the
History about the Pharos: at the end of the section he
will find references to Fort Kait Bey where the Pharos
stood, to Abousir where there is a miniature replica of
it, and to the Coin Room in the Museum, where it appears on the moneys of Domitian and Hadrian. Or
again, suppose that the tragic fate of Hypatia has
touched him: at the end will be references to the
Caesareum, where Hypatia was murdered, and to the
Wady Natrun, where the monks who murdered her
generally resided. Or the British victories of 1801: he
will be referred to the country over which our troops
marched, to the Abercrombie Monument at Sidi Gaber,
and to a tombstone in the courtyard of the Greek
Patriarchate. The "sights" of Alexandria are in themselves not interesting, but they fascinate when we approach them through the past, and this is what I have
tried to do by the double arrangement of History and
Guide.

The "Guide" calls for no introduction. It is written
from the practical standpoint, and is intended to be
used on the spot.‡ Maps and plans accompany it. The
city is divided into sections, the visitor in every case
starting from the Square. Other sections deal with the
environs, and with the surrounding country as far as
Rosetta on the east and Abousir on the west. In trans-
literating Arabic names I have preferred the French
system: there are three English systems, each backed
by a rival government department, so the French seems

the safer course, and if I have not kept to it rigidly, I am only following, though at a respectful distance, the example of the Alexandria Municipality. Here and there some History has crept into the Guide—notably in the case of Aboukir, whose fortunes, though dependent on Alexandria's, present features of their own.

AUTHORITIES

There is, so far as I know, no monograph on Alexandria, and though the present little book makes no claim to original research, it has drawn together much information that was hitherto scattered. The following works, among others, have been consulted: those marked with an asterisk are published locally.

(A). History:—

Ptolemaic Period: — *Bouché-Leclercq, Histoire des Lagides.* A scholarly and delightful work. 4 vols.

Ptolemaic Literature:—*A. Couat, La Poésie Alexandrine;* well written. *Theocritus,* translated A. Lang.

Christian Period: — No satisfactory work. *S. Sharpe, History of Egypt until the Arab Conquest,* vol. 2 may be consulted; also *Gibbon,* chs. 21 and 47. *Mrs. Butcher, The Story of the Church in Egypt* is full of information, but uncritical and diffuse.

Arab Conquest:—*A. J. Butler, The Arab Conquest of Egypt.* A monograph of the highest merit, brilliantly written and practically reconstructing the episode.

Jewish Thought:—*E. Herriot, Philon le Juif.*

Neo-Platonism:—Various works. There is a lucid introduction to Plotinus in *S. McKenna, Translation of the Enneads,* vol. 1; this admirable translation is still in progress. *Porphyry's Letter to Marcella* (translated, A. Gardner) is also interesting.

Christian Theology:—See under "Christian Period." The Fathers can be read in the *Ante-Nicene Christian Library.*

Arab Period:—Too obscure to possess a history.

Napoleonic Wars:—*Mahan, Influence of Sea Power upon the French Revolution,* chs. 9 and 10. R. T. Wilson, *History of the British Expedition to Egypt.* See also below, under Aboukir.

General Modern History:—*D. A. Cameron, Egypt in the Nineteenth Century.* A well-written book by the late Consul General at Alexandria; contains good account of Mohammed Ali. The works of Lord Cromer, W. S. Blunt and Sir V. Chirol are also useful.

Events of 1882:—*C. Royle, The Egyptian Campaigns.*

One or two novels and plays dealing with the History may here be mentioned. The career of Cleopatra has inspired two noble tragedies, Shakespeare's *Antony and Cleopatra,* and Dryden's *All for Love;* extracts from them are given on p. 231. Dryden's masterpiece should be better known; it is most moving, admirably constructed, and contains some magnificent scenes. A novel by Pierre Loüys, *Aphrodite,* also treats of the period, but in a scented Parisian way.—Anatole France, *Thais,* pictures life in the 4th cent. A.D.; the details are both vivid and accurate, and build up a perfect work of art.—For the early 5th cent. there is Charles Kingsley's *Hypatia,* a rousing yarn about the final contest between Paganism and Christianity; Kingsley is always readable, but his bluff burly mind was incapable of understanding Alexandria.—Two good novels by Marmaduke Pickthall, *Said the Fisherman* and *Children of the Nile* touch upon events in the modern period.

(B). GUIDE:—

E. Breccia, Alexandrea ad Aegyptum. In French: English translation announced. Deals mainly with Classical Antiquities. Two sections— the first dealing with the remains in the city and environs, the second with the Greco-Roman Museum, of which Professor Breccia is the distinguished Curator. I am under much obligation to this fine scholarly book, especially in the following sections:—Greco-Roman Museum, Catacombs of Anfouchi and Kom es Chogafa, Serapeum, Abousir.

Prehistoric Harbour:—*E. Jondet, Les Ports submergés de l'ancienne Isle de Pharos.* A monograph by the discoverer. Magnificent Maps.

Pharos and Fort Kait Bey:—*H. Thiersch, Pharos, antike Islam und Occident.* A standard monograph, but exhibiting the defects as well as the merits of German Scholarship.

Canopus and Aboukir:—*J. Faivre, Canopus, Menouthis, Aboukir.* Published in French and English. *R. D. Downes, A History of Canopus.* These excellent pamphlets supplement one another, the first dealing with the literary evidence, the second with the typography.

Rosetta:—*Max Herz Bey, Les Mosquées de Rosette* (various articles in the *Comptes Rendus* of the Comité de Conservation des Monuments Arabes).

St. Menas:—*C. M. Koufmann, La Decouverte des Sanctuaires de Menas.* By the Excavator.

Natrun Monasteries:—*A. J. Butler, Ancient Coptic Churches.*

Many friends have also helped me, among whom I would particularly thank the following:—Mr. George Antonius for his assistance with those interesting but little known buildings, the Alexandria Mosques; Mr.

M. S. Briggs for his help in the Rosetta section; Dr. A. J. Butler for permission to reproduce two plans of the Natrun Churches; Mr. C. P. Cavafy for permission to publish one of his poems, and Mr. G. Valassopoulo for translating the same; the Rev. R. D. Downes for his help at Aboukir; Mr. R. A. Furness for his verse translations from Callimachus and other Greek poets; M. E. Jondet, Director of Ports and Lights, for taking me to see his fascinating discovery, the Prehistoric Harbour, and for placing at my disposal his unrivalled collection of Maps and Views, two of which I have reproduced; and above all Mr. G. H. Ludolf, to whose suggestion this book is due, and without whose help it would never have been completed. I shall never forget the kindness that I have received at Alexandria, and in no wise endorse the verdict of my predecessor the poet Gelal ed Din ben Mokram who monstrously asserts that:—

> The visitor to Alexandria receives nothing in the way
>   of hospitality
> Except some water and an account of Pompey's
>   Pillar.
> Those who wish to treat him very well go so far as to
>   offer some fresh air
> And to tell him where the Lighthouse is.
> They also instruct him about the sea and its waves,
> Adding a description of the large Greek boats.
> The visitor need not aspire to receive any bread,
> For to a request of this sort there is no reply.

Circumstances which I could not control have delayed the publication of the book, but, with the help of friends, I have tried to bring the "Guide" up to date as far as possible.

PART I
HISTORY

MEDITERRANEAN SEA

Anfouchi Tom

Military Hospital

PREHISTORIC HARBOUR

RUE RAS EL T

Breakwater

Lighthouse

Ras el Tin Palace

WESTERN HARBOUR (EUNOSTOS)

Franciscan C

MINET E

BASSAL

to Mex

GABBARI

Kom es Chogafa

to Mex & the Western Desert

Fishing Village

Plan of
ALEXANDRIA

LAKE MARIOUT

The Ptolemaic lighthouse at Abousir, 24 kilometres west of Alexandria, and first of a chain that stretched from the Pharos all down the North African Coast to Cyrene. It was modelled on its gigantic contemporary, but only one-tenth its size. (See page 207.)

SECTION I

Greco-Egyptian Period

THE LAND AND THE WATERS

The situation of Alexandria is most curious. To understand it we must go back many thousand years.

Ages ago, before there was civilisation in Egypt, or the delta of the Nile had been formed, the whole of the country as far south as Cairo lay under the sea. The shores of this sea were a limestone desert. The coastline was smooth as a rule, but at the north-west corner an extraordinary spur jutted out from the main mass. It was not more than a mile wide, but many miles long. Its base is not far from the modern Bahig. Alexandria is built half-way down it, and its tip is the headland of Aboukir. On each side of it there used to be deep salt water.

Centuries passed, and the Nile, issuing out of his crack above Cairo, kept carrying down the muds of Upper Egypt, and dropping them as soon as his current slackened. In the north-west corner they were arrested by this spur, and began to silt up against it. It was a shelter not only from the outer sea, but from the prevalent wind. Alluvial land appeared; the huge shallow lake of Mariout was formed; and the current of the Nile, unable to escape through the limestone barrier, rounded the headland of Aboukir, and entered the outer sea by what was known in historical times as the "Canopic" Mouth.

This explains one characteristic of Alexandrian scenery—the long narrow ridge edged on the north by the sea and on the south by a lake and flat fields. But it does not explain why Alexandria has a harbour.

To the north of the spur, and more or less parallel to it, runs a second limestone range. It is much shorter than the spur and much lower, being often below the surface of the sea in the form of reefs. It seems unimportant. But without it there would have been no harbour (and consequently no town), because it breaks the force of the waves. Starting at Agame it continues as a series of rocks across the entrance of the modern harbour. Then it re-emerges to form the hammer-headed promontory of Ras-el-Tin, disappears into a second series of rocks that close the entrance of the Eastern Harbour, and makes its final appearance at the promontory of Silsileh, after which it rejoins the big spur.

Such are the main features of the situation; a limestone ridge, with harbours on one side of it, and alluvial country on the other. It is a situation unique in Egypt, and the Alexandrians have never been truly Egyptian.

BEST SURVEY POINTS ON RIDGE ARE:

    QUARRIES BEYOND MEX: p. 185.
    HILL OF ABOU EL NAWATIR: p. 180.
    MONTAZAH: p. 186.
    HEADLAND OF ABOUKIR: p. 196.

PHAROS, RHAKOTIS, CANOPUS

Who first settled on this remarkable stretch of coast? There seem to have been three early centres.

(i)   Homer (Odyssey, Book iv) says:—

"There is an island in the surging sea, which they call
Pharos, lying off Egypt. It has a harbour with good anchorage, and hence they put out to sea after drawing water."

Homer's island is now the promontory of Ras-el-Tin;
the intervening channel has silted up. There are no
traces of any early settlement on its soil, but in the sea
to its north and west the masonry of a prehistoric harbour has been found. Homer goes on to tell how Menelaus was becalmed on Pharos as he returned from Troy,
and how he could not get away until he had entrapped
Proteus, the divine king of the island, and exacted a
favourable wind. A similar legend has been found in
an ancient Egyptian papyrus. There the King is called
the "Prouti" or "Pharaoh." "Prouti" is probably the
original of Homer's "Proteus," "Pharaoh" of his "Pharos."
It is significant that our first glimpse of the coast should
be through the eyes of a Greek sailor.

(ii)   But our historical survey must begin with
Rhakotis. Rhakotis was a small Egyptian town built on
the rise where "Pompey's Pillar" stands now, and it existed as long ago as 1,300 B.C., for statues of that time
have been found here. The people were coast-guards
and goat herds. Their chief god was Osiris. Rhakotis
was never important in itself. But it is important as an
element in the great Greek city that was built up round
it. It was a little lump of Egypt. Compare it to the Arab
villages and slums that have been embedded in the
scheme of the modern town—to Mazarita or to Kom-el-
Dik. Rhakotis was like one of these. The native and
conservative element naturally rallied to it, and it became the site for Alexandria's great religious effort—
the cult of Serapis.

(iii)   At the tip of the limestone ridge, where the
Nile once entered the sea, was another early settle-

ment. It also appears in Greek legend. In historical
times, it was known as Canopus.

ALEXANDER THE GREAT (B.C. 331)

Few cities have made so magnificent an entry into
history as Alexandria. She was founded by Alexander
the Great.

When he arrived here he was only twenty-five years
old. His career must be sketched. He was a Macedonian and had begun by destroying the city-civilisation
of ancient Greece. But he did not hate the Greeks, no,
he admired them immensely and desired to be treated
as if he was one, and his next exploit was to lead a
crusade against Greece's traditional enemy, Persia, and
to defeat her in two tremendous battles, one at the
Dardanelles and one in Asia Minor. As soon as he conquered Syria, Egypt fell into his hands, and fell will-
ingly, for she too hated the Persians. He went to
Memphis (near modern Cairo). Then he descended
the Nile to the coast, and ordered his architect Dinocrates to build round the nucleus of Rhakotis a magnificent Greek city. This was not mere idealism on his part,
or rather idealism was happily combined with utility.
He needed a capital for his new Egyptian kingdom,
and to link it with Macedonia that capital had to be
on the coast. Here was the very place—a splendid harbour, a perfect climate, fresh water, limestone quarries, and easy access to the Nile. Here he would per-

petuate all that was best in Hellenism, and would create a metropolis for that greater Greece that should consist not of city-states but of kingdoms, and should include the whole inhabited world.

Alexandria was founded.

Having given his orders, the young man hurried on. He never saw a single building rise. His next care was a visit to the temple of Ammon in the Siwan Oasis, where the priest saluted him as a god, and henceforward his Greek sympathies declined. He became an Oriental, a cosmopolitan almost, and though he fought Persia again, it was in a new spirit. He wanted to harmonise the world now, not to Hellenise it, and must have looked back on Alexandria as a creation of his immaturity. But he was after all to return to her. Eight years later, having conquered Persia, he died, and his body, after some vicissitudes, was brought to Memphis for burial. The High Priest refused to receive it there. "Do not settle him here," he cried, "but at the city he has built at Rhakotis, for wherever this body must lie the city will be uneasy, disturbed with wars and battles." So he descended the Nile again, wrapped in gold and enclosed in a coffin of glass, and he was buried at the centre of Alexandria, by her great cross roads, to be her civic hero and tutelary god.

COIN OF ALEXANDER: Museum, Room 3.
STATUES OF HIM: Museum, Rooms 12, 16.
HIS TOMB (Soma): p. 112.
TOMBSTONE OF MACEDONIAN OFFICER: Museum, Room 20.

THE FOUNDATION PLAN
(*See Map of Ancient City p.* 106)

Before dissecting Alexander's plan we must remember three differences in the configuration of the soil as it existed in his day.

(i)   As already pointed out, Ras-el-Tin was then an island. He thought of building here, but rejected the site as too cramped. A shrine to his dead friend Hephaestion rose here, that was all.

(ii)   Lake Mariout was much deeper then than now, and directly connected with the Nile. Consequently it was almost as important a water-way as the sea, and a lake harbour was an integral part of the plan.

(iii)   There was then through water-connection between the Mediterranean and the Red Sea. The ancient Egyptians had cut a canal from the Nile at Memphis down to the salt lakes that begin by the modern Ismailia. Thus Alexandria stood in the position of Port Said to-day; a maritime gate-way to India and the remoter east.

The city was oblong, and filled up the strip between the lake and the sea; she was laid out in rigidly straight lines. Her main street (the "Canopic") still exists in part as the Rue Rosette. It ran almost due east and west—a bad direction because it was cut off from the cool north wind that is the real tutelary god of Alexandria, but, owing to the site, nothing else could be contrived. Westward it terminated in the sea; eastward it proceeded to Canopus (Aboukir). It was the natural highway along the limestone spur, and no doubt existed long before Alexander came.

Crossing the Canopic Street, and following the line of the present Rue Nebi Daniel, was the second main artery, the street of the Soma. It started at the Lake Harbour and ran northward to the sea. Where it intersected the Canopic Street stood the Soma, or burial place of Alexander—close to the present Mosque. Parallel to these two streets ran others, dividing the city into blocks of an American regularity. It could not have been picturesque, but the Greeks did not desire picturesqueness. They liked to lay their towns out evenly —Rhodes and Halicarnassus had just been laid out on the same lines—and the only natural feature they cared to utilise was the sea. The blocks were labelled according to the letters of the Greek alphabet.

Of the sea front magnificent use was to be made. Only one feature shall be mentioned here: the dyke Heptastadion (seven stades long) which was built to connect the island of Pharos and the mainland. It performed two functions; it enlarged the city area, and it broke the force of the currents and created a double harbour—the Great Harbour to the east and the Eunostos ("Safe Return") to the west. In the Arab period the Heptastadion silted up and became the neck of land that leads to Ras-el-Tin.

The course of the walls is uncertain. Perhaps their eastern course was from the promontory of Silsileh to the lake, and their western from the modern Gabbari to the lake. Their foundations were accompanied by a portent of the usual type. There was not enough chalk to mark the outlines, so meal had to be substituted, and a number of birds flew out of the lake and ate it all up. The Greeks interpreted the portent satisfactorily: to the Egyptians it might well have symbolised the advent of the hungry foreigner. We are not told what was substituted for the meal, but somehow or other the walls were built and were studded at frequent intervals with towers.

LAKE MARIOUT: p. 204.
RUE ROSETTE, (Canopic Street): p. 111.
RUE NEBI DANIEL (Street of Soma): p. 112.

THE FIRST THREE PTOLEMIES†

PTOLEMY I., SOTER, 323–285.
PTOLEMY II., PHILADELPHUS, 285–247.
PTOLEMY III., EUERGETES, 247–222.

(See Genealogical Tree p. 14)

When Alexander died the empire was divided among his generals, who ruled for a little in the name of his half-brother or of his son, but who soon proclaimed themselves as independent kings. Egypt fell to the ablest and most discreet of these generals, a Macedonian named Ptolemy. Ptolemy was no soaring idealist. He desired neither to Hellenise the world nor to harmonise it. But he was no cynic either. He respected mental as well as material activity. He had been present at the foundation of Alexandria, and had evidently decided that the place would suit him, and now, taking up his abode in the unfinished city, he began to adorn her with architecture and scholarship and song. Rival generals, especially in Asia Minor and Macedonia, occupied much of his energy. At the very beginning of his rule he was involved in a curious war for the possession of the corpse of Alexander, which he had kidnapped as it was on its way from Persia to the Oasis of Ammon. Ptolemy annexed the corpse and much else. Before he died he had assumed the titles of King and of Soter (saviour), and had added to his kingdom Cyrene, Palestine, Cyprus, and parts of the Asia Minor coast. Of this substantial domain Alexandria was the capital, and also the geographic centre. Then, as now, she belonged not so much to Egypt as to the Mediterranean, and the Ptolemies realised this. Up in Egypt

GENEALOGICAL TREE OF THE PTOLEMIES†

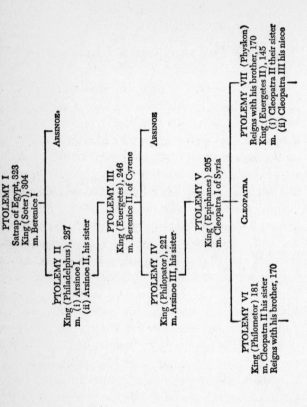

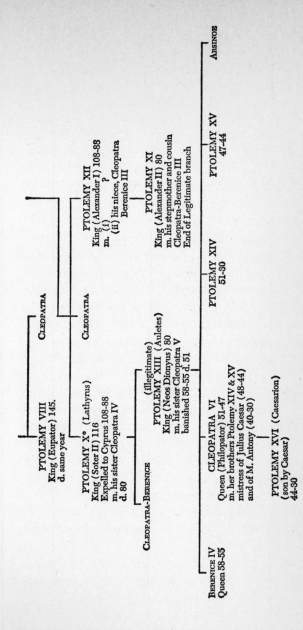

PTOLEMY VIII
King (Eupator) 145.
d. same year

CLEOPATRA

CLEOPATRA

PTOLEMY X* (Lathyrus)
King (Soter II) 116
Expelled to Cyprus 108-88
m. his sister Cleopatra IV
d. 80

PTOLEMY XII
King (Alexander I) 108-88
m. (i) ?
(ii) his niece, Cleopatra
Berenice III

PTOLEMY XI
King (Alexander II) 80
m. his stepmother and cousin
Cleopatra-Berenice III
End of Legitimate branch

CLEOPATRA-BERENICE

(Illegitimate)
PTOLEMY XIII (Auletes)
King (Neos Dionysus) 80
m. his sister Cleopatra V
banished 58-55 d. 51

BERENICE IV
Queen 58-55

CLEOPATRA VI
Queen (Philopator) 51-47
m. her brothers Ptolemy XIV & XV
mistress of Julius Caesar (48-44)
and of M. Antony (40-30)

PTOLEMY XVI (Caesarion)
(son by Caesar)
44-30

PTOLEMY XIV
51-30

PTOLEMY XV
47-44

ARSINOE

*Ptolemy IX is omitted from this list; he was probably a dead son of Ptolemy VII and Cleopatra II, whom
they inserted posthumously in the annals as "Neos Philopator."

they played the Pharaoh, and built solemn archaistic temples like Edfu and Kom Ombo. Down in Alexandria they were Hellenistic.

The second Ptolemy, Philadelphus, (Friend of his Sister), was a more pretentious person than his father. He is famous through the praises of the poets whom he patronised and of the Jews whom he invited, but his personal achievements were slight. Indeed the chief event of his reign is domestic rather than military—in 277 he married his sister Arsinoe. This was as startling to Greek feelings as it is to Christian, but in Egypt he had a prototype in the god Osiris who had married his sister Isis, and he justified the union on the highest sacerdotal grounds. He and Arsinoe were deified as the "Adelphian Gods," in whose equal veins flowed the un-contaminated blood of their divine father, the general, and their example was followed, when possible, by their successors. It was the pride of race carried to an extreme degree. The royalties of to-day, for fear of de-basing their stock, marry first cousins; the Ptolemies, more logical, tried to propagate within even narrower limits. In flesh, as in spirit, the dynasty claimed to be apart from common men, and to appear as successive emanations of the Deity, in pairs of male and female. Arsinoe—to come back to earth—was a domineering and sinister woman. She was seven years older than her brother, and when they married he had already a wife, whom she drove from Alexandria by her in-trigues. However, he liked her and when, a martyr to indigestion, she died, he was so far inconsolable that he did not marry again.

The closing years of his reign were divided between his mistresses and the gout. During a respite from the latter he looked out of his palace window on some pub-lic holiday, and saw beneath him the natives picnicking on the sand, as they do at the feast of Shem-el-Nessem to-day. They were obscure, they were happy. "Why can I not be like them?" sighed the old king, and burst into tears. His reign had been imposing rather than beautiful and had initiated little in Alexandrian civilisation beyond the somewhat equivocal item of a mystic marriage. He could endow and patronise. But, unlike Alexander, unlike his father, he could not create. He completed what they had laid down, and appropriated the praise.

Ptolemy Euergetes (Well-doer) was the son of Philadelphus by his first wife. In character he resembled his grandfather. He was a sensible and successful soldier, with a taste for science. By marrying his cousin Berenice, he secured Cyrene which had lapsed—Berenice the most highly praised of all the Ptolemaic Queens, though we know nothing of her character. In their reign the power of Egypt and the splendour of Alexandria came to their height. It is now time to examine that splendour. One hundred years have passed since Alexander laid the foundations. What has been built upon them?

COINS OF FIRST THREE PTOLEMIES: Museum, Room 3.
INSCRIPTIONS: Museum, Rooms 6, 22.
PTOLEMY EUERGETES, STATUES: Museum, Room 12.
BERENICE, STATUES: Museum, Rooms 4, 12.

THE PTOLEMAIC CITY
(*See Map of Ancient City p.* 106)

The following were the most important buildings in the Ptolemaic city.

(i). THE LIGHTHOUSE.
The Egyptian coast, being mainly alluvial, is difficult

to sight from the sea. It was therefore imperative to
indicate, by some great monument, where the new city
stood. It was desirable too to provide a guide for sailors
through the limestone reefs that line the shore. For
these reasons the Ptolemies built a lighthouse over four
hundred feet high on the Eastern end of Pharos Island
(present Fort Kait Bey). Full details are given later
(p. 144); here it is enough to note that the Pharos (as
it was called) was the greatest practical achievement
of the Alexandrian mind and the outward expression
of the mathematical studies carried on in the Mouseion;
Sostratus, its architect, was contemporary with Eratosthenes and Euclid.

A fortress as well as a beacon, the Pharos was the
pivot of the city's naval defences. It dominated both
the harbours, and kept special watch over the more
precious of them—the Eastern, which held the Royal
fleet. Here the promontory of the Palace stretched towards it. Westward, it could signal over the other harbour to the Chersonese (present Fort Agame). And
further west, the system was prolonged into a long line
of watch towers and beacons that studded the north
African coast, and connected Egypt with her daughter
kingdom of Cyrene. One of these towers (that at Abousir) still remains, and shows in miniature what the
Pharos must once have been.

FORT KAIT BEY (Pharos): p. 144.
COINS ILLUSTRATING PHAROS: Museum, Room 2.
TOWER OF ABOUSIR: p. 207.

(ii). THE PALACE.

We can locate one point in the Palace, or rather
palace-system: it certainly covered the Promontory of
Silsileh, which was then both longer and broader than
now. But no one knows how far the buildings stretched

inland, or along the shore, nor what the architecture was. Each Ptolemy made additions, and the whole formed a special quarter, somewhat like the Imperial City at Pekin. Egypt being an autocracy, the Palace was the seat of government as well as royal residence; clerks had their offices there. There was a palace-harbour (left of Silsileh), and an Island Palace or Kiosk called Antirrhodus, which rivalled the glories of Rhodes; Antirrhodus lay in the Eastern Harbour, and rocks, now deep below the surface of the sea, have been identified with it.

Inland, the Palace connected with another great system—that of the Mouseion. On its seaward side, it was prolonged by breakwaters towards the Pharos.

SILSILEH (Site of Palace): p. 178.
COLUMNS FROM LOCALITY: Museum, Room 16.

(iii). THE MOUSEION.

The Mouseion at Alexandria was the great intellectual achievement of the dynasty. Not only did it mould the literature and science of its day, but it has left a permanent impress upon thought. Its buildings have all disappeared, and the very site is conjectural; perhaps it had a façade opposite the Soma, west of the present Rue Nebi Daniel. In its vast areas were lecture halls, laboratories, observatories, a library, a dining hall, a park, and a zoo.

It was founded by Ptolemy Soter, who summoned a follower of Aristotle, Demetrius Phalerus, and ordered him to organise an institution on the lines of the Athenian Mouseion—a philosophic establishment that had contained the library of Aristotle. But the Alexandrian Mouseion soon diverged widely from its model. It was far richer and larger for one thing; the funds being administered by a priest who was appointed by the King. And it was essentially a court institution, under palace control, and knew both the advantages and disadvantages of royal patronage. In some ways it resembled a modern university, but the scholars and scientists and literary men whom it supported were under no obligation to teach; they had only to pursue their studies to the greater glory of the Ptolemies.

The most famous element in this enormous institution was the Library—sometimes called the "Mother" library to distinguish it from a later and even greater collection. 500,000 books, and a catalogue that occupied 120. The post of "Librarian" was of immense importance and its holder was the chief official in the Mouseion.

The actual literary and scientific output of the Mouseion will be considered elsewhere (p. 31).

RUE NEBI DANIEL (Site of Mouseion ?): p. 112.

(iv). THE TEMPLE OF SERAPIS.

The idea that one religion is false and another true is essentially Christian, and had not occurred to the Egyptians and Greeks who were living together at Alexandria. Each worshipped his own gods, just as he spoke his own language, but he never thought that the gods of his neighbour had no existence, and he was willing to believe that they might be his own gods under another name. The Greeks in particular held this view and had already identified Osiris, god of the world beyond death, with their Dionysus, who was a god of mysteries and also of wine. So when Ptolemy Soter decided to compound a god for his new city, he was only taking advantage of this tendency, and giving a local habitation and a name and a statue to sentiments that already existed.

Osiris was the main ingredient. He was already worshipped on the hill of Rhakotis, and he was the most celebrated of the Egyptian deities. To him was added the bull god Apis, of Memphis, whose cult had been recently revived, and out of their names was formed the compound, "Serapis." But while the origins and title of the new god were Egyptian, his appearance and attributes were Greek. His statue—ascribed to the Greek sculptor Bryaxis—showed him seated in Greek garments upon a classic throne. His features were those of the bearded Zeus, but softened and benign; indeed he more closely resembled Aesculapius, god of Healing, to whom in a civilised age men naturally turned. The basket on his head showed that he was a harvest god, the three-headed Cerberus stood by his side to show that he represented Pluto, god of the underworld.

The Ptolemies could launch such a being without any fear of wounding religious susceptibilities. What they could not have foreseen was his success. Serapis not only fulfilled their immediate political aim of providing the Alexandrians with a common cult. He spread beyond the city, beyond Egypt, and shrines to him arose all over the Mediterranean world. Osiris-Apis-Dionysus-Zeus-Aesculapius-Pluto may seem to us an artificial compound, but it stood the test of time, it satisfied men's desires, and was to be the last stronghold of Paganism against Christianity.

The Temple stood on the old citadel of Rhakotis, where "Pompey's Pillar" rises to-day. It was in the midst of a cloister, and colonnades connected it with each of the cloister's sides. The architecture was Greek: a large hall, and, at the end, the shrine with the god's statue. As the centuries passed, other buildings were added, and the second and greater of the two Alexandrian libraries—the "Daughter"—was arranged in them.

(v). The Royal Tombs.

The "Soma" of Alexander became so famous that the earlier Ptolemies were buried close to it, and a mass of building—probably Greek in architecture—arose where the present Rue Rosette and Rue Nebi Daniel intersect. Later on, the burial place seems to have been in the Palace enclosure, and perhaps the "Mausoleum" where Cleopatra died was on the promontory of Silsileh, by a little Temple of Isis, within sound of the sea.

(vi). Other Buildings.

Theatre and Racecourse. Both were near the Palace: the former was probably on the site of the present Egyptian Government Hospital. Their architecture was Greek.

The Dyke of the Heptastadion was part of Alexander's scheme. But the Ptolemies completed it and fortified it where it rested on the Island of Pharos.

Such were the chief buildings and institutions that arose during the first hundred years of the city's life. Additions were made—notably the "Caesareum," begun by Cleopatra. But on the whole it may be said that Alexandria was the product of a single scheme, laid down by Dinocrates and executed by the first three

Ptolemies, and that she exhibited all the advantages, and perhaps some of the drawbacks, of a town that has been carefully planned. There was the majesty of well considered effects; but there also may have been a little dullness, and there were certainly none of the mysterious touches that reminded Athens and even Rome of an unanalysable past. In one sense the place was more Greek than Greece—built at a date when the Hellenic spirit had freed itself from many illusions and was winning a command over material forces that it had never possessed before. To her also Romance was added in time; but she started brand new, gleaming white, a calculated marvel of marble. Everything in her had been thought out—even her religion.

THE LATER PTOLEMIES (B.C. 221–51)
(*See Genealogical Tree p.* 14)

After the death of Euergetes, the dynasty declines. Some of his successors were able men, but a type evolved that made neither for morality nor for success. The average later Ptolemy is soft; he has the artistic temperament but no passionate love of art; he is born in the Palace at Alexandria and spends all his time there—so much so that it was not known for a year that Ptolemy IV had died; not naturally cruel, he is easily hurried into cruelty; he is unexpectedly shy; in his old age he grows fat, so that the Roman envoy murmurs "at all events the Alexandrians have seen their king walk" when Ptolemy VII comes puffing to greet him along the quay. And as the men soften, the women harden. The dynasty is interwoven with terrific queens. There is the Arsinoe whom Philadelphus married; there is Arsinoe III who faced the Syrian army

at Rafa; there is Cleopatra III who murdered her son;
and there is the last and greatest Cleopatra, with
whom the tangled race expires.

In contrast to this confusion there rises the solid but
unattractive figure of Rome (first embassy B.C. 273,
first intervention B.C. 200). Her advance was postponed until she had gained the Western Mediterranean by defeating Carthage. She then came forward
with studied politeness as the protector of liberty and
morals in the East. Legal and self-righteous, she struck
a chill into the whole Hellenistic world. She was hor-
rified at its corruption—a corruption of which she never
failed to take advantage, and the shattered empire of
Alexander fell piece by piece into her hands. The Ptolemies were the allies of this impeccable creature—a curious alliance, but it lasted over 200 years. As the
Egyptian fleet and army decayed, Rome's ministra-
tions multiplied. She declared herself guardian of the
dynasty; then that one of the Ptolemies had be-
queathed Egypt to her in a will that she never produced. The dynasty became, with Ptolemy XIII, illegitimate, and Rome made him pay her to recognise his
legitimacy. When he was driven from Egypt (B.C. 89)
she made him pay her to restore him. He was escorted
back by an army of creditors, and to raise the necessary
sum of ten thousand talents he had to grind down the
people with taxes. Rome was shocked, but firm.

Against this relentless advance Alexandria could do
nothing. She was the brain of Egypt, and its five senses
too and, as each embassy touched her quays, she realised, as the priest-ridden towns of the interior could
not, that the glory was departing from the Nile. There
was only one hope. Would Rome, before she could an-
nex Egypt, fall to pieces herself? There were signs of
it. The victorious republic had absorbed more plunder
and more ideas than she could conveniently digest.

She had always found it particularly difficult to digest
an idea. Rival Ptolemies had contended in Alexandria.
But rival Romans were now contending in Rome.
Might it be possible to play off against one the other,
and so win through to safety? The scheme commended
itself to the Alexandrians. It also occurred to the daughter of the bankrupt Ptolemy XIII, a beautiful and
amusing princess called Cleopatra.

COINS OF LATER PTOLEMIES: Museum, Room 3.
PORTRAIT OF PTOLEMY IV: Museum, Room 12.
INSCRIPTION TO PTOLEMY VII: Museum, Garden Court.
CARICATURE OF ROMAN SENATOR as a rat: Museum,
   Room 13.

CLEOPATRA (B.C. 51–30)
(*See Genealogical Tree p.* 14)

The girl who came to the throne as Cleopatra VI
Philopater was only seventeen. Her brother and husband Ptolemy XIV was ten; her younger brother eight,
her sister fifteen. The Palace at Alexandria became a
nursery, where four clever children watched the duel
that was proceeding between Pompey and Caesar beyond the seas. Pompey was their guardian, but they
had no illusions, either about him or one another. All
they cared for was life and power. Cleopatra failed in
her first intrigue, which was directed against her husband. He expelled her, and in her absence the duel
was concluded. Pompey, defeated by Caesar, drifted
to Egypt, threw himself on the mercy of his wards, and
was murdered by their agents as he disembarked.

With the arrival of Caesar, Cleopatra's triumphs began. She did not differ in character from the other able
and unscrupulous queens of her race, but she had one

source of power that they denied themselves—the power of the courtesan—and she exploited it professionally. Though passionate, she was not the slave of passion, still less of sentimentality. Her safety, and the safety of Egypt were her care; the clumsy and amorous Romans, who menaced both, were her natural prey. In old times, a queen might rule from her throne. Now she must descend and play the woman. Having heard that Caesar was quartered at the Palace, Cleopatra returned to Alexandria, rolled herself up in a bale of oriental carpets and was smuggled to him in this piquant wrapper. The other children protested, but her first victory had been won; she could count on the support of Julius Caesar against her husband.

Caesar's own position, was, however, most insecure. He was Lord of the World, but in his haste to catch Pompey he had hurried ahead of his legions. When the glamour of .his arrival had worn off the Alexandrians realised this, and in a fierce little war (Aug. 48–Jan. 47) tried to crush him before reinforcements arrived. He held the Palace (near Chatby); the Theatre (Egyptian Government Hospital); also part of the Eastern Harbour where his small fleet lay. They held the rest of the town, including the Western Harbour and the Island, and they had with them Cleopatra's sister who had escaped from the Palace and, later, Ptolemy XIV himself,—so that they could claim to represent the dynasty.

It was indeed a national rising against the Romans and ably conducted. Five stages (*see* Map, p. 106).

(1). *Siege of the Palace.*—This was succeeding by land but failed by sea, when Caesar, making a sudden excursion down the docks of the Eastern Harbour, set fire to the Alexandrian fleet. The flames spread to the Mouseion and the Library ("Mother" Library) was burnt.† An attempt to contaminate the Palace water supply also failed; when the

Alexandrians pumped salt water into the conduit, the be-
sieged Romans bored wells in the Palace enclosure.

(2). *First Naval Engagement.*—Caesar's reinforcements
had begun to arrive, and a heavy east wind had carried them
past the entrance of his harbour. He went out to tow them
in, and the Alexandrians issued from their own harbour—
the Western—to intercept him. They failed.

(3). *Second Naval Engagement and loss of the Island
of Pharos.*—Issuing from his harbour, Caesar rounded Ras-
el-Tin and deployed outside the line of reefs that stretch
from it to Agame and guard the entrance to the Western
Harbour. The Alexandrians waited inside. Dashing through
the entrance he pressed them against the quays of Rhakotis
and defeated them. Now he could attack the Island on both
sides. On the following day it fell and he made it his headquarters, thus changing the strategy of the war.

(4). *Battle of the Dyke.*—Caesar now blocked up the
arches that penetrated the Heptastadion so that the Alexandrians could not manœuvre from harbour to harbour.
Then he tried to force his way into the town. He employed too many troops, and landing in his rear the Alexandrians threw him into confusion. He himself had to jump
from the dyke and swim to a boat. Victory. They recaptured the whole of the Heptastadion and reopened its
arches.

(5). *Battle by the Nile.*—The war was after all decided
outside Alexandria. More reinforcements were coming to
Caesar down the Canopic mouth of the Nile and the
Alexandrians marched out to intercept them there. The
young Ptolemy XIV was their general now. He was defeated and drowned, his army was destroyed, and Caesar
returned in triumph to its city and to Cleopatra.

Cleopatra's fortune now seemed assured. Having
married her younger brother (as Ptolemy XV) she
went for a trip with Caesar up the Nile to show him its
antiquities. The Egyptians detested her as their be-
trayer but she was indifferent. She bore Caesar a son
and followed him to Rome, there to display her inso-

lence. She was at the height of her beauty and power when the blow fell. On the Ides of March, B.C. 44, Caesar was murdered. She had chosen the wrong lover after all.

Back in Alexandria again, she watched the second duel—that between Mark Antony and Caesar's murderers. She helped neither party, and when Antony won he summoned her to explain her neutrality. She came, not in a carpet but in a gilded barge, and her life henceforward belongs less to history than to poetry. It is almost impossible to think of the later Cleopatra as an ordinary person. She has joined the company of Helen and Iseult. Yet her character remained the same. Voluptuous but watchful, she treated her new lover as she had treated her old. She never bored him, and since grossness means monotony she sharpened his mind to those more delicate delights, where sense verges into spirit. Her infinite variety lay in that. She was the last of a secluded and subtle race, she was a flower that Alexandria had taken three hundred years to produce and that eternity cannot wither, and she unfolded herself to a simple but intelligent Roman soldier.

Alexandria, now reconciled to her fate and protected by the legions of Antony, became the capital of the Eastern world. The Western belonged to Octavian, Caesar's nephew, and a third duel was inevitable. It was postponed for some years, during which Antony acquired and deserted a Roman wife, and Cleopatra bore him several children. Her son by Julius Caesar was crowned as Ptolemy XVI, with the additional title of King of Kings. Antony himself became a God, and she built a temple to him, afterwards called the Caesareum, and adorned by two ancient obelisks (Cleopatra's Needles). This period of happiness and splendour ended in the naval disaster of Actium in the

Adriatic, where Octavian defeated their combined
fleets. The defeat was hastened by Cleopatra's cowardice.† At the decisive moment she fled with sixty ships,
actually breaking her way through Antony's line from
the rear, and throwing it into confusion. He followed
her to Alexandria, and there, when the recriminations
had ceased, they resumed their life of pleasures that
were both shadowed and sharpened by the approach
of death. They made no attempt to oppose the pur-
suing Octavian. Instead, they formed a Suicide Club,
and Antony, to imitate the misanthrope Timon, built
a hermitage in the Western Harbour which he called
Timonium. Nor was religion silent. The god Hercules,
whom he loved and who loved him, was heard passing
away from Alexandria one night in exquisite music and
song.

Arrival of Octavian. He is one of the most odious of
the world's successful men and to his cold mind the
career of Cleopatra could appear as nothing but a vulgar debauch. Vice, in his opinion, should be furtive. At
his approach, Antony after resisting outside the Canopic Gate (at "Caesar's Camp") retreated into the city
and fell upon his sword. He was carried, dying, to Cleopatra, who had retired into their tomb, and their story
now rises to the immortality of art. Shakespeare drew
his inspiration from Plutarch, who was himself inspired, and it is difficult through their joint emotion
to realise the actual facts. The asp, for example,
is not a certainty. It was never known how Cleopatra
died. She was captured and taken to Octavian, with
whom even in Antony's life-time she had been intri-
guing, for the courtesan in her persisted. She appeared
this time not in a carpet nor yet in a barge, but upon a
sofa, in the seductive negligence of grief. The good
young man was shocked. Realising that he intended
to lead her in his triumph at Rome, realising too that

she was now thirty-nine years old, she killed herself. She was buried in the tomb with Antony; and her ladies Charmion and Iras, who died with her, guarded its doors as statues of bronze. Alexandria became the capital of a Roman Province.

COIN OF CLEOPATRA: Museum, Room 3.

PORTRAIT OF CLEOPATRA (?): Museum, Room 12.

DEATH OF CLEOPATRA in Plutarch, Shakespeare and Dryden: Appendix p. 231.

INSCRIPTION TO ANTONY: Museum, Room 6.

COLOSSUS OF ANTONY: Museum, Garden Court.

SITE OF CAESAREUM: p. 175.

SHRINE OF POMPEY (?): p. 171.

DEPARTURE OF THE GOD HERCULES: p. 104.

Thus the career of the Greco-Egyptian city closes, as it began, in an atmosphere of Romance. Cleopatra is of course a meaner figure than Alexander the Great. Ambition with her is purely selfish; with Alexander it was mystically connected with the welfare of mankind. She knows nothing beyond the body and so shrinks from discomfort and pain: Alexander attained the strength of the hero. Yet for all their differences, the man who created and the woman who lost Alexandria have one element in common: monumental greatness; and between them is suspended, like a rare and fragile chain, the dynasty of the Ptolemies. It is a dynasty much censored by historians, but the Egyptians, who lived under it, were more tolerant. For it had one element of greatness: it did represent the complex country that it ruled. In Upper Egypt it carried on the tradition of the Pharaohs: on the coast it was Hellenistic and in touch with Mediterranean culture. After its extinction, the vigour of Alexandria turns inwards. She is to do big things in philosophy and religion. But she is no longer the capital of a kingdom, no longer Royal.

PTOLEMAIC CULTURE

Before leaving the Ptolemies, let us glance back at their civilisation. We have seen how they founded two great institutions, the Palace and the Mouseion, which communicated with one another, and which stretched from the promontory of Silsileh to some point inland— as far as the modern railway station, perhaps. It was in this area, among gardens and colonnades, that the culture of Alexandria came into being. The Palace provided the finances and called the tune: the Mouseion responded with imagination or knowledge; the connection between them was so intimate as almost to be absurd. When, for instance, Queen Berenice the wife of Euergetes lost her hair from the temple where she had dedicated it, it was the duty of the court astronomer to detect it as a constellation and of the court poet to write an elegy thereon. And Stratonice, who was perfectly bald, presented an even more delicate problem; she sent over· a message to the Mouseion that something must be written about her hair also. Victory odes, Funeral dirges, Marriage hymns, jokes, genealogical trees, medical prescriptions, mechanical toys, maps, engines of war: whatever the Palace required it had only to inform the Mouseion, and the subsidised staff set to work at once. The poets and scientists there did nothing that would annoy the Royal Family and not much that would puzzle it, for they knew that if they failed to give satisfaction they would be expelled from the enchanted area, and have to find another patron or starve. It was not an ideal arrangement, as outsiders were prompt to point out, and snobbery and servility taint the culture of Alexandria from the first.

It sprang up behind walls, it never knew loneliness, nor the glories and the dangers of independence, and the marvel is that it flourished as well as it did. At all events it is idle to criticise it for not being different, for if it had been different it would not have been Alexandrian. In spirit as in fact the Palace and the Mouseion touched, and the Palace was the stronger and the older. The contact strangled Philosophy and deprived Literature of such sustenance as Philosophy can bring to her. But it encouraged Science and gave even to Literature certain graces that she had hitherto ignored.

TEMPLE WHERE BERENICE DEDICATED HER HAIR: p. 196.

(A) LITERATURE

CALLIMACHUS, about 310–240.
APOLLONIUS OF RHODES, 260–188.
THEOCRITUS, about 320–250.

The literature that grew up in the Mouseion had no lofty aims. It was not interested in ultimate problems nor even in problems of behaviour, and it attempted none of the higher problems of art. To be graceful or pathetic or learned or amusing or indecent, and in any case loyal—this sufficed it, so that though full of experiments it is quite devoid of adventure. It developed when the heroic age of Greece was over, when liberty was lost and possibly honour too. It was disillusioned, and we may be glad that it was not embittered also. It had strength of a kind, for it saw that out of the wreck of traditional hopes three good things remained —namely the decorative surface of the universe, the delights of study, and the delights of love, and that of these three the best was love. Ancient Greece had also sung of love, but with restraint, regarding it as one activity among many. The Alexandrians seldom sang of anything else: their epigrams, their elegies and idylls, their one great epic, all turn on the tender passion, and celebrate it in ways that previous ages had never known, and that future ages were to know too well. Darts and hearts, sighs and eyes, breasts and chests, all originated in Alexandria and from the intercourse between Palace and Mouseion—stale devices to-day, but then they were fresh.

Who sculptured Love and set him by the pool,
thinking with water such a fire to cool?*

runs a couplet ascribed to one of the early Librarians, and containing in brief the characteristics of the school —decorative method, mythological allusiveness, and the theme of love. Love as a cruel and wanton boy flits through the literature of Alexandria as through the thousands of terra cotta statuettes that have been exhumed from her soil; one tires of him, but it is appropriate that he should have been born under a dynasty that culminated in Cleopatra.

Literature took its tone from Callimachus—a fine poet, though not as fine as his patrons supposed. He began life as a schoolmaster at Eleusis (the modern Nouzha) and then was called to the Mouseion, where he became Librarian under Euergetes. His learning was immense, his wit considerable, his loyalty untiring. It was he who wrote the poem about Berenice's hair. Dainty and pedantic in all that he did, he announced that "a big book is a big nuisance" and cared more about neatness of expression than depth of feeling, though the feeling emerges in his famous epigram:

Someone told me, Heracleitus, of your end;
and I wept, and thought how often you and I

---

* Translated by R. A. Furness.

*sunk the sun with talking. Well! and now you lie
antiquated ashes somewhere, Carian friend.
But your nightingales, your songs, are living still;
them the death that clutches all things cannot kill.**

Only once was this exquisite career interrupted.
There was among his pupils a young man from Rhodes
with thin legs, by name Apollonius. Apollonius was
ambitious to write an Epic—a form of composition detested by Callimachus, and opposed to all his theories.
In vain he objected; Apollonius, then only eighteen,
gave in the Mouseion a public reading of the preliminary draft of his poem. A violent quarrel was the result,
Apollonius was expelled, and Callimachus wrote a sat-
ire called the Ibis, in which his rival's legs and other
deficiencies were exposed. The friends of Apollonius
retorted with equal spirit, and the tranquillity of the
Mouseion was impaired. Callimachus won, but his victory was not eternal; after his death Apollonius was
recalled to Alexandria, and in time became Librarian
there in his turn.

The Epic Apollonius insisted on writing has survived. It is modelled on Homer and deals with the voy-
age of the Argo to recover the Golden Fleece. But
there is nothing Homeric in the treatment and though
we are supposed to be in barbaric lands we never
really leave the cultivated court of the Ptolemies. Love
is still the ruling interest. He slips, the naughty little
boy, into the Palace of Medea, and shoots his tiny dart
at her, to inspire her with passion for Jason. So might
he have inspired Queen Berenice or Arsinoe. Pains,
languors, and raptures succeed, and the theme of the
heroic quest is forgotten. Callimachus can have found
nothing to object to in such a poem except its length,
for it is typical of his school. Its pictorial method is also
characteristic of Alexandria; many of the episodes

---

* Translated by R. A. Furness.

might be illustrated by terra cotta statues and gems.

But one of the poets who worked in the Mouseion—Theocritus—was a genius of a very different kind, a genius that Alexandria matured but cannot be said to have formed. Theocritus came here late in his career. He had been born at Cos and had lived in Sicily, and he arrived full of memories that no town-dweller could share—memories of fresh air and the sun, of upland meadows and overhanging trees, of goats and sheep, of the men and the women who looked after them, and of all the charm and the coarseness that go to make up country life. He had thrown these memories into poetical form, sometimes idealising them, sometimes giving them crudely, and he had called these poems Idylls—little pictures of rural existence. Love, mythological fancies, decorative treatment—he liked these things too, but he backed them with a width of experience and a zest for it that Callimachus and Apollonius never knew. While they are "Classics" who have to be studied, Theocritus appeals to us at once; his Fifteenth Idyll, describing life in the Greek Quarter at Alexandria, is as vivid now as when he wrote it. The dialogue with which it opens can be heard to-day in any of the little drawing rooms of Camp de César or Ibrahimieh. Praxinoe, a lady of the middle classes, is discovered seated, doing nothing in particular. In comes Gorgo, her friend.

Gorgo. Is Praxinoe at home?

Praxinoe. Oh my dear Gorgo, it's ages since you were here. She *is* at home. The wonder is that you've come even now. (calls to the maid). Eunoe, give her a chair and put a cushion on it.

Gorgo. Oh it does beautifully as it is.

Praxinoe. Sit down!

G. My nerves are all to bits—Praxinoe, I only just got here alive . . . . what with the crowd, what with the carriages . . . soldiers' boots—soldiers' great-coats, and the street's endless—you really live too far.

P.   That's my insane husband. We took this hut—one can't call it a house—at the ends of the earth so that we shouldn't be neighbours. Mere jealousy. As usual.

G.   But, dear, don't talk about your husband when the little boy's here—he's staring at you. (to the little boy) Sweet pet—that's all right—she isn't talking about papa.—Good Heavens, the child understands.—Pretty papa!

P.   The other day, papa—we seem to call every day the other day—the other day he went to get some soda at the Baccal and brought back salt by mistake—the great overgrown lout.

G.   Mine's exactly the same, he . . . . *

And so on. But Gorgo wants to go out again, in spite of her nerves. It is the Feast of the Resurrection—the Resurrection of Adonis—and there is to be a magnificent service inside the Palace, with a special singer. Praxinoe decides to venture too, and puts on the dress with the full body, that cost "at least eight pounds," excluding embroidery. They are ready at last and then the little boy begins to scream; he wishes to be of the party. But his mother remarks, "cry as much as you like, I cannot have you lamed," and takes Eunoe instead. In the street the crush is terrific, they are terrified of the Egyptians (just like Greek ladies to-day) and Eunoe, who is always awkward, nearly falls under a horse. The battle at the Palace Gate is worse still, Praxinoe's best muslin veil is torn, and she is more thankful than ever that she did not bring her little boy. But for a kind gentleman in the crowd, they would never have got in. Once inside, all is enjoyment. The draperies are gorgeous as might be expected when the Queen Arsinoe is paying for them—Arsinoe the wife of

* Adapted from Andrew Lang's Translation.

Philadelphus. And here is a Holy Sepulchre on which lies an image of Adonis, the down of early manhood just showing on his cheeks! The ladies are in ecstasies and can scarcely quiet themselves to listen to the Resurrection Hymn. In this Hymn Theocritus displays the other side of his genius—the "Alexandrian" side. He is no longer the amusing realist, but an erudite poet, whose chief theme is love.

> O Queen that lovest Golgi and Idalium and Eryx, O Aphrodite that playest with gold—lo from the everlasting stream of Hades they have brought thee back Adonis. . . . . . A bridegroom of eighteen or nineteen years is he, his kisses are not yet rough, the golden down being yet on his lips. . . . . Thou only, dear Adonis, so men tell, visitest both this world and the stream of Hades. For Agamemnon had no such fate, nor Ajax the wrathful, nor Hector the first-born of Hecuba, nor Patroclus, nor Pyrrhus that returned out of Troy, nor the heroes of yet more ancient days. . . . . Be gracious now, dear Adonis, and bless us in the coming year. Dear has thy resurrection been, and dear shall it be when thou comest again.

A beautiful hymn; but as Gorgo remarks "all the same it's time to be getting home; my husband hasn't had his dinner and when he's kept waiting for his dinner he's as sour as vinegar." They salute the risen god, and go.

This delightful Idyll is not quite characteristic of Theocritus—he generally sings of Shepherds and their flocks. But it is his great contribution to the literature of Alexandria, and our chief authority for daily life under the Ptolemies. History is too much an affair of armies and kings. The Fifteenth Idyll corrects the error. Only through literature can the past be recovered and here Theocritus, wielding the double spell of realism and of poetry, has evoked an entire city from the dead and filled its streets with men. As Praxinoe remarks of the draperies "Why the figures seem to stand up and to move, they're not patterns, they are alive."

The Mouseion was at its best under the first three Ptolemies. Then it declined—at least in its literary output—and though Alexandria turned out poems, etc., for several hundred years, few of them merit attention. With the coming of the Romans her genius took a new line, and essayed the neglected paths of philosophy and religion. But she remained attractive to men of letters, and nearly every writer of note visited her in the course of his travels.

STATUETTES OF LOVES: Museum, Room 18.
NOUZHA (birthplace of Callimachus): p. 172.

(B) SCHOLARSHIP

In the Mouseion at Alexandria Greece first became aware of her literary heritage, and the works of the past were not only collected in the Library but were codified, amended, and explained. Scholarship dates from Zenodotus, the first Librarian. He turned his attention to Homer, divided the Iliad and Odyssey into "Books," struck out spurious verses from the text, marked doubtful ones, and introduced new readings. He gave a general impulse to research. Hitherto the Greek language had developed unnoticed. Now it was consciously examined, and the result of the examination was the first Greek Grammar (about 100 B.C.). Grammar is a valuable subject but also a dangerous one, for it naturally attracts pedants and schoolmasters and all who think that Literature is an affair of rules. And the Grammarians of Alexandria forgot that they were merely codifying the usages of the past, and presumed to dictate to the present, and to posterity; they set a bad example that has been followed for nearly 2,000 years. Greek accents—another doubtful boon— were also invented in the Mouseion. Indeed the whole of literary scholarship, as we know it, sprang up, including that curious by-product the Scholarly Joke. For instance: one learned man wrote a poem that had, when transcribed, the shape of a bird, another wrote a poem in the shape of a double-headed axe, and a third re-wrote the whole of the Odyssey without using the letter S. The donnish wit of the Mouseion infected the Palace, and was practiced by the Ptolemies themselves. One scholar, Sosibius by name, complained to King Philadelphus that he had not received his salary. The King replied, "The first syllable of your name occurs in Soter, the second in Sosigenes, the third in Bion, and the fourth in Apollonius; I have paid these four gentleman, and therefore I have paid you."

(C) ART

Unimportant. Alexandria had her special industries —*e.g.* glass, terra cotta, "Egyptian Queen" pottery, and woven stuffs, and her mint was famous; but for creative artists the Ptolemies looked over seas. Greek and Egyptian motives did not blend in Art as they did in Religion; attempts occur, but they are not notable and on the whole the city follows the general Hellenistic tendencies of the time. These tendencies led as we have seen away from the ideal and the abstract, and towards portraiture and the dainty and the picturesque. Men had lost for the time many illusions, both religious and political, and were trying to beautify their private lives, and the tombs of those whom they had loved.

GLASS AND "EGYPTIAN QUEEN" POTTERY: Museum, Room 17.

TERRA COTTAS: Museum, Room 18.

PTOLEMAIC COINS: Museum, Room 3.

BLEND OF GREEK AND EGYPTIAN MOTIVES: Museum, Rooms 11 and 15; also Kom es Chogafa Catacombs, (p. 163).

TOMB ORNAMENTS: Museum, Rooms 17–22.

(D) PHILOSOPHY

Unimportant. The Ptolemies imported some second-rate disciples of Aristotle to give tone to the Mouseion, but took no interest in the subject, and were indeed averse to it, since it might lead to freedom of thought. It was not until their dynasty was extinct that the great school of Alexandrian Philosophy arose. (See p. 64, under heading "The Spiritual City.")

(E) SCIENCE

The Ptolemies were more successful over Science than over Literature. They preferred it, for it could not criticise their divine right. Its endowment was the greatest achievement of the dynasty and makes Alexandria famous until the end of time. Science had been studied in Ancient Greece, but sporadically: there had been no co-ordination, no laboratories, and though important truths might be discovered or surmised, they were in danger of oblivion because they could not be popularised. The foundation of the Mouseion changed all this. Working under royal patronage and with every facility, science leapt to new heights, and gave valuable gifts to mankind. The third century B.C. is (from this point of view) the greatest period that civilisation has ever known—greater even than the nineteenth century A.D. It did not bring happiness or wisdom: science never does. But it explored the physical universe and harnessed many powers for our use. Mathematics, Geography, Astronomy, Medicine, all grew to maturity in the little space of the land between the present Rue Rosette and the sea, and if we had any sense of the fitting, some memorial to them would arise on the spot to-day.

(i). MATHEMATICS.

Mathematics begin with the tremendous but obscure career of Euclid. Nothing is known about Euclid: indeed one thinks of him to-day more as a branch of knowledge than as a man. But Euclid was once alive, landing here in the reign of Ptolemy Philadelphus, and informing that superficial monarch that there is "no royal road to geometry." Here he composed, among other works, his "Elements" in which he incorporated all previous knowledge, and which have remained the world's text book for Geometry almost down to the present day. Here he founded a mathematical school that lasted 700 years, and acknowledged his leadership to the last. Apollonius of Perga, who inaugurated the study of Conic Sections, was his immediate pupil: Hyspicles added to the thirteen books of his "Elements" two books more: and Theon—father to the martyred Hypatia—edited the "Elements" and gave them their present form, so that from first to last the mathematicians of Alexandria were preoccupied with him. An in-

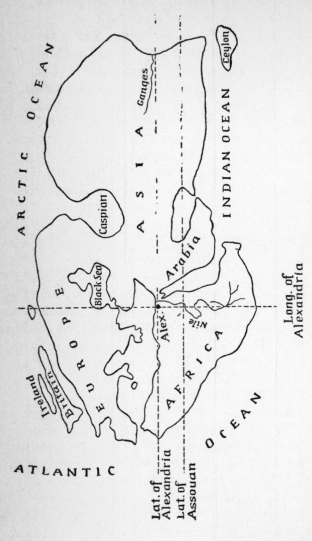

THE WORLD ACCORDING TO ERATOSTHENES

B.C. 250

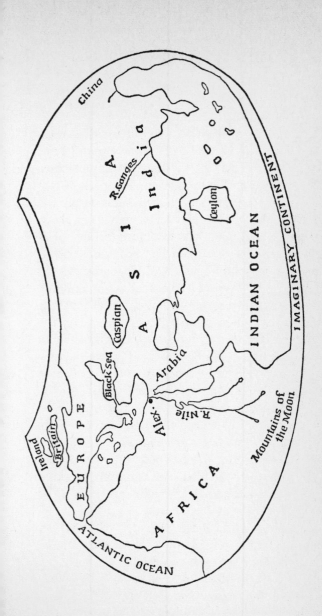

THE WORLD ACCORDING TO CLAUDIUS PTOLEMY
A.D. 100

significant man, according to tradition, and very shy;
his snub to Philadelphus seems to have been excep-
tional.

(ii). GEOGRAPHY.

In Geography there are two leading figures—Eratosthenes and Claudius Ptolemy. Eratosthenes is the
greater. He seems to have been an all round genius,
eminent in literature as well as science. He was born
at Cyrene in B.C. 276 and, on the death of Callimachus,
was invited to Alexandria to become librarian. It was
in the Mouseion observatory that he measured the
Earth—perhaps not the greatest achievement of Alexandrian science, but certainly the most thrilling. His
method was as follows. He knew that the earth is
round, and he was told that the midsummer sun at
Assouan in Upper Egypt cast no shadow at midday.
At Alexandria, at the same moment, it did cast a
shadow, Alexandria being further to the north on the
same longitude. On measuring the Alexandria shadow
he found that it was 7.⅕ degrees—*i.e.* ¹⁄₅₀th of a complete circle—so that the distance from Alexandria to
Assouan must be ¹⁄₅₀th the circumference of the
Earth. He estimated the distance at 500 miles, and
consequently arrived at 25,000 miles for the complete
circumference, and 7,850 for the diameter; in the latter calculation he is only 50 miles out. It is strange that
when science had once gained such triumphs mankind
should ever have slipped back again into fairy tales
and barbarism.

The other great work of Eratosthenes was his "Ge-
ographies," including all previous knowledge on the
subject, just as the "Elements" of Euclid had included
all previous mathematical knowledge. The "Geogra-
phies" were in three books, and to them was attached
a map of the known world. (See p. 42.) It is, of course,

full of inaccuracies—*e.g.* Great Britain is too large, India fails to be a peninsula and the Caspian Sea connects with the Arctic Ocean. But it is conceived in the scientific spirit. It represents the world as Eratosthenes thought it was, not as he thought it ought to be. When he knows nothing, he inserts nothing; he is not ashamed to leave blank spaces. He bases it on such facts as he knew, and had he known more facts he would have altered it.

The other great geographer, Claudius Ptolemy, belongs to a later period (A.D. 100) but it is convenient to notice him here. Possibly he was a connection of the late royal family, but nothing is known of his life. His fame has outshone Eratosthenes', and no doubt he was more learned, for more facts were at his disposal. Yet we can trace in him the decline of the scientific spirit. Observe his Map of the World (p. 43). At first sight it is superior to the Eratosthenes Map. The Caspian Sea is corrected, new countries—*e.g.* China—are inserted, and there are (in the original) many more names. But there is one significant mistake. He has prolonged Africa into an imaginary continent and joined it up to China. It was a mere flight of his fancy: he even scattered this continent with towns and rivers. No one corrected the mistake and for hundreds of years it was believed that the Indian Ocean was land bound. The age of enquiry was over, and the age of authority had begun, and it is worth noting that the decline of science at Alexandria exactly coincides with the rise of Christianity.

(iii). ASTRONOMY AND THE CALENDAR.

Astronomy develops on the same lines as Geography. There is an early period of scientific research under Eratosthenes, and there is a later period in which Claudius Ptolemy codifies the results and dictates his

opinions to posterity. He announced, for example, that
the Universe revolves round the Earth, and this "Ptolemaic" Theory was adopted by all subsequent astrono-
mers until Galileo, and supported by all the thunders
of the Church. Yet another view had been put forward,
though Ptolemy ignores it. Aristarchus of Samos, working at Alexandria with Eratosthenes, had suggested
that the earth might revolve round the sun, and it is
only a chance that this view was not stamped as official
and imposed as orthodox all through the Middle Ages.
We do not know what Aristarchus' arguments were,
for his writings have perished, but we may be sure that,
working in the 3rd century B.C., he had arguments and
did not take refuge in authority. Astronomy under the
Ptolemies was a serious affair—lightened only by the
episode of Berenice's Hair.

As to the Calendar. The Calendar we now use was
worked out in Alexandria. The Ancient Egyptians had
calculated the year at 365 days. It is actually 365¼,
so before long they were hopelessly out; the official
Harvest Festival, for instance, only coincided with the
actual harvest once in 1,500 years. They were aware of
the discrepancy, but were too conservative to alter it:
that was left to Alexandria. In B.C. 239 the little daughter of Ptolemy Euergetes died, and the priests of
Serapis at Canopus passed a decree making her a goddess. A reformer even in his grief, the King induced
them to rectify the Calendar at the same time by de-
creeing the existence of a Leap Year, to occur every
four years, as at present; he attempted to harmonise
the traditions of Egypt with the science of Greece. The
attempt—so typical of Alexandria—failed, for though
the priests passed the decree they kept to their old
chronology. It was not until Julius Caesar came to
Egypt that the cause of reform prevailed. He established the "Alexandrian Year" as official, and modelled

on it the "Julian," which we use in Europe to-day; the two years were of the same length, but the "Alexandrian" retained the old Egyptian arrangement of twelve equal months.

(iv). MEDICINE.

Erasistratus (3rd. cent. B.C.) is the chief glory of the Alexandrian medical school. In his earlier life he had been a great practitioner, and had realised the connection between sexual troubles and nervous breakdowns. In his old age he settled in the Mouseion, and devoted himself to research. He practised vivisection on animals, and possibly on criminals, and he seems to have come near to discovering the circulation of the blood. Less severely scientific were the healing cults that sprang up in the great temples of Serapis, both at Alexandria and at Canopus;—cults that were continued into Christian times under other auspices.

SITE OF MOUSEION: p. 113.
MAP OF ERATOSTHENES: p. 42.
MAP OF CLAUDIUS PTOLEMY: p. 43.
TEMPLE OF SERAPIS AT CANOPUS: p. 190.
        "   "   ALEXANDRIA: p. 157.

Christian Period

THE RULE OF ROME (B.C. 30–A.D. 313)

Octavian (Augustus) the founder of the Roman Empire, so disliked Alexandria that after his triumph over Cleopatra he founded a town near modern Ramleh— Nicopolis, the "City of Victory." He also forbade any Roman of the governing classes to enter Egypt without his permission, on the ground that the religious orgies there would corrupt their morals. The true reason was economic. He wanted to keep the Egyptian corn supply in his own hands, and thus control the hungry populace of Rome. Egypt, unlike the other Roman provinces, became a private appanage of the Emperor, who himself appointed the Prefect who governed it, and Alexandria turned into a vast imperial granary where the tribute, collected in kind from the cultivators, was stored for transhipment. It was an age of exploitation. Octavian posed locally as the divine successor of the Ptolemies, and appears among hieroglyphs at Dendyra and Philae. But he had no local interest at heart.

After his death things improved. The harsh ungenerous Republic that he had typified passed into Imperial Rome, who, despite her moments of madness, brought happiness to the Mediterranean world for two hundred years. Alexandria had her share of this happiness. Her new problem—riots between Greeks and Jews—was solved at the expense of the latter; she

gained fresh trade by the improved connections with
India (Trajan A.D. 115, recut the Red Sea Canal); she
was visited by a series of appreciative Emperors on
their way to the antiquities of Upper Egypt.

In about A.D. 250 she, with the rest of the Empire,
re-entered trouble. The human race, as if not designed
to enjoy happiness, had slipped into a mood of envy
and discontent. Barbarians attacked the frontiers of
the Empire, while within were revolts and mutinies.
The difficulties of the Emperors were complicated by
a religious problem. They had, for political reasons,
been emphasising their own divinity—a divinity that
Egypt herself had taught them: it seemed to them that
it would be a binding force against savagery and
schism. They therefore directed that everyone should
worship them. Who could have expected a protest, and
a protest from Alexandria?

RAMLEH (Nicopolis): p. 181.
STATUE OF EMPEROR (Marcus Aurelius): Museum,
    Room 12.
IMPERIAL COINS: Museum, Room 2.
CERTIFICATES TO ROMAN SOLDIERS: Museum, Room 6.

THE CHRISTIAN COMMUNITY

According to the tradition of the Egyptian Church,
Christianity was introduced into Alexandria by St.
Mark, who in A.D. 45 converted a Jewish shoemaker
named Annianus, and who in 62 was martyred for pro-
testing against the worship of Serapis. There is no
means of checking this tradition; the origins of the
movement were unfashionable and obscure, and the
authorities took little notice of it until it disobeyed their

regulations. Its doctrines were confounded partly with
the Judaism from which they had sprung, partly with
the other creeds of the city. A letter ascribed to the
Emperor Hadrian (in Alexandria, 134) says, "Those
who worship Serapis are Christians, and those who call
themselves bishops of Christ are devoted to Serapis,"
showing how indistinct was the impression that the
successors of St. Mark had made. The letter continues,
"As a race of men they are seditious, vain, and spiteful;
as a body, wealthy and prosperous, of whom nobody
lives in idleness. Some blow glass, some make paper,
and others linen. Their one God is nothing peculiar;
Christians, Jews, and all nations worship him. I wish
this body of men was better behaved."

The community was organised under its "overseer"
or bishop, who soon took the title of patriarch, and appointed bishops elsewhere in Egypt. The earliest centres were (i) the oratory of St. Mark which stood by
the sea shore—probably to the east of Silsileh—and was
afterwards enlarged into a Cathedral; (ii) a later cathedral church dedicated (285) by the Patriarch Theonas to the Virgin Mary; it was on the site of the
present Franciscan Church by the Docks; (iii) a Theological College—the "Catechetical School," founded
about 200, where Clement of Alexandria and Origen
taught—site unknown.

It was its "bad behaviour," to use Hadrian's term,
that brought the community into notice—that is to say,
its refusal to worship the Emperors. To the absurd
spiritual claims of the state, Christianity opposed the
claims of the individual conscience, and the conflict
was only allayed by the state itself becoming Christian.
The conflict came to its height in Alexandria, which,
more than any other city in the Empire, may claim to
have won the battle for the new religion. Persecution,
at first desultory, grew under Decius, and culminated

in the desperate measures of Diocletian (303)—demolition of churches, all Christian officials degraded, all
Christian non-officials enslaved. Diocletian, an able
ruler—the great column miscalled Pompey's is his memorial—did not persecute from personal spite, but
the results were no less appalling and definitely discredited the pagan state. While we need not accept the
Egyptian Church's estimate of 144,000 martyrs in nine
years, there is no doubt that numbers perished in all
ranks of society. Among the victims was St. Menas, a
young Egyptian soldier who became patron of the desert west of Lake Mariout, where a great church was
built over his grave. St. Catherine of Alexandria is also
said to have died under Diocletian, but it is improbable
that she ever lived; she and her wheel were creations
of Western Catholicism, and the land of her supposed sufferings has only recognised her out of politeness to the French. The persecution was vain, the state
was defeated, and the Egyptian Church, justly triumphant, dates its chronology, not from the birth of
Christ, but from the "Era of Martyrs" (A.D. 284). A few
years later the Emperor Constantine made Christianity
official, and the menace from without came to an end.

COIN OF HADRIAN AT ALEXANDRIA: Museum, Room 2.
SITE OF ST. MARK'S: p. 178.
CAPITAL FROM ST. MARK'S: Museum, Room 1.
SITE OF ST. THEONAS: p. 184.
COLUMN FROM ST. THEONAS: p. 177.
STATUE OF DIOCLETIAN: Museum, Room 17.
COINS OF DIOCLETIAN: Museum, Room 4.
"POMPEY'S (Diocletian's) Pillar": p. 157.
CHURCH OF ST. MENAS: p. 210.
REMAINS FROM ST. MENAS: Museum, Rooms 1, 2, 5.
MODERN CHURCH OF ST. CATHERINE: p. 155.
PILLAR OF ST. CATHERINE: p. 114.

CERTIFICATE OF HAVING WORSHIPPED THE GODS: Museum, Room 6.

ARIUS AND ATHANASIUS (4th Cent. A.D.)

It was natural that Alexandria, who had suffered so much for Christianity, should share in its triumph, and as soon as universal toleration was proclaimed her star re-emerged. Rome, as the stronghold of Paganism, was discredited, and it seemed that the city by the Nile might again become Imperial, as in the days of Antony. That hoped was dashed, for Constantine, a very cautious man, thought it safer to found a new capital on the Bosphorus, where no memories from the past could intrude. But Alexandria was the capital spiritually, and at least it seemed that she, who had helped to free imprisoned Christendom, would lead it in harmony and peace to its home at the feet of God. That hope was dashed too. An age of hatred and misery was approaching. The Christians, as soon as they had captured the machinery of the pagan state, turned it against one another, and the century resounds to a dispute between two dictatorial clergymen.

Both were natives of Alexandria. Arius, the older, took duty at St. Mark's—the vanished church by the sea at Chatby where the Evangelist was said to have been martyred. Learned and sincere, tall, simple in his dress, persuasive in his speech, he was accused by his enemies of looking like a snake, and of seducing, in the theological sense, 700 virgins. Athanasius, his opponent, first appears as a merry little boy, playing with other children on the beach below St. Theonas—on the shore of the present western harbour, that is to say. He was playing at Baptism, which not being in orders he

had no right to do, and the Patriarch, who happened
to be looking out of the palace window, tried to stop
him. No one ever succeeded in stopping St. Athanasius.
He baptised his playmates, and the Patriarch, struck
by his precocity, recognised the sacrament as valid
and engaged the active young theologian as his secre-
tary. Physically Athanasius was blackish and small, but
strong and extremely graceful—one recognises a modern street type. His character can scarcely be discerned
through the dust of the century, but he was certainly
not loveable, though he lived to be a popular hero. His
powers were remarkable. As a theologian he knew
what is true, and as a politician he knew how truth
can be enforced, and his career blends subtlety with
vigour and self-abnegation with craft in the most remarkable way.

The dispute—Arius started it—concerned the nature
of Christ. Its doctrinal import is discussed below (p.
80); here we are only dealing with the outward results. Constantine who was no theologian and dubi-
ously Christian, was appalled by the schism which rap-
idly divided his empire. He wrote, counselling charity,
and when he was ignored summoned the disputants to
Nicaea on the Black Sea (325). Two hundred and fifty
bishops and many priests attended, and amid great
violence the *Nicene Creed* was passed, and Arius condemned. Athanasius who was still only a deacon, returned in triumph to Alexandria, and soon afterwards
became Patriarch here. But his troubles were only beginning. Constantine, still obsessed with hopes of toleration, asked him to receive Arius back. He refused,
and was banished himself.

He was banished five times in all—once by the orthodox Constantine (335), twice by the Arian Constantius (338 and 356), once by the pagan Julian (362),
and once, shortly before his death, by the Arian Valens.

Sometimes he hid in the Libyan desert, sometimes he escaped to Rome or Palestine and made Christendom ring with his grievances. Twice he came near to death in church—once in the Caesareum where he marched processionally out of one door as the enemy came in at the other, and once in St. Theonas at night, where he escaped from the altar just before the Arian soldiers attacked him there. He always returned, and he had the supreme joy of outliving Arius, who fell down dead one evening, while walking through Alexandria with a friend. To us, living in a secular age, such triumphs appear remote, and it seems better to die young, like Alexander the Great, than to drag out this arid theological Odyssey. But Athanasius has the immortality that he would have desired. Owing to his efforts the Church has accepted as final his opinion on the nature of Christ, and, duly grateful, has recognised him as a doctor and canonised him as a saint. In Alexandria a large church was built to commemorate his name. It stood on the north side of the Canopic Street; the Attarine Mosque occupies part of its site to-day.

St. Mark's: p. 178.
St. Theonas': p. 184.
Council of Nicaea, picture of: p. 114.
Nicene Creed: original text containing Clause against Arius: Appendix p. 236.
Caesareum: p. 175.
Attarine Mosque (Church of St. Athanasius): p. 155.

THE RULE OF THE MONKS
(4th and 5th Cents.)

Theophilus.
Cyril.
Dioscurus.

After the exploits of Athanasius the Patriarchate of Alexandria became very powerful. In theory Egypt belonged to the Emperor, who sent a Prefect and a garrison from Constantinople; in practise it was ruled by the Patriarch and his army of monks. The monks had not been important so long as each lived alone, but by the 4th cent. they had gathered into formidable communities, whence they would occasionally make raids on civilisation like the Bedouins to-day. One of these communities was only nine miles from Alexandria (the "Ennaton"), others lay further west, in the Mariout desert; of those in the Wady Natrun, remnants still survive. The monks had some knowledge of theology and of decorative craft, but they were averse to culture and incapable of thought. Their heroes were St. Ammon who deserted his wife on their wedding eve, or St. Antony, who thought bathing sinful and was consequently carried across the canals of the delta by an angel. From the ranks of such men the Patriarchs were recruited.

Christianity, which had been made official at the beginning of the 4th century, was made compulsory towards its close, and this gave the monks the opportunity of attacking the worship of Serapis. Much had now taken refuge in that ancient Ptolemaic shrine—philosophy, magic, learning, licentiousness. The Patriarch Theophilus led the attack. The Serapis temple at Canopus (Aboukir) fell in 389, the parent temple at Alexandria two years later; great was the fall of the latter, for it involved the destruction of the Library whose books had been stored in the cloisters surrounding the buildings; a monastery was installed on the site. The persecution of the pagans continued, and culminated in the murder of Hypatia (415). The achievements of Hypatia, like her youthfulness, have been exaggerated; she was a middle-aged lady who taught mathematics at the Mouseion and though she was a

philosopher too we have no record of her doctrines.
The monks were now supreme, and one of them had
murdered the Imperial Prefect, and had been canonised for the deed by the Patriarch Cyril. Cyril's wild
black army filled the streets, "human only in their
faces," and anxious to perform some crowning piety
before they retired to their monasteries. In this mood
they encountered Hypatia who was driving from a lecture (probably along the course of the present Rue
Nebi Daniel), dragged her from the carriage to the
Caesareum, and there tore her to pieces with tiles. She
is not a great figure. But with her the Greece that is a
spirit expired—the Greece that tried to discover truth
and create beauty and that had created Alexandria.

The monks however, have another aspect. They
were the nucleus of a national movement. Nationality
did not exist in the modern sense—it was a religious
not a patriotic age. But under the cloak of religion racial passions could shelter, and the monks killed Hypatia not only because they knew she was sinful but also
because they thought she was foreign. They were anti-
Greek, and later on they and their lay adherents were
given the name of Copts. "Copt" means "Egyptian."
The language of the Copts was derived from the ancient Egyptian, their script was Greek, with the addition of six letters adapted from the hieroglyphs. The
new movement permeated the whole country, even
cosmopolitan Alexandria, and as soon as it found a theological formula in which to express itself, a revolt
against Constantinople broke out.

That formula is known as "Monophysism." Its theological import—it concerns the Nature of Christ—is discussed below (p. 81); here we are concerned with its
outward effects. The Patriarch Dioscurus, successor
and nephew to Cyril, is the first Monophysite hero and

the real founder of the Coptic Church. The Emperor
took up a high and mighty line, and at the Council of
Chalcedon near Constantinople Dioscurus was exiled
and his doctrines condemned (451). From that moment no Greek was safe in Egypt. The racial trouble,
which had been averted by the Ptolemies, broke out
at last and has not even died down to-day. Before long
Alexandria was saddled with two Patriarchs. There
was (i) The Orthodox or "Royal" Patriarch, who upheld the decrees of Chalcedon. He was appointed by
the Emperor and had most of the Church revenues.
But he had no spiritual authority over the Egyptians;
to them he was an odious Greek official, disguised as a
priest. (ii) The Monophysite or Coptic Patriarch, who
opposed Chalcedon—a regular Egyptian monk, poor,
bigoted and popular. Each of these Patriarchs claimed
to represent St. Mark and the only true church; each
of them is represented by a Patriarch in Alexandria to-
day. Now and then an Emperor tried to heal the
schism, and made concessions to the Egyptian faith.
But the schism was racial, the concessions theological,
so nothing was effected. Egypt was only held for the
Empire by Greek garrisons, and consequently when
the Arabs came they conquered her at once.

TOMBSTONES FROM THE ENNATON: Museum, Room 1.
WADY NATRUN: p. 216.
TEMPLE OF SERAPIS AT CANOPUS: p. 190.
TEMPLE OF SERAPIS AT ALEXANDRIA: p. 157.
CAESAREUM: p. 175.
ORTHODOX AND COPTIC PATRIARCHATES: pp. 227, 228.
PORTRAIT OF DIOSCURUS: p. 223.

THE ARAB CONQUEST (641)

We are now approaching the catastrophe. Its details though dramatic are confusing. It took place during the reign of the Emperor Heraclius, and we must begin by glancing at his curious career.

Heraclius was an able and sensitive man—very sensitive, very much in the grip of his own moods. Sometimes he appears as a hero, a great administrator; sometimes as an apathetic recluse. He won his empire (610) by the sword; then the reaction came and he allowed the Persians to occupy Syria and Egypt almost without striking a blow. Alexandria fell by treachery. She was safe on the seaward side, for the Persians had no fleet, and her immense walls made her impregnable by land; their army (which was encamped near Mex) could burn monasteries but do nothing more. But a foreign student—Peter was his name—got into touch with them and revealed the secrets of her topography. A canal ran through her from the Western Harbour, rather to the north of the present (Mahmoudieh) canal, and it passed, by a bridge, under the Canopic Way (present Rue Sidi Metwalli). The harbour end of the canal was unguarded, and a few Persians, at Peter's advice, disguised themselves as fishermen and rowed in; then walked westward down the Canopic Way and unbarred the Gate of the Moon to the main army (617). Their rule was not cruel; though sun-worshippers, they persecuted neither orthodox Christians nor Copts. For five years Heraclius did nothing; then shook off his torpor and performed miracles. Marching against the armies of the Persians in Asia, he defeated them and recovered the relic of the True Cross, which they had taken from Jerusalem. Alexandria and Egypt were freed, and at the festival of the Exaltation of the Cross—his coins comemmorate it—the Emperor appeared as the champion of Christendom and the greatest ruler in the world. It is unlikely that in the hour of his triumph he paid any attention to the envoys of an obscure Arab Sheikh named Mohammed, who came to congratulate him on his victory and to suggest that he should adopt a new religion called "Peace" or "Islam." But he is said to have dismissed them politely. The same Sheikh also sent envoys to the Imperial Viceroy at Alexandria. He too was polite and sent back a present that included an ass, a mule, a bag of money, some butter and honey, and two Coptic maidens. One of the latter, Mary, became the Sheikh's favourite concubine. Amidst such amenities did our intercourse with Mohammedanism begin.

Heraclius, now at the height of his power and with a mind now vigorous, turned next to the religious problem. He desired that his empire should be spiritually as it was physically one, and in particular that the feud in Egypt should cease. He was not a bigot. He believed in tolerance, and sought a formula that should satisfy both orthodox and Copts—both the supporters and the opponents of the Council of Chalcedon. A disastrous search. He had better have let well alone. The formula that he found—Monothelism—was so obscure that no one could understand it, and the man whom he chose as its exponent was a cynical bully, who did not even wish that it should be understood. This man was Cyrus, sometimes called the Mukaukas, the evil genius of Egypt and of Alexandria. Cyrus was made both Patriarch and Imperial Viceroy. He landed in 631, made no attempt to conciliate or even to explain, persecuted the Copts, tried to kill the Coptic Patriarch and at the end of ten years' rule had ripened Egypt for its fall. There was a Greek garrison in Alexandria and another to the south of the present Cairo in a fort called "Babylon." And there were some other forces in the Delta and the fleet held the sea. But the mass of the people were hostile. Heraclius ruled by violence, though he did not realise it; the reports that Cyrus sent him never told the truth. Indeed, he paid little attention to them; he was paralysed by a new terror: Mohammedanism. His nerve failed him again, as at the Persian invasion. Syria and the Holy Places were again lost to the Empire, this time for ever. Broken in health and spirits, the Emperor slunk back to Constantinople, and there, shortly before he died, Cyrus arrived with the news that Egypt had been lost too.

What happened was this. The Arab general Amr had invaded Egypt with an army of 4,000 horse. Amr was not only a great general. He was an administrator, a delightful companion, and a poet—one of the ablest and most charming men that Islam ever produced. He would have been remarkable in any age; he is all the more remarkable in an age that was petrified by theology. Riding into Egypt by the coast where Port Said stands now, he struck swiftly up the Nile, defeated an Imperial army at Heliopolis and invested the fort of Babylon. Cyrus was inside it. His character, like the Emperor's, had collapsed. He knew that no native Egyptian would resist the Arabs, and he may have felt, like many of his contemporaries, that Christianity was doomed, that its complexities were destined to perish before the simplicity of Islam. He negotiated a peace, which the Emperor was to ratify. Heraclius was furious and recalled him to Constantinople. But the mischief had been done; all Egypt, with the exception of Alexandria, had been abandoned to the heathen.

Alexandria was surely safe. In the first place the Arabs had no ships, and Amr, for all his courage, was not the man to build one. "If a ship lies still," he writes, "it rends the heart; if it moves it terrifies the imagination. Upon it a man's power ever diminishes and calamity increases. Those within it are like worms in a log, and if it rolls over they are drowned." Alexandria had nothing to fear on the seaward side from such a foe and on the landward what could he do against her superb walls, defended by all the appliances of military science? Amr, though powerful, had no artillery. His was purely a cavalry force. And there was no great alarm when, from the southeast, the force was seen approaching and encamping somewhere beyond the present Nouzha Gardens. Moreover the Patriarch Cyrus was back, and had held a great service in the Caesareum and exhorted the Christians to arms. Indeed it is not easy to see why Alexandria did fall. There was no physical reason for it. One is almost driven to say that she fell because she had no soul. Cyrus, for the second time, betrayed his trust. He negotiated again with the Arabs, as at Babylon, and signed (Nov. 8th, 641) an armistice with them, during which the Imperial garrison evacuated the town. Amr did not make hard terms; cruelty was neither congenial to him nor politic. Those inhabitants who wished to leave might do so; the rest might worship as they wished on payment of tribute.

The following year Amr entered in triumph through the Gate of the Sun that closed the eastern end of the Canopic Way. Little had been ruined so far. Colonnades of marble stretched before him, the Tomb of Alexander rose to his left, the Pharos to his right. His sensitive and generous soul may have been moved, but the message he sent to the Caliph in Arabia is sufficiently prosaic. "I have taken," he writes, "a city of which I can only say that it contains 4,000 palaces, 4,000 baths, 400 theatres, 1,200 greengrocers and 40,-

ooo Jews." And the Caliph received the news with equal calm, merely rewarding the messenger with a meal of bread and oil and a few dates. There was nothing studied in this indifference. The Arabs could not realise the value of their prize. They knew that Allah had given them a large and strong city. They could not know that there was no other like it in the world, that the science of Greece had planned it, that it had been the intellectual birthplace of Christianity. Legends of a dim Alexander, a dimmer Cleopatra, might move in their minds, but they had not the historical sense, they could never realise what had happened on this spot nor how inevitably the city of the double harbour should have arisen between the lake and the sea. And so though they had no intention of destroying her, they destroyed her, as a child might a watch. She never functioned again for over 1,000 years.†

One or two details are necessary, to complete this sketch of the conquest. It had been a humane affair, and no damage had been done to property; the Library which the Arabs are usually accused of destroying had already been destroyed by the Christians. A few years later, however, some damage was done. Supported by an Imperial fleet, the city revolted, and Amr was obliged to re-enter it by force. There was a massacre, which he stayed by sheathing his sword; the Mosque of Amr or of Mercy was built upon the site. As governor of Egypt, he administered it well, but his interests lay inland not on the odious sea shore, and he founded a city close to the fort of Babylon—Fostat, the germ of the modern Cairo. Here all the life of the future was to centre. Here Amr himself was to die. As he lay on his couch a friend said to him: "You have often remarked that you would like to find an intelligent man at the point of death, and to ask him what his feelings were. Now I ask *you* that question." Amr replied, "I feel as if the heaven lay close upon the earth and I between the two, breathing through the eye of a needle."† There is something in this dialogue that transports us into a new world; it could never have taken place between two Alexandrians.

CoIN OF HERACLIUS, SHOWING CROSS: Museum, Room 4.
ROSETTA GATE (Gate of the Sun): p. 132.
MOSQUE OF AMR: p. 157.

Such were the chief physical events in the city during the Christian Period. We must now turn back to consider another and more important aspect: the spiritual.

SECTION III

The Spiritual City

INTRODUCTION

When Cleopatra died and Egypt became part of the Roman Empire, it seemed that the career of Alexandria was over. Her life had centred round the Ptolemies who had adorned her with architecture and scholarship and song, and when they were withdrawn what remained? She was just a provincial capital. But the vitality of a city is not thus measured. There is a splendour that kings do not give and cannot take away, and just when she lost her outward independence she was recompensed by discovering the kingdom that lies within. Three sections of her citizens—Jews, Greeks and Christians—were attracted by the same spiritual problem, and tried to solve it in the same way.

The Problem. It never occurred to these Alexandrian thinkers, as it had to some of their predecessors in ancient Greece, that God might not exist. They assumed that he existed. What troubled them was his relation to the rest of the universe and particularly to man. Was God close to man? Or was he far away? If close, how could he be infinite and eternal and omnipotent? And if far away, how could he take any interest in man, why indeed should he have troubled to create him? They wanted God to be both far and close.

The Solution. Savages solve such a problem by

having two gods—a pocket fetich whom they beat
when he irritates them, and a remote spirit in the sky,
and they do not try to think out any connection between the two. The Alexandrians, being cultivated,
could not accept such crudities. Instead, they assumed
that between God and man there is an intermediate
being or beings, who draw the universe together, and
ensure that though God is far he shall also be close.
They gave various names to this intermediate being,
and ascribed to him varying degrees of dignity and
power. But they became as certain of his existence as
of God's, for in philosophy their temperament was mystic rather than scientific, and as soon as they hit on an
explanation of the universe that was comforting, they
did not stop to consider whether it might be true.

After this preliminary, let us approach the three
great sections of Alexandrian thought.

I. THE JEWS

THE SEPTUAGINT—about B.C. 200.
THE WISDOM OF SOLOMON—about B.C. 100.
PHILO—cont. with Christ.

The seat of the Jews was Jerusalem, where they had
evolved their cult of Jehovah and built him his unique
temple. But as soon as Alexandria was founded they
began to emigrate to the lucrative and seductive city,
and to take up their quarters near the modern Ibrahimieh. Soon a generation arose that was Greek in
speech. The Hebrew Scriptures had to be translated
for their benefit, and seventy rabbis—so the legend
goes—were shut up by Ptolemy Philadelphus in seventy huts on the island of Pharos, whence they simul-

taneously emerged with seventy identical translations of the Bible. This was the famous Septuagint version —made as a matter of fact over many years, and not completed till B.C. 130.

But the new generation was Greek in spirit as well as speech, and diverged increasingly from the conservative Jews at Jerusalem. Both sections worshipped Jehovah, but the Alexandrian grew more and more conscious of the churlishness and inaccessibility of his national god. Thought mingled with his adoration. How could he link Jehovah to man? And, utilising a few hints in the orthodox scriptures, he produced as his first attempt a fine piece of literature called "The Wisdom of Solomon"; it is at present included in the Apocrypha. The author—his name is unknown—not only wrote in Greek but had studied Stoic and Epicurean Philosophy and Egyptian rites. He had the cosmopolitan culture of Alexandria. And, solving his problem in the Alexandrian way, he conceived an intermediate between Jehovah and man whom he calls Sophia or Wisdom.

> Wisdom is more moving than any motion: she goeth through all things by reason of her pureness. Being but one she can do all things and in all ages entering into holy souls she makes them friends of God, and prophets. She is more beautiful than the sun and all the order of stars: being compared with the light she is found beyond it. For after this cometh night, but vice shall not prevail against wisdom.

In such a passage Wisdom is more than "being wise." She is a messenger who bridges the gulf and makes us friends of God.

In Philo the Jewish school of Alexandria reaches its height. Little is known of his life. His brother was head

of the Jewish community here and he himself was sent
(A.D. 40) on a disastrous embassy to the mad Emperor
Caligula at Rome.

Being an orthodox Jew, he states his philosophic
problem in the language of the Old Testament. Thus:—

Jehovah had said I AM THAT I AM—that is to say,
nothing can be predicated about God except existence.
God has no qualities, no desires, no form, and no home.
We cannot even call God "God" because "God" is a
word, and no word can describe God. While to regard
him as a man is to commit "an error greater than the
sea." GOD IS, and no more can be said of him.

Yet this unapproachable being has created us. How?
And why?

Through his Logos or Word. This Logos of Philo is,
like "Wisdom," a messenger who bridges the gulf. He
is the outward expression of God's existence. He created and he sustains the world, and Philo uses the actual language of devotion concerning him, calling him
Israel the Seer, the Dove, the Dweller in the Inmost,
—language which naturally recalls and possibly suggested the opening of St. John's Gospel. "In the beginning was the Word, and the Word was with God."
Philo might have written this. But he could not have
written "the Word was God" nor "the Word was made
flesh" for it was, as we shall see, the distinction of
Christianity to conceive that the link between man
and God should be himself both God and man.

By this doctrine of the Logos, Philo made the Hebrew Jehovah intelligible and acceptable to the Alexandrian Jews. It is a doctrine not found in the Old Testament, and to extract it he had to employ allegory and
to wrest words from their natural meanings. This gives
his philosophy a frigid timid air, and obscures its real
sublimity. Only once or twice does he break loose, and
declare that the path to truth lies not through alle-

gory but through vision. "Those who can see" he exclaims, "lift their eyes to heavens, and contemplate the Manna, the divine Logos. Those who cannot see, look at the onions in the ground." After his death, the Jews of Alexandria accomplished no more in philosophy. They had stated the problem. The restatement was for the Greeks and the Christians.

JEWISH INSCRIPTIONS FROM IBRAHIMIEH: Museum, Room 21.

II.   NEO-PLATONISM

PLOTINUS (204–262).
PORPHYRY (233–306).
HYPATIA (d. 415).

The Ptolemies had imported some Greek philosophers, as part of the personnel of the Mouseion, but they were second-rate, and it was not until the Ptolemies had passed away, and the city herself was declining, that philosophy took root and bore the white mystic rose of Neo-Platonism. It developed out of a doctrine of Plato's. Six hundred years before, Plato had taught at Athens that the world we live in is an imperfect copy of an ideal world. He had also taught other things, but this was the doctrine that the "New Platonists" of Alexandria took up and pursued to sublime and mystic conclusions. Whatever Plato had thought of this world as a philosopher, he had enjoyed it as a citizen and a poet, and has left delightful accounts of it in his dialogues. The Neo-Platonists were more logical. Since this world is imperfect, they regarded it as negligible, and excluded from their writings all references to daily life. They might be disembodied spirits, freed from locality and time, and it is only after careful study that we realise that they too were human,—nay, that they were typically Alexandrian, and that in them the later city finds her highest expression.

The School was founded by Ammonius Saccas, who had begun life as a porter in the docks, and as a Christian, but abandoned both professions for the study of Plato. Nothing is known of his teaching, but he produced great pupils—Longinus, Origen, and, greatest of all, Plotinus. Plotinus was probably born at Assiout; probably; no one could find out for certain because he was reticent about it, saying that the descent of his soul into his body had been a great misfortune, which he did not desire to discuss. He completed his main training at Alexandria, and then took part in a military expedition against Persia, in order to get into touch with Persian thought (Zoroastrianism), and with Indian thought (Hinduism, Buddhism). He must have made a queer soldier and he was certainly an unsuccessful one, for the expedition suffered defeat, and Plotinus was very nearly relieved of the disgrace of having a body. Escaping, he made his way to Rome, and remained there until the end of his life, lecturing. In spite of his sincerity, he became fashionable, and the psychic powers that he had acquired not only gained him, on four occasions, the Mystic Vision which was the goal of his philosophy, but also discovered a necklace which had been stolen from a rich lady by one of her slaves. He was indifferent to literary composition; after his death his pupil Porphyry collected his lecture-notes and published them in nine volumes—the "Enneads." The Enneads are ill arranged and often obscure. But they contain a logical system of thought, some account of which must be attempted—Alexandria produced nothing greater. And they deal with the usual Alexandrian problem—the linking up of God and man.

Like Philo, and like the Christians, Plotinus believes in God, and since his God has three grades, we may almost say that he believes in a Trinity. But it is very different to the Christian Trinity, and even more difficult to understand. The first and highest grade in it he calls the One. The One is—Unity, the One. Nothing else can be predicated about it, not even that it exists; it is more incomprehensible than the Jehovah of Philo; it has no qualities, no creative force, it is good only as the goal of our aspirations. But though it cannot create, it overflows (somewhat like a fountain), and from its overflow or emanation is generated the second grade of the Trinity—the "Intellectual Principle." The Intellectual Principle is a little easier to understand than the "One" because it has a remote connection with our lives. It is the Universal mind that contains—not all things, but all thoughts of things, and by thinking it creates. It thinks of the third grade—the All Soul—which accordingly comes into being. With the All Soul we near the realm of the comprehensible. It is the cause of the Universe that we know. All that we grasp through the senses was created by it—the Gods of Greece, etc., in the first place, then the demi-gods and demons, then, descending in the scale, ourselves, then animals, plants, stones; matter, that seems so important to us, is really the last and feeblest emanation of the All Soul, the point at which creative power comes to a halt.—And these three grades, the "One," the "Intellectual Principle," and the "All Soul," make up between them a single being, GOD; who is three in one and one in three, and the goal of all creation.

Thus far the system of Plotinus may appear unattrac-

tive as well as abstruse; we must now look at the other
and more emotional side. Not only do all things flow
from God; they also strive to return to him; in other
words, the whole Universe has an inclination towards
good. We are all parts of God, even the stones, though
we cannot realise it; and man's goal is to become actually, as he is potentially, divine. Therefore rebirth is
permitted, in order that we may realise God better in
a future existence than we can in this; and therefore
the Mystic Vision is permitted, in order that, even in
this existence we may have a glimpse of God. God is
ourself, our true self, and in one of the few literary passages in the Enneads, the style of Plotinus catches fire
from his thought and we are taught in words of immortal eloquence, how the Vision may be obtained.

But what must we do? How lies the path? How come
to vision of the inaccessible Beauty, dwelling as if in consecrated precincts, apart from the common ways where
all men may see?

"Let us flee to the beloved Fatherland." This is the
soundest counsel. But what is the flight? How are we to
gain the open sea?

The Fatherland is There whence we have come, and
There is the Father.

What then is our course, what the manner of our
flight? This is not a journey for the feet; the feet bring
us only from land to land; all this order of things you
must set aside and refuse to see; you must close the eyes
and call instead upon another vision which is to be
waked within you, a vision the birth-right of all, which
few can see. . . . .

Withdraw into yourself and look. And if you do not
find yourself beautiful yet, act as does the creator of a
statue that is to be made beautiful; he cuts away here,
he smooths there, he makes this line lighter, that purer,
until a lovely face has grown upon his work.

When you know that you have become this perfect

work, when you are self-gathered in the purity of your being, nothing now remaining that can shatter that inner unity—when you perceive that you have grown to this, you are now become very vision; now call up all your confidence, strike forward yet a step—you need a guide no longer—forward yet a step—you need a guide no longer —strain and see.

This is the only eye that sees the mighty Beauty. If the eye that ventures the vision be dimmed by vice, impure or weak, then it sees nothing even though another point to what lies plain before it. To any vision must be brought an eye adapted to what is to be seen, and having some resemblance to it. Never did eye see the sun unless it had first become sunlike, and never can the soul have vision of the first Beauty unless itself be beautiful.*

This sublime passage suggests three comments, with which our glance at Plotinus must close. In the first place its tone is religious, and in this it is typical of all Alexandrian philosophy. In the second place it lays stress on behaviour and training; the Supreme Vision cannot be acquired by magic tricks—only those will see it who are fit to see. And in the third place the vision of oneself and the vision of God are really the same, because each individual *is* God, if only he knew it. And here is the great difference between Plotinus and Christianity. The Christian promise is that a man shall see God, the Neo-Platonic—like the Indian—that he shall be God. Perhaps, on the quays of Alexandria, Plotinus talked with Hindu merchants who came to the town. At all events his system can be paralleled in the religious writings of India. He comes nearer than any other Greek philosopher to the thought of the East.

Porphyry, the pious disciple of Plotinus, was himself a philosopher of note, and the Neo-Platonic School

* S. McKenna's Translation.

continued to flourish all through the 4th cent. Its main temper kept the same; it was pessimistic as regards the actual world and actual men, but optimistic as regards the future because it believed that the world and all in it has emanated from God and has been granted the means of reverting to him. It recognised the presence of Evil but not its eternal existence, and consequently it was a practical support to its believers, and upheld the last of them, Hypatia, through martyrdom.

> When I do contemplate your words and you
> revered Hypatia, then I kneel to view
> the Virgin's starry home; there in the skies
> your works and perfect words I recognise,
> a star unsullied of instruction wise.*

Thus wrote an unknown admirer at the beginning of the 5th century. None of Hypatia's discourses have been preserved, but we know that with her and with her father, Theon, the great tradition of Plotinus expired at Alexandria.

III. CHRISTIANITY

INTRODUCTION

Percolating through the Jewish Communities, the Christian religion reached Egypt as early as the 1st cent. A.D. On its arrival, it found, already established there, two distinct forms of spiritual life.

The first was the spiritual life of Ancient Egypt, which had clung to the soil of the Nile valley for over 4,000 years. It had existed so long that though Chris-

* Translated by R. A. Furness.

tianity could close its temples she never quite up-
rooted it from the heart of the people. The resurrection
of Osiris as Sun God; the partaking of him as Corn God
by the blessed in the world below; the beneficent
group of the mother Isis with Horus her child; the same
Horus as a young warrior slaying the snaky Set; the
key-shaped "ankh" that the gods and goddesses carried
as a sign of their immortality:—these symbols had sunk
too deeply into the minds of the native Egyptians to
be removed by episcopal decrees. Consequently there
were cases of reversion—e.g. at Menouthis (near Aboukir) in 480, when some villagers were discovered
worshipping the ancient deities in a private house. And
there were also cases of confusion, where the old religion passed imperceptibly into the new. Did Christianity borrow from the Osiris cult her doctrines of the
Resurrection and Personal Immortality, and her sacrament of the Eucharist? The suggestion has been made.
It is more certain that she borrowed much of her sym-
bolism and popular art. Isis and Horus become the
Virgin and Child, Horus and Set St. George and the
Dragon, while the "ankh" appears unaltered on some
of the Christian tombstones as a looped cross, and
slightly altered on others as a cross with a handle.

The second form of spiritual life was the life of Alexandria. Its quality (mainly Hellenic and philosophic)
has already been indicated. Christianity, to begin with
was not philosophic, being addressed to poor and
unfashionable people in Palestine. But as soon as it
reached Alexandria its character altered, the turning
point in its worldly career arrived. The Alexandrians
were highly cultivated, they had libraries where all the
wisdom of the Mediterranean was accessible, and their
faith inevitably took a philosophic form. Occupied by
their favourite problem of the relation between God
and man, they at once asked the same question of the

new religion as they asked the Jews and the Greeks—
namely, What is the link? Philo said the Logos, Plotinus
the Emanations. The new religion replied "Christ."
There was nothing startling to the Alexandrians in such
a reply. Christ too was the Word, he too proceeded
from the Father. His incarnation, his redemption
of mankind through suffering—even these were not
strange ideas to people who were accustomed to "divine" kings, and familiar with the myths of Prometheus
and Adonis. Alexandrian orthodoxy, Alexandrian heresies, both centred round the problem that was familiar to Alexandrian paganism—the relation between
God and man.

Thus Christianity did not burst upon Egypt or upon
Alexandria like a clap of thunder, but stole into ears
already prepared. Neither on her popular nor on her
philosophic side was she a creed apart. Only politically
did she stand out as an innovator, through her denial of
divinity to the Imperial Government at Rome.

ANKH: Museum, Room 8.
EARLY CHRISTIAN CROSSES: Museum, Room 1.
ISIS AND HORUS: Museum, Room 10.
MENOUTHIS: p. 197.

(1).   GNOSTICISM (Esoteric knowledge)

CERINTHUS—About 100 A.D.
BASILIDES—120.
VALENTINUS—140.

Gnosticism taught that the world and mankind are
the result of an unfortunate blunder. God neither created us nor wished us to be created. We are the work
of an inferior deity, the Demiurge, who wrongly be-

lieves himself God, and we are doomed to decay. But
God, though not responsible for our existence, took
pity on it, and has sent his Christ to counteract the
ignorance of the Demiurge and to give us Gnosis
(knowledge). Christ is the link between the divine
and that unfortunate mistake the human.

The individual Gnostics played round this idea. Cerinthus (educated here) taught that Jesus was a man,
and Christ a spirit who left him at death. Basilides (a
Syrian visitor) that there were three dispensations,
pre-Jewish, Jewish, and Christian, each of whose rulers
had a son, which son comprehended more of God than
did his father. The Ophites worshipped snakes because
the serpent in Eden was really a messenger from God,
who induced Eve to disobey the Demiurge Jehovah.
Consequently if we wish to be good we must be bad
—a conclusion that was also reached, though by a different route, by Carpocrates, who organised an Abode
of Love on one of the Greek islands. These are unsa-
voury charlatans. But one of the Gnostics—Valentinus
—was a man of another stamp, and his system has a
tragic quality most rare in Alexandria.

Valentinus (probably an Egyptian; educated here;
taught mainly at Rome) held the usual Gnostic doctrine that creation is a mistake. But he tried to explain
how the mistake came about. He imagines a primal
God, the centre of a divine harmony, who sent out
manifestations of himself in pairs of male and female.
Each pair was inferior to its predecessor, and Sophia
("wisdom") the female of the thirtieth pair, least perfect of all. She showed her imperfection not, like Lucifer, by rebelling from God, but by desiring too ardently
to be united to him. She fell through love.† Hurled from
the divine harmony, she fell into matter, and the universe is formed out of her agony and remorse. She herself was rescued by the first Christ but not before she

had borne a son, the Demiurge, who rules this world of sadness and confusion, and is incapable of realising anything beyond it. In this world there are three classes of men, all outwardly the same, men of the Body, the Spirit, and the Soul. The first two belong to the Demiurge and ought to obey him. The third are really the elect of his mother Sophia. He rules them but cannot make them obey. It was for their salvation that the Christ whom we call Jesus descended straight from the primal God and left with his twelve disciples the secret tradition of the Gnosis.

With Valentinus the Gnosticism of Alexandria reaches its height. Further east it took other forms. It had spread by 150 A.D. all round the Mediterranean, and threatened to defeat orthodox Christianity. But it was pessimistic, imaginative, esoteric—three great obstacles to success. It was not a creed any society could adopt, being anti-social, and by the time of Constantine its vogue was over.

GNOSTIC AMULETS: Museum, Room 17.

(II). ORTHODOXY (Early)

CLEMENT OF ALEXANDRIA—about 200.
ORIGEN—185–253.

Orthodoxy at Alexandria did not begin on clear-cut lines; indeed the more we look at it the more it melts into its surroundings. It adapted from Philo his doctrine of the Logos, and identified the Logos with Christ. It shared with Gnosticism the desire for knowledge of God, while declaring that such knowledge need not be esoteric. It has its special Gospel—St. Mark's—but other Gospels, since condemned as uncanonical, were equally read in its churches, e.g. the Gospels of the

Hebrews and of the Egyptians. It was permeated by Greek thought—Neo-Platonists became Christians, and vice versa. But one distinguishing doctrine it did have —the supreme value of Christ. Christ was the "Word" incarnate, through whom the love and power of God could alone be "known." Problems as to Christ's nature did not trouble the earlier theologians. Their impulse was to testify, not to analyse. A feeling of joy inspires their interminable writings, and it is possible to detect through their circumlocution the faith that steeled the martyrs, their contemporaries.

Clement of Alexandria (probably a Greek from Athens) was head of the big Theological College here. His problem, like that of the Jews before him, was to recommend his religion to a subtle and philosophic city, and his methods forestall those of the advanced missionary to-day. He does not denounce Greek philosophy. His line is that it is a preparation for the Gospel, that the Jewish law was also a preparation, and that all that happened before the birth of Christ is indeed a divine approach to that supreme event. Learned and enlightened, he set Christianity upon a path that she did not long consent to follow. He raised her from intellectual obscurity, he lent her for a little Hellenic persuasion, and the graciousness of Greece seems in his pages not incompatible with the Grace of God.

> He is the greatest in the Kingdom of Heaven who shall do and teach in imitation of God by showing free Grace like His; for the bounties of God are for the common benefits.

Only in Alexandria could such a theologian have arisen.

His work was carried on by his pupil Origen, the strangest and most adventurous of the Early Fathers. Gentle and scholarly by nature, Origen had an instinct

for self-immolation that troubled his life and the lives
of his friends. He was an Egyptian (the name is connected with Horus), and he was born here of Christian
parents and tried as a boy to share his father's martyrdom at the Temple of Serapis. Calmed for a while, he
supported his mother and brothers, and was fellow pupil with Plotinus. Then he became head of the Theological College, and having attained fame as a teacher
and lay preacher, castrated himself (a "Eunuch for the
Kingdom of Heaven's sake."—Matt. xix, 12). His patron, the Bishop of Alexandria, disowned him for this,
and ruled that he could not now take orders; other
bishops declared that he could, and the Christian communities were divided by the grotesque controversy.
Origen was considerate and even repentant; he had no
wish to cause scandal, and when ordered to leave Alexandria he obeyed. But his opinions ever verged towards the incorrect; he believed, like Plotinus, in pre-
existence, he disbelieved in the eternity of punishment,
and it is with the greatest hesitation that orthodoxy has
received him to her bosom. In the main he developed
the theory of his master Clement—that Christianity is
the heir of the past and the interpreter of the future,
—and he taught that Christ has been with mankind not
only at his incarnation but since the beginning of creation, and has in all ages linked them, according to their
capacity, with God.

Thus the characteristic of early orthodoxy was a belief in Christ as the link between God and man. A hu-
manising belief; the work of the Greek scholars who
had subtilised and universalised the simpler faith of
Palestine, and had imparted into it doctrines taught by
Paganism. We must now watch it harden and trans-
form. Several causes transformed it—*e.g.* the growth
of an ignorant monasticism in Egypt, the growth in

Northern Africa, of a gloomier type of Christianity under Tertullian, and the general spirit of aggression the
new religion everywhere displayed as soon as Constantine labelled it as official. But there was one cause that
was inherent in the belief itself, and that alone concerns us here. Christ was the Son of God. All agreed.
But what was the *Nature* of Christ? The subtle Alexandrian intellect asked this question about the year
300, and the Arian heresy was the result. It asked it
again about 400 and produced the Monophysite heresy. And a third query about 600 produced a third heresy, the Monothelite. Let us glance at these three in
turn. Heresies to others, they were of course orthodox
in their own eyes. Each believed itself the only interpreter of the link that binds God to man.

UNCANONICAL GOSPELS: Appendix p. 235.

(III). ARIANISM

Christ is the Son of God. Then is he not younger
than God? Arius held that he was and that there was
a period before time began when the First Person of
the Trinity existed and the Second did not. A typical
Alexandrian theologian, occupied with the favourite
problem of linking human and divine, Arius thought
to solve the problem by making the link predominately
human. He did not deny the Godhead of Christ, but
he did make him inferior to the Father—of *like* substance, not of the *same* substance, which was the view
held by Athanasius, and stamped as orthodox by the
Council of Nicaea. Moreover the Arian Christ, like the
Gnostic Demiurge, made the world;—creation, an inferior activity, being entrusted to him by the Father,
who had Himself created nothing but Christ.

It is easy to see why Arianism became popular. By

making Christ younger and lower than God it brought him nearer to us—indeed it tended to level him into a mere good man and to forestall Unitarianism. It appealed to the untheologically minded, to emperors and even more to empresses. But St. Athanasius, who viewed the innovation with an expert eye, saw that while it popularised Christ it isolated God, and he fought it with vigour and venom. His success has been described (p. 52). It was condemned as heretical in 325, and by the end of the century had been expelled from orthodox Christendom. Of the theatre of this ancient strife no trace remains at Alexandria; the church of St. Mark where Arius was presbyter has vanished: so have the churches where Athanasius thundered—St. Theonas and the Caesareum. Nor do we know in which street Arius died of epilepsy. But the strife still continues in the hearts of men, who always tend to magnify the human in the divine, and it is probable that many an individual Christian to-day is an Arian without knowing it.

NICENE CREED (original text): Appendix p. 236.
PICTURE OF. COUNCIL OF NICAEA: p. 114.

(IV). MONOPHYSISM ("Single Nature")

Christ is the Son of God, but also the Son of Mary. Then has he two natures or one? The Monophysites said "One." They did not deny Christ's incarnation, but they asserted that the divine in him had quite absorbed the human. The question was first raised in clerical circles in Constantinople, but Alexandria took it up hotly, and "Single Nature" became the national cry of Egypt. We have already seen (p. 56) the political importance of this heresy, how it was connected with a racial movement against the Greeks, how when it was condemned at Chalcedon (451) Egypt slipped into permanent mutiny against the Empire. The Council announced that Christ had two natures, unmixed and unchangeable but at the same time indistinguishable and inseparable. This is the orthodox view—the one we hold. The Copts (and Abyssinians) are still Monophysites, and consequently not in communion with the rest of Christendom.

COPTIC CHURCH: pp. 175, 229.

(v). MONOTHELISM ("Single Will")

As the minds of the Alexandrians decayed, their heresies became more and more technical. Arianism enshrines a real problem which the layman as well as the cleric can apprehend. Monophysism is more remote. And Monothelism is difficult to state in the language of theology, and almost impossible to state in the language of common sense. Perhaps it bears in it the signs of carelessness, for as we have seen (p. 59) it was the invention of the Emperor Heraclius in the last desperate days when he was trying to conciliate Egypt.

If Christ has one Nature he has of course one will. But suppose he has two Natures. How many wills has he then? The Monothelites said "One." The orthodox view—the one we hold—is "Two, one human the other divine, but both operating in unison." Obscure indeed is the problem, and we can well believe that the Alexandrians, against whom the Arabs were then marching, did not understand Monothelism when it was hurriedly explained to them by a preoccupied general. But it was not without a future. It failed as a compromise but survived as a heresy, and long after the Imperial Government had disowned it and Egypt had fallen to

Islam, it was cherished in the uplands of Syria by the Maronite Church.

MARONITE CHURCH: pp. 153, 229.

CONCLUSION: ISLAM

We have now seen Alexandria handle one after another the systems that entered her walls. The ancient religion of the Hebrews, the philosophy of Plato, the new faith out of Galilee—taking each in turn she has left her impress upon it, and extracted some answer to her question, "How can the human be linked to the divine?"

It may be argued that this question must be asked by all who have the religious sense, and that there is nothing specifically Alexandrian about it. But no; it need not be asked; it was never asked by Islam, by the faith that swept the city physically and spiritually into the sea. "There is no God but God, and Mohammed is the Prophet of God," says Islam, proclaiming the needlessness of a mediator; the man Mohammed has been chosen to tell us what God is like and what he wishes, and there all machinery ends, leaving us to face our Creator. We face him as a God of power, who may temper his justice with mercy, but who does not stoop to the weakness of Love, and we are well content that, being powerful, he shall be far away. That old dilemma, that God ought at the same time to be far away and close at hand, cannot occur to an orthodox Mohammedan. It occurs to those who require God to be loving as well as powerful, to Christianity and to its kindred growths, and it is the weakness and the strength of Alexandria to have solved it by the conception of a link. Her weakness: because she had always to be shifting the link up and down—if she got it too near God it was too far from man, and *vice versa*. Her strength: because she did cling to the idea of Love, and much philosophic absurdity, much theological aridity, must be pardoned to those who maintain that the best thing on earth is likely to be the best in heaven.

Islam, strong through its abjuration of Love, was the one system that the city could not handle. It gave no opening to her manipulations. Her logoi, her emanations and aeons, her various Christs, orthodox, Arian, Monophysite, or Monothelite—it threw them all down as unnecessary lumber that do but distract the true believer from his God. The physical decay that crept on her in the 7th century had its counterpart in a spiritual decay. Amr and his Arabs were not fanatics or barbarians and they were about to start near Cairo a new Egypt of their own. But they instinctively shrank from Alexandria; she seemed to them idolatrous and foolish; and a thousand years of silence succeeded them.

INSCRIPTION FROM KORAN (Terbana Mosque): p. 136.

SECTION IV

Arab Period

THE ARAB TOWN (7th–16th Cents.)

During the thousand years and more that intervene between the Arab conquest of Egypt and its conquest by Napoleon, the events in the history of Alexandria are geographic rather than political. Neglected by man, the land and the waters altered their positions, and could Alexander the Great have returned he would have failed to recognise the coast. (i) The fundamental change was in the 12th cent., when the Canopic mouth of the Nile silted up. Consequently the fresh water lake of Mariout, being no longer fed by the Nile floods, also silted and ceased to be navigable. Alexandria was cut off from the entire river system of Egypt, and could not flourish until it was restored; she has always required the double nourishment of fresh water and salt. (ii) There was also a change in the outline of the city: the dyke Heptastadion, built by the Ptolemies to connect the mainland with the island of Pharos, fell into ruin and became a backbone along which a broad spit of land accreted; and so Pharos turned from an island into a peninsula—the present Ras-el-Tin.

The Arabs, though they let the city fall out of repair, admired it greatly. One of them writes as follows:—

The city was all white and bright by night as well as by day. By reason of the walls and pavements of white marble the people used to wear black garments; it was the glare of the marble that made the monks wear black. So too it was painful to go out by night . . . . . . a tailor could see to thread his needle without a lamp. No one entered without a covering over his eyes.

A second writer describes the green silk awnings that were spread over the Canopic Way. A third, even more enthusiastic exclaims:—

> I have made the Pilgrimage to Mecca sixty times, but if Allah had suffered me to stay a month at Alexandria and pray on its shores, that month would be dearer to me.

The Arabs were anything but barbarians; their own great city of Cairo is a sufficient answer to that charge. But their civilisation was Oriental and of the land; it was out of touch with the Mediterranean civilisation that has evolved Alexandria. At first they made some effort to adapt it to their needs. The church of St. Theonas became part of the huge "Mosque of the 1,000 Columns"; the church of St. Athanasius also became a Mosque—the present Attarine Mosque occupies part of its site; and a third Mosque, that of the Prophet Daniel, rose on the Mausoleum of Alexander. But the Caesareum, the Mouseion, the Pharos, the Ptolemaic Palace, all became ruinous. So did the walls. And though the Arabs built new walls in 811, their course is so short that they vividly illustrate the decline of the town and of the population. (See map p. 106). They only enclosed a fragment of the ancient city.

In 828 the Venetians, according to their own account, stole from Alexandria the body of St. Mark, concealing it first in a tub of pickled pork in order to repel the attentions of the Moslem officials on the quay. The theft was a pardonable one, for the Arabs never seemed to know that it had been made; it occasioned much satisfaction in Venice and no inconvenience in Alex-

andria. St. Mark procured, there was little to attract
the European world; the ports of Egypt were now Rosetta (Bolbitine Mouth of the Nile), and Damietta
(Phatnitic Mouth); there was no reason to approach
Alexandria now that her water system had collapsed.
Towards the end of the Arab rule she did indeed re-
gain some slight importance; the Mameluke Sultan of
Cairo, Kait Bey, built on the ruins of the Pharos the
fine fort that bears his name (1480). He built it as a
defence against the growing naval power of the Turks.
The Turks conquered Egypt in 1517, and a new but
equally unimportant chapter in the history of Alexandria begins.

ST. THEONAS: p. 184.
ATTARINE MOSQUE: p. 155.
MOSQUE OF THE PROPHET DANIEL: p. 112.
FRAGMENT OF ARAB WALL: pp. 113, 170.
FORT KAIT BEY: p. 144.

THE TURKISH TOWN (16th–18th Cents.)

Under the Turks the population continued to shrink,
so that eventually the narrow enclosure of the Arab
walls became too large. A new settlement sprang up
on the neck of land that had formed between the two
harbours. It still exists and is known as the "Turkish
Town." A second-rate affair; little more than a strip of
houses intermixed with small mosques; a meagre copy
of Rosetta, where the architecture of these centuries
can best be studied. So unimportant a place can have
no connected history. All that one can do is to quote
the isolated comments of a few travellers. (i) The
English sailor, John Foxe, (1577) has a lively tale to

tell. He had been caught by the Turkish corsairs and imprisoned with his mates. With the connivance of a friendly Spaniard he organised a mutiny, recaptured his ship and in true British style worked it out of the Eastern Harbour under the fire of the guns on Kait Bey. (ii) John Sandys (1610) gives a quaint but impressive description of the decay:—

> Such was this Queen of Cities and Metropolis of Africa: who now hath nothing left her but ruins; and those ill witnesses of his perished beauties: declaring rather that towns as well as men have the ages and destinies . . . . . Sundry Mountains were raised of the ruins, by Christians not to be mounted; lest they should take too exact a survey of the city: in which are often found, (especially after a shower) rich stones and medals engraven with the figure of their Gods and men with such perfection of Art as these now cut seeme lame to those and unlively counterfeits.

(iii) Captain Norden, a Dane, (1757) was in an irritable mood, as the Turks would not let him sketch the fortifications. The English community was already in existence, and the Captain's account of it makes interesting if painful reading:—

> They keep themselves quiet and conduct themselves without making much noise. If any nice affair is to be undertaken they withdraw themselves from it and leave to the French the honour of removing all difficulties. When any benefits result from it they have their share and if affairs turn out ill they secure themselves in the best manner they can.

(iv) Another irritable visitor landed here in 1779— the lively but spiteful Mrs. Eliza Fay. Being a Christian, she was not allowed to disembark in the Western Harbour nor to ride any animal nobler than a donkey. She visited Cleopatra's Needles and "Pompey's Pillar,"

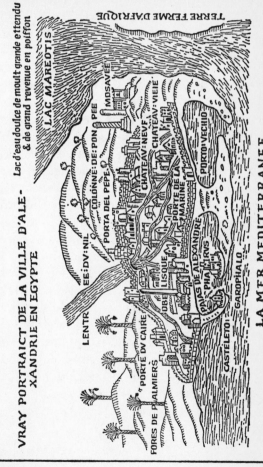

VRAY PORTRAICT DE LA VILLE D'ALE-
XANDRIE EN EGYPTE

Lac d'eau doulce de moult grande e'tendu
& de grand revenue en poisson

LAC MAREOTIS

TERRE FERME D'AFRIQUE

LENTR EE∶DV∶NIL

COLÖNNE∶DE∶PON∶PEE

MDSAVEE

PORTA DEL PEPE

CHATEAV∶NEVF

CHATEAV∶VIEIE

PORTE DE LA MARINE

PORTE DE ALEXANDRE

PHAL'IRVS

PORTO∶VECHIO

GAROPHIALO

OBELISQUE

PAIAS DE AL

CASTELETO∶

PORTE DV CAIRE

FORES DE PHALMIERS

LA MER MEDITERRANEE

Calque par E.Zaccar.
Calque par R.Palacios

Extrait des *Observations de plvsieurs singvlaritez etc.*
par Pierre Belon du Mans

Paris 1554

then writes to her sister, "I certainly deem myself very fortunate in quitting this place so soon." She makes no mention of the English community, but was entertained by the Prussian Consul, and has left an unflattering account of his stout wife.

There are some old maps, compiled from the accounts of travellers, but bearing little reference to reality. That of Pierre Belon (1554) is reproduced on p. 89. Its main errors are the introduction of the Nile, and the outflow of Lake Mariout to the sea. It shows the two harbours, the Arab walls, Cleopatra's Needles, "Pompey's Pillar" and the Canopic or Rosetta Gate (Porte du Caire). The Turkish town has not yet been built. De Monconys' map of 1665—*see* frontispiece—is in some ways still more absurd; Cleopatra's Needle has turned into a pyramid. The mound in the right centre is meant for Fort Cafarelli. The beginnings of the Turkish Town appear on Ras-el-Tin. In 1743 Richard Pocock published the first scientific map in his "Description of the East"; measurements and soundings are given. Captain Norden the Dane brought out a good pictorial plan of the "New," *i.e.* Eastern Harbour, showing the seamarks. And the exact extent of Alexandria's decay is shown in the magnificent map published by the French expedition under Napoleon. There we see that the Arab enclosure is empty except for a few houses on Kom-el-Dik and by the Rosetta Gate, and that the population—only 4,000—is huddled into the wall-less Turkish Town.

With Napoleon a new age begins.

TURKISH TOWN: p. 134.
ROSETTA: p. 199.
CLEOPATRA'S NEEDLES: p. 175.
"POMPEY'S PILLAR": p. 157.
FORT CAFARELLI: p. 183.

SECTION V

Modern Period

NAPOLEON (1798–1801)

On July 1st 1798 the inhabitants of the obscure town saw that the deserted sea was covered with an immense fleet. Three hundred sailing ships came out from the west to anchor off Marabout Island, men disembarked all night and by the middle of next day 5,000 French soldiers under Napoleon had occupied the place. They were part of a larger force, and had come under the pretence of helping Turkey, against whom Egypt was then having one of her feeble and periodic revolts. The future Emperor was still a mere general of the French Republic, but already an influence on politics, and this expedition was his own plan. He was in love with the East just then. The romance of the Nile valley had touched his imagination, and he knew that it was the road to an even greater romance—India. At war with England, he saw himself gaining at England's expense an Oriental realm and reviving the power of Alexander the Great. In him, as in Mark Antony, Alexandria nourished imperial dreams. The expedition failed but its memory remained with him: he had touched the East, the nursery of kings.

Leaving Alexandria at once, he marched on Cairo and won the battle of the Pyramids. Then an irreparable disaster befell him. He had left his admiral, Brueys, with instructions to dispose the fleet as safely as possible, since Nelson was known to be in pursuit. Under modern conditions Brueys would have sailed into the Western Harbour, but in 1798 the reefs that cross the entrance had not been blasted away, and though the transports got in the passages were rather dangerous for the big men of war. Brueys was nervous and thought he had better take them round to an anchorage, supposed impeccable, in the Bay of Aboukir. Nelson followed him, attacked him unexpectedly and destroyed his fleet. Details of this famous engagement, the so-called "Battle of the Nile," are given in another place (p. 191); its result was to lose for Napoleon the command of the sea. The French expedition took Cairo and remained powerful on land, but could receive no reinforcements, no messages, and withered away like a plant that has been cut at the root. Turkey declared against it, and a Turkish force, supported by British ships, landed at Aboukir (July 1799). Here Napoleon was successful. He commanded in person and in a series of brilliant engagements drove the invaders into the sea: this is the "Land" battle of Aboukir (described in detail p. 192). But his dreams had been shattered by Nelson. He saw that his destiny, whatever it was, would not be accomplished in the East, and meanly deserting his army he slipped back to France.

We now come to the first British expedition, and to its successful and interesting campaign. In March 1801 Sir Ralph Abercrombie landed with 1,500 men at Aboukir. His aim was not to occupy Egypt, but to induce the French armies to evacuate it. He marched westward against Alexandria, keeping close to the sea. The country on his left was very different to what it is now, and to understand his operations two of the differences must be remembered. (i) The "Lake of Aboukir," since drained, stretched from Aboukir Bay almost as far as Ramleh. As it connected with the sea, it was full of salt

water. (ii) The present Lake Mariout was almost dry.
It contained a little fresh water, but most of its enormous bed was under cultivation. It lay twelve feet below the waters of Lake Aboukir, and was protected
from them by a dyke. Thus Abercrombie saw water
where we see land, and vice versa. He advanced with
success as far as Mandourah, because his left flank was
protected by Lake Aboukir. But when he wanted to
attack the French position at Ramleh he feared they
would outflank him over the dry bed of Mariout. His
losses had been heavy, his advance was held up;
wounded in the thigh by a musket shot, he had to abandon the command, and was carried on to a boat where
he died; a small monument at Sidi Gaber commemorates him to-day. His successor, Hutchinson, took dras-
tic measures. At the advice of his engineers he cut the
dyke that separated Lake Aboukir from Mariout. The
salt water rushed in, to the delight of the British soldiers, and in a month thousands of acres had been
drowned, Alexandria was isolated from the rest of
Egypt, and the left flank of the expedition was protected all the way up to the walls of the town. Later
in the year a second British force landed to the west
of Alexandria, at Marabout, and, caught between two
fires, the French were obliged to surrender. They were
given easy terms, and allowed to leave Egypt with all
the honours of war. The British followed them; we had
accomplished our aim, and had no reason to remain in
the country any longer; we left it to our allies the Turks.
But the sleep of so many centuries had been broken.
The eyes of Europe were again directed to the deserted shore. Though Napoleon had failed and the
British had retired, a new age had begun for Alexandria. Life flowed back into her, just as the waters, when
Hutchinson cut the dyke, flowed back into Lake Mariout.

MOHAMMED ALI (1805-1848)

When Napoleon drove the Turks into the sea at Aboukir, among the fugitives was Mohammed Ali, the founder of the present reigning house of Egypt. Little is known of his origin. He was an Albanian, but born at Cavala in Macedonia where he is said to have distinguished himself as a tax collector in his earlier youth. His education was primitive; he was ignorant of history and economics and only learnt the Arabic alphabet late in life. But he was a man of great ability and power and an acute judge of character. He reappears in Egypt in 1801, still obscure, and fights under Abercrombie. When the English withdrew he profited by the internal disturbances and became in 1805 Viceroy of the country under the Sultan of Turkey.

His power was consolidated by the disastrous British expedition of 1807—General Frazer's "reconnoitering" expedition, as it is officially termed. England was hostile to Turkey now, and Frazer was sent to see whether a diversion could be created in Egypt. He landed, like Napoleon before him, at Marabout, but with no more than the following regiments;—the 31st, the 35th, the 78th, and a foreign legion: 4,000 men in all. He occupied Alexandria and Rosetta, but before long Mohammed Ali had killed or captured half his force and

he was obliged to ask for terms. They were readily
granted. The "reconnoitering" expedition was allowed
to re-embark, and the only trace it has left of its presence in Alexandria is a tombstone of a soldier of the
78th, in the courtyard of the Greek Patriarchate.

For thirty years the power of Mohammed Ali grew,
and with it the importance of Alexandria, his virtual
capital. He freed the Holy Places of Arabia from a heretical sect, he interfered in Greece, he revolted against
his suzerain the Sultan of Turkey, and invading Syria
added it to his dominions. A kingdom, comparable in
extent to the Ptolemaic, had come into existence with
Alexandria as its centre, and it seemed that the dreams
of Napoleon would be realised by this Albanian adven-
turer, and that the English would be cut off from India.
England took alarm. And suddenly the Empire of Mohammed Ali fell. Syria revolted (1840), supported
by a British fleet, and soon the English admiral, Sir
Charles Napier, was at Alexandria, and compelled the
Viceroy to confine himself to Egypt. According to tradition the interview took place in the new Ras-el-Tin
Palace, and Napier exclaims, "If Your Highness will not
listen to my unofficial appeal to you against the folly of
further resistance, it only remains for me to bombard
you, and by God I will bombard you and plant my
bombs in the middle of this room where you are sitting." Anyhow Mohammed Ali gave in. He had failed
as a European power, but he had secured for his family a comfortable principality in Egypt, where he was
king in all but name.

His internal policy was rather disreputable. He admired European civilisation because it made people
aggressive and gave them guns, but he had no sense of
its finer aspects, and his "reforms" were mainly veneer
to impress travellers. He exploited the fellahin by buy-
ing grain from them at his own price: the whole of

Egypt became his private farm. Hence the importance of the foreign communities at Alexandria at this date: he needed their aid to dispose of the produce in European markets. He won over the British and other consuls to be his agents by giving them licences to export Egyptian antiquities, which were then coming into fashion; our own Consul Henry Salt—his tomb is here —was a particular offender in this. He also gave away "Cleopatra's Needles" to the British and American Governments respectively; the obelisks that still remained on their original sites outside the vanished Caesareum, and would have lent such dignity to our modern sea front. Still, with all his faults, he did create the modern city, such as she is. He waved his wand, and what we see arose from the aged soil. Let us examine it for a moment.

THE MODERN CITY

During the years 1798–1807 as many as four expeditions had landed at or near Alexandria—one French, one Turkish, and two English. Egypt had again been drawn into the European system. A maritime capital was necessary, and the genius of Mohammed Ali realised that it could be found not in the mediaeval ports of Damietta and Rosetta, but in a restored Alexandria. The city that we know to-day has followed the lines

that he laid down, and it is interesting to compare his
dispositions with those of Alexander the Great, over
two thousand years before.

The main problem was the waters. The English, by
cutting the dykes in 1801, had refilled Lake Mariout
so that it had suddenly regained its ancient area. But
it was too shallow for navigation and they had filled
it with salt water instead of the former fresh: it gave
no access to the system of the Nile. That system had
to be tapped. Alexander could find the Nile at Aboukir
(Canopic Mouth): now it was as far off as Rosetta
(ancient Bolbitic Mouth). Consequently Mohammed
Ali had to construct a canal 45 miles long. This canal,
called the Mahmoudieh after Mahmoud, the reigning
Sultan of Turkey, was completed in 1820. It was badly
made and the sides were always falling in, but it led to
the immediate rise of Alexandria and to the decay of
Rosetta. Alexandria now had water communications
with Cairo, to which was added communication by
rail. The Harbour followed. Mohammed Ali developed
the Western which had been the less important in classical times. The present docks and arsenals were built
for him (1828–1833) by the French engineer De
Cerisy. A fleet was added. To the same scheme belongs
the impressive Ras-el-Tin Palace, which standing on a
rise above the Harbour dominated it as the Ptolemaic
Palace had once dominated the Eastern; the favourite
residence of the Viceroy, it indicated that his new kingdom was no mere oriental monarchy, but a modern
power with its face to the sea.

Meanwhile the town started its development, but
not on very regal lines. Houses began to run up and
streets to sprawl over the deserted area inside the Arab
Walls. It did not occur either to Mohammed Ali or to
his friends the Foreign Communities that a city ought
to be planned. Their one achievement was a Square

and certainly quite a fine one—the Place des Consuls,
now Place Mohammed Ali. The English were granted
land to the north of the Square, on part of which they
built their church, the French and the Greeks land to
the south; areas were also acquired by other communities, *e.g.* by the Armenians. But there was no attempt
to co-ordinate the various enterprises, or to utilise the
existing features of the site. These features were: the
sea, the lake, "Pompey's Pillar," the forts of Kom-el-Dik
and Cafarelli, and the Arab Walls. The sea was ignored
except for commercial purposes; the main thorough-
fares still keep away from its shores, and even the fine
New Quays are attracting no buildings to their curve.†
The lake was ignored even more completely—the lake
whose delicate pale expanse might so have beautified
the southern quarters; many people do not know that
a lake exists. "Pompey's Pillar," instead of being the
centre of converging roads, has been left where it will
least be seen; only down the Rue Bab Sidra does one
get a distant view of it. Similarly with the two forts;
huddled behind houses. The Arab walls have been
finally destroyed—remnants surviving in the eastern
reach where they have been utilised (and well utilised) in the Public Gardens.

As Alexandria grew in size and wealth she required
suburbs. The earliest development was along the line
of the Mahmoudieh Canal, where the Villa Antoniadis
and a few other fine houses have been built. But with
the improvement of communications the rich merchants were able to live further afield. Two alternatives
were open to them—Mex and Ramleh—and rather re-
grettably they selected the latter. Mex, with its fine
natural features, might have developed into a very
beautiful place: as it is a belt of slums have parted it
from the town, and an execrable tram service has removed it even further. The town has spread to the east

instead, to Ramleh, served at first by a railway and
now by good electric trams.

Such are the main features of Alexandria as it has
evolved under Mohammed Ali and his successors. It
does not compare favourably with the city of Alexander the Great. On the other hand it is no worse than
most nineteenth-century cities. And it has one immense advantage over them—a perfect climate.

MAHMOUDIEH CANAL: p. 167.
MODERN HARBOUR: p. 141.
RAS-EL-TIN PALACE: p. 140.
SQUARE: p. 109.
ENGLISH CHURCH: p. 110.
FORT KOM-EL-DIK: p. 113.
FORT CAFARELLI: p. 183.
"POMPEY'S PILLAR": p. 157.
PUBLIC GARDENS: p. 170.
VILLA ANTONIADIS: p. 172.
MEX: p. 184.
RAMLEH: p. 181.

THE BOMBARDMENT OF
ALEXANDRIA (1882)

Thus the city develops quietly under Mohammed
Ali and his successors—one of whom, Said Pasha, is
buried here. Attention was rather diverted from her by
the cutting of the Suez Canal, and it is not until 1882
that anything of note occurs. She is in this year connected with the rebellion of Arabi, the founder of the
Egyptian Nationalist Party. Arabi, then Minister of
War, was endeavouring to dominate the Khedive Tewfik, and to secure Egypt for the Egyptians. Alexandria,
which had held a foreign element ever since its foun-

dation, was therefore his natural foe, and it was here that he opened the campaign against Europe that ended in his failure at Tel-el-Kebir. The details—like Arabi's motives—are complicated. But four stages may be observed.

(i). Riot of June 11th.

This began at about 1.0 p.m. in the Rue des Soeurs; it is said that two donkey boys, one Arab and one Maltese, had a fight in a café, and that others joined in. The rioters moved down towards the Square, and at some cross roads near the Laban Caracol the British Consul was nearly killed. They were joined in the Square by two other mobs, one from the Attarine Quarter and one from Ras-el-Tin. British and other warships were in the harbour, but took no action, and the Egyptian troops in the city refused to intervene without orders from Arabi, who was in Cairo. At last a telegram was sent to him. He responded and the disorder ceased. There is no reason to suppose that he planned the riot. But naturally enough he used it to increase his prestige. He had shown the foreign communities, and particularly the British, that he alone could give them protection. In the evening he came down in triumph from Cairo. About 150 Europeans are thought to have been killed that day, but we have no reliable statistics.

(ii). Bombardment of July 11th.

British men-of-war under Admiral Seymour had been in the harbour during the riot, but it was a month before they took action. In the first place the British residents had to be removed, in the second the fleet required reinforcing, in the third orders were awaited from home. As soon as Seymour was ready he picked a quarrel with Arabi and declared he should bombard the city if any more guns were mounted in the forts.

Since Arabi would not agree he opened fire at 7.0 a.m. July 11th. There were eight iron-clads—six of them the most powerful in our navy. They were thus distributed: —*Monarch, Invincible* and *Penelope* close inshore off Mex; *Alexandria, Sultan* and *Superb* off Ras-el-Tin; while the two others the *Temeraire* and *Inflexible* were in a central position outside the harbour reef, half way between Ras-el-Tin and Marabout; and off Marabout were some gun-boats, under Lord Charles Beresford. The bombardment succeeded, though Arabi's gunners in the forts fought bravely. In the evening the *Superb* blew up the powder magazine in Fort Adda. Fort Kait Bey was also shattered and the minaret of its 15th cent. Mosque was seen "melting away like ice in the sun." The town, on the other hand, was scarcely damaged, as our gunners were careful in their aim. Arabi and his force evacuated it in the evening, marching out by the Rue Rosette to take up a position some miles further east, on the banks of the Mahmoudieh Canal.

(iii). *Riot of July 12th.*

Unfortunately Admiral Seymour, after his success, never landed a force to keep order, and the result was a riot far more disastrous than that of June. With the withdrawal of Arabi's troops the native population lost self-control. The Khedive had now broken with Arabi, but during the bombardment he had moved from Ras-el-Tin Palace to Ramleh and his authority was negligible. Pillaging went on all day on the 12th, and by the evening the city had been set on fire. The damage was material rather than artistic, the one valuable object in the Square, the statue of Mohammed Ali, fortunately escaping. Rues Chérif and Tewfik Pacha—indeed all the roads leading out of the Square—were destroyed, and nearly every street in the European quarter was impassable through fallen and falling houses. Empty jewel cases and broken clocks lay on the pavements. Every shop was looted, and by the time Admiral Seymour did land it was impossible for his middies to buy any jam; one of them has recorded this misfortune, adding that in other ways Alexandria, then in flames, was "well enough." Meanwhile the Khedive had returned to his Palace, and order was slowly restored. It is not known how many lives were lost in this avoidable disaster.

(iv). *Military Operations.*

A large British force was despatched under Lord Wolseley to the Suez Canal—the force that finally defeated Arabi at Tel-el-Kebir. But, until it reached Egypt, Alexandria remained in danger, for Arabi might attack from his camp at Kafr-el-Dawar. So the city had to be defended on the east. In the middle of July General Alison arrived with a few troops, including artillery, and occupied the barracks at Mustapha Pacha, the hill of Abou-el-Nawatir, and the water works down by the canal. He could thus watch Arabi's movements. And he had a second strongly fortified position at the gates of the Antoniadis Gardens, in case he was attacked from the south. Here he was able to hold on and to harry the enemy's outposts until pressure was relieved. His losses were slight; the regiments involved are commemorated by tablets in the English church. Next month Wolseley arrived, and having inspected the position re-embarked his troops and pretended that he was going to land at Aboukir. Arabi was deceived and prepared resistance there. Wolseley steamed past him, and landed at Port Said instead. Arabi then had to break up his camp, and the danger for Alexandria was over.

Rue des Sœurs: p. 183.

Fort Adda: p. 144.

Fort Kait Bey: p. 144.

Gun on Abou-el-Nawatir: p. 180.

Antoniadis Gardens: p. 172.

Tablets in English Church: p. 110.

Howitzer of Arabi; at Egyptian Government Hospital: p. 177.

CONCLUSION †

Since the bombardment of 1882, the city has known other troubles, but they will not be here described. Nor will any peroration be attempted, for the reason that Alexandria is still alive and alters even while one tries to sum her up. Politically she is now more closely connected with the rest of Egypt than ever in the past, but the old foreign elements remain, and it is to the oldest of them, the Greek, that she owes such modern culture as is to be found in her. Her future like that of other great commercial cities is dubious. Except in the cases of the Public Gardens and the Museum, the Municipality has scarcely risen to its historic responsibilities. The Library is starved for want of funds, the Art Gallery cannot be alluded to, and links with the past have been wantonly broken—for example the name of the Rue Rosette has been altered and the exquisite Covered Bazaar near the Rue de France destroyed. Material prosperity based on cotton, onions, and eggs, seems assured, but little progress can be discerned in other directions, and neither the Pharos of Sostratus nor the Idylls of Theocritus nor the Enneads of Plotinus are likely to be rivalled in the future. Only the climate, only the north wind and the sea remain as pure as when Menelaus, the first visitor, landed upon Ras-el-Tin, three thousand years ago; and at night the constellation of Berenice's Hair still shines as brightly as when it caught the attention of Conon the astronomer.

THE GOD ABANDONS ANTONY

When at the hour of midnight
an invisible choir is suddenly heard passing
with exquisite music, with voices—
Do not lament your fortune that at last subsides,
your life's work that has failed, your schemes that have
    proved illusions.
But like a man prepared, like a brave man,
bid farewell to her, to Alexandria who is departing.
Above all, do not delude yourself, do not say that it is a
    dream,
that your ear was mistaken.
Do not condescend to such empty hopes.
Like a man for long prepared, like a brave man,
like to the man who was worthy of such a city,
go to the window firmly,
and listen with emotion,
but not with the prayers and complaints of the coward
(Ah! supreme rapture!)
listen to the notes, to the exquisite instruments of the
    mystic choir,
and bid farewell to her, to Alexandria whom you are
    losing.

                                        C. P. CAVAFY.*

* The local reference of this exquisite poem is to the omen that
heralded the defeat of Mark Antony (p. 29). The poet is eminent
among the contemporary writers of Greece; he and his translator,
Mr. George Valassopoulo, are both residents of Alexandria.

PART II
GUIDE

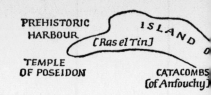

M E D I T E R R A N E A N

PREHISTORIC
HARBOUR

ISLAND o

[Ras el Tin]

TEMPLE
OF POSEIDON

CATACOMBS
[of Anfouchy]

E U N O S T O S   H A R B O U R

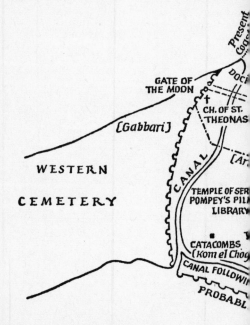

Present
Coast

DOC

GATE OF
THE MOON

CH. OF ST.
THEONAS

[Gabbari]

CANAL

[Ar

WESTERN

CEMETERY

TEMPLE OF SER
POMPEY'S PIL
LIBRARY

CATACOMBS
[Kom el Chog

CANAL FOLLOWIN

PROBABL

L A K E   M A R E O T I S

A L E X A N D R I A
H I S T O R I C A L   M A P

Ancient Sites in CAPITALS
Modern Sites bracketed []

SEA

PHAROS · LIGHTHOUSE
[Fort Kait Bey]

TEMPLE OF
ISIS ON PHAROS

AROS

GREAT HARBOUR

ROYAL HARBOUR

CAPE LOCHIAS
(Silsileh)
TEMPLE OF ISIS

HEPTASTADION DYKE

Present Coastline

Place
(Mohammed Ali)

ISLAND PALACE

ANTIRRHODOS

AREA OF PALACE

CH. OF
ST. MARK

CONVENT OF ST.
CATHERINE
CH. OF ST.
ATHANASIUS

CLEOPATRA'S
NEEDLES
CAESAREUM
THEATRE

(Chatby)

JEWISH
QUARTER

CANOPIC STREET

RACE
COURSE
(Arab Walls)

AREA OF MOUSEION
LIBRARY (Now Rue Rosette)
SOMA

Walls of A.D. 811

GATE OF THE SUN
TO CANOPUS
(Porte Rosette)

SHRINE OF
POMPEY

PARK OF PAN

STREET OF THE SOMA
(Now Rue Nebi Daniel)

KOTIS

RACE
COURSE

CANAL

URSE

URSE

LAKE HARBOUR

OF MAHMOUDIEH

OF WALLS B.C. 331

TO CANOPUS
AND NILE

[Lake Mariout]

EASTERN CEMETERIES

In Rue Lepsius, now Sharia Sharm el Sheikh, a dusty plaque above the sign for the Pension Amir reads in Arabic and Greek. "In this house for the last twenty-five years of his life lived the Alexandrian poet Constantine Cavafy (1863–1933)."

SECTION I

From the Square to
the Rue Rosette

ROUTE:—Square, Rue Chérif Pacha, Rue Rosette, leading through the most modern section of the town. No tram line.

CHIEF POINTS OF INTEREST:—Square and Statue of Mohammed Ali; Banco di Roma; Mosque of the Prophet Daniel; St. Saba; Greco-Roman Museum.

THE SQUARE†

The Square (officially, Place Mohammed Ali; formerly Place des Consuls; known to cabmen as "Menschieh" from the adjoining Police Station) was laid out by Mohammed Ali as the centre of his new city. (About 1830; *see* p. 97). In Ptolemaic times the ground here was under the sea. The Square is over 100 yds. broad and nearly 500 long and well planted, but unworthy buildings surround it. It suffered in the riots of 1882 (p. 101); everything was then burnt excepting the statue of Mohammed Ali and the Church of St. Mark.

In the Centre:—*Equestrian Statue of Mohammed Ali,* an impressive specimen of French Sculpture, by Jacquemart; exhibited in the Salon of 1872. Orthodox Mohammedans were hostile to its erection, and even now there is no inscription on it. Its presence is the more welcome since it is one of the few first class objects in the city. It should be studied from every point of view.

Right as one faces the Statue:—*The Mixed Tribunals*, where, in accordance with arrangements dating from 1875, civil and commercial cases between Egyptians and Europeans are tried.

Left:—*The French Gardens*, a pleasant strip, stretching at right angles from the Square to the New Quays, (p. 153).

Also left:—*Anglican Church of St. Mark*, which with the adjacent St. Mark's Buildings was built on land granted to the English by Mohammed Ali. Looking through the railings of the churchyard is the funny little bust of General Earle (k. 1885 at Kirbekan in the Soudan). It was erected by the European Community, and represents their chief incursion into the realms of art. The Church itself, considering its date (1855), and its pseudo-Byzantine architecture, is however a tolerable building. The interior is restful and the stained glass and triptych in the chancel strike a pleasing note of colour. Historically, its only associations are with the fighting against Arabi in 1882 (p. 99). The Regiments it commemorates are the 2nd Bn. Duke of Cornwall's Light Infantry (on the scroll by the entrance stairs); 2nd Bn. Derbyshires; Royal Marine Artillery; 1st Bn. London Division; Royal Artillery 1st Bn. Royal West Kents (in the Nave). In the churchyard trees multitudinous, sparrows gather at sunset, and fill the Square with their chatter.

End of the Square:—*The Bourse*, with arcaded exterior and clock. Inside is the Cotton Exchange, the chief in the Egyptian trade; the howls and cries that may be heard here of a morning proceed not from a menagerie but from the wealthy merchants of Alexan-

dria as they buy and sell. At the other end of the same
hall is the Stock Exchange. The whole scene is well
worth a visit (introduction necessary).

Rue Chérif Pacha, a smart little street bristling with
flag staffs, leads out of the Square to the left of the
Bourse. Here are the best shops. Towards the end, left,
at the entrance of the Rue Toussoum Pacha, is the
Banco di Roma, the finest building in the city. Architect, Gorra. A modified copy of the famous Palazzo
Farnese, which Antonio da San Gallo and Michelan-
gelo built in the 16th cent., at Rome. The materials are
artificial stone and narrow bricks of a charming pale
red. It has two stories as against the Farnese's three,
but there is a sort of half storey up under the heavy
cornice. Each side of the door are elaborate torch hold-
ers of bent iron; over door, the Wolf of Rome. In a
cosmopolitan city like Alexandria, which has never
evolved an architecture of its own, there is nothing in-
congruous in this copy of the Italian Renaissance. A
little further up Rue Toussoum Pacha is the *Land Bank
of Egypt*, with a good semicircular portico.
Rue Chérif Pacha then joins the Rue Rosette.

RUE ROSETTE†

This street, despite its modern appearance, is the
most ancient in the city. It runs on the lines of the
Canopic Way, the central artery of Alexander's town,
(p. 10), and under the Ptolemies it was lined from end
to end with marble colonnades. Its full title is "Rue de
la Porte Rosette" from the Rosetta Gate in the old Arab
walls through which it passed out eastwards (p. 86).
The Municipality have recently changed its name to

the unmeaning Rue Fouad Premier, thus breaking one of the few links that bound their city to the past.

At its entrance, right, are:—the Caracol Attarine (British Main Guard); the Rue de la Gare du Caire, leading to the main railway station; and the Mohammed Ali Club, the chief in the town—a small temple to Serapis once stood on its site. Here too is Cook's office.

100 yds. down it is crossed by the Rue Nebi Daniel and by a tramway. Here, in ancient times, was the main crossway of the ancient city—one of the most glorious places in the world (p. 10). Achilles Tatius, a bishop who in A.D. 400 wrote a somewhat foolish and improper novel called Clitophon and Leucippe, thus describes it:—

> The first thing one noticed in entering Alexandria by the Gate of the Sun (i.e. by the Rosetta Gate) was the beauty of the city. A range of columns went from one end of it to the other. Advancing down them, I came in time to the place that bears the name of Alexander, and there could see the other half of the town, which was equally beautiful. For just as the colonnades stretched ahead of me, so did other colonnades now appear at right angles to them.

Thus the tramway was also lined with marble once.

Turning to the right, a few yards up the Rue Nebi Daniel, we come to:—*The Mosque of the Prophet Daniel* which stands on the site of Alexander's tomb—the "Soma" where he and some of the Ptolemies lay, buried in the Macedonian fashion (p. 22). The cellars have never been explored, and there is a gossipy story that Alexander still lies in one of them, intact: a dragoman from the Russian Consulate, probably a liar, said in 1850 that he saw through a hole in a wooden door "a human body in a sort of glass cage with a diadem on its head and half bowed on a sort of elevation or throne.

A quantity of books or papyrus were scattered around."
The present Mosque, though the chief in the city, is
uninteresting; a paved approach, a whitewashed door,
a great interior supported by four colonnades with
slightly pointed arches. The praying niche faces south
instead of the usual east. All has been mercilessly restored. Stairs lead down to two tombs, assigned to the
Prophet Daniel and to the mythical Lukman the Wise;
it is uncertain why or when such a pair visited our city.
The tombs stand in a well-crypt of cruciform shape,
above which is a chapel roofed by a dome and entered from the Mosque through a door. Here and there
some decorations struggle through the whitewash.

In a building to the right of the approach to the
Mosque are the *Tombs of the Khedivial Family*, worth
seeing for their queerness; there is nothing like them in
Alexandria. The Mausoleum is cruciform, painted to
imitate marble, and covered with Turkey carpets. Out
of the carpet rise the tombs, of all sizes but of similar
design, and all painted white and gold. A red tarboosh
indicates a man, a crown with conventionalised hair a
woman. The most important person buried here is Said
Pacha—third tomb on the right. He was the son of Mohammed Ali and ruled Egypt 1854–1863: Mohammed
Ali himself lies at Cairo.

Between the Mausoleum and the street:—a fountain
with eaves and a dome; Turkish style.

Opposite the Mosque:—some antique columns used
as gate posts; perhaps the façade of the Mouseion
stretched along here (p. 19).

Behind the Mosque:—Fort of Kom-el-Dik. View.
Site of ancient Paneum or Park of Pan—the summit of
the hill was then carved into a pinecone, which a
spiral path ascended.—In Arab times the walls of the
shrunken city passed to the south of Kom-el-Dik, (p.
86), and a fine stretch of them still survives, half way

between the base of the Fort and the railway station; they border the road, but cannot be seen from it, being sunken; they include a moat.—Beyond the Fort the high ground continues; the little Arab quarter of Kom-el-Dik is built along its crest, and the winding lanes, though insignificant, contrast pleasantly with the glare of the European town.

We return to the Rue Rosette.

A little further down the Rue Rosette a turning on the left leads to the *Church and Convent of St. Saba*, the seat of the Greek Orthodox Patriarch. (For history of Patriarchate, *see* p. 227.) A church was founded here in 615, on the site of a Temple of Apollo. The present group dates from 1687, and has an old world atmosphere that is rare in Alexandria. In the quiet court of the Convent are three tombstones of British soldiers, dating from Napoleonic times: Colonel Arthur Brice of the Coldstreams, k. in the Battle of Alexandria, 1801 (p. 93); Thomas Hamilton Scott of the 78th, and Henry Gosle, military apothecary, who both died during General Frazer's disastrous "reconnoitering" expedition, 1807, (p. 94).—From the court, steps descend to the church which has been odiously restored. In the nave, eight ancient columns of granite, now smeared with chocolate paint. In the apse of the sanctuary, fresco of the Virgin and Child. Right—Chapel of St. George with a table said to be 4th cent., and an interesting picture of the Council of Nicaea (p. 53); the Emperor Constantine presides with the bishops around him and the heretic Arius at his feet. Left—Chapel of St. Catherine of Alexandria, with a block of marble purporting to come from the column where the saint was martyred.—Hanging outside the church, three fine bells.

At the top of the street, to left, is the Greek Hospital, a pleasant building that stands in a garden.

The Rue Rosette now passes the Native Courts (left) and reaches the Municipal Buildings. Behind the latter, a few yards up the Rue du Musée, is the Municipal Library; go up the steps opposite the entrance gate; push the door. The Library is good considering its miserable endowment; the city that once had the greatest Library in the world now cannot afford more than £300 per annum for the combined purchase and binding of her books.

Beyond the Library is a far more adequate institution—the Greco-Roman Museum.

THE GRECO-ROMAN MUSEUM†

The collection was not formed until 1891, by which time most of the antiques in the neighbourhood had passed into private hands. It is consequently not of the first order and little in it has outstanding beauty. Used rightly, it is of great value, but the visitor who "goes through" it will find afterwards that it has gone through him, and that he is left with nothing but a vague memory of fatigue. The absence of colour, the numerous small exhibits in terra cotta and limestone, will tend to depress him, and to give a false impression of a civilisation which, whatever its defects, was not dull. He should not visit the collection until he has learned or imagined something about the ancient city, and he should visit certain definite objects, and then come away—a golden rule indeed in all museums. He may then find that a scrap of the past has come alive.

The collection is well housed (date of building 1895) and well catalogued. There is a Guide (in French) by the Director, Professor Breccia, extracts from which are pasted up about the rooms. On this scholarly work

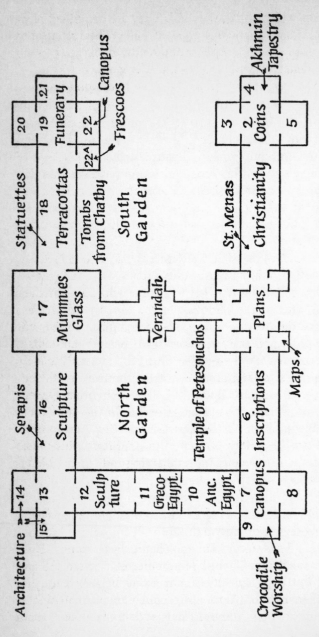

PLAN OF GRECO-ROMAN MUSEUM

the following notes are based. They are compiled, however, from a particular point of view. They attempt to illustrate the historical section of the book (p. 5), and are connected with it by cross references.

For arrangement of exhibits, *see* Plan opposite.

INTRODUCTION

The Museum mainly illustrates the civilisation of Ancient Alexandria. There are some portraits—not satisfactory—of the Founder (Room 12), and magnificent coins of the Ptolemies (Room 3); also sculptures of them (Rooms 4, 12). Their religious policy appears in the statues of Serapis (Room 16). As for the Roman Emperors, we have besides their coins (Room 2) colossal statues of Marcus Aurelius (Room 12), and of Diocletian (?) (Room 17); then some gold coins of their Byzantine successors (Room 5). Meanwhile the career of the private citizen is also being illustrated, but mainly in his grave. Masses and masses and masses of funerary stuff (Rooms 6, 13–15, 17–21), mostly dull, but attaining great beauty in the terra cotta statuettes of women (Room 18). The "Egyptian Queen" pottery (Room 17) is more cheerful. In the same room is lovely glass. With Christianity, the Alexandrian, though still mainly presented to us through his tombs (Room 1), develops the interesting cult of St. Menas (Rooms 1, 5, 22A).

The Museum also exhibits, though imperfectly, other aspects of Egyptian life.

(i). PHARAONIC EGYPT:—There are some mummies, etc., from Thebes, Heliopolis, etc. (Rooms 8 and 10), but they have the air of being here because not good enough for Cairo; also a collection of small objects (Room 10), and Rameses statues from Aboukir (Room

9 and North Garden). The blend of Pharaonic and Hellenistic is shown in Room 11.

(ii). THE FAYOUM:—This is the most important non-Alexandrian section in the Museum. The Fayoum, an irrigated depression south-west of Cairo, was developed by Ptolemy II Philadelphus, and, as in Alexandria, Greek and Egyptian mingled, but with different results. It was barbaric and provincial. Note especially crocodile worship (North Garden, Rooms 9, 22A). Mummies of quite a new type (Room 17). Black basalt statues (Room 11). It is a pity that the Fayoum exhibits cannot all be shown together.

(iii). AKHMIN:—An early Christian Necropolis in Upper Egypt. Hence come the robed mummies (Room 1), and the fragments of tapestry (Rooms 1, 2, 4), whose beauty will linger when many a grandiose statue has been forgotten.

VESTIBULE.

PLANS, PHOTOGRAPHS, ETC.

Note especially (1) Thiersch's reconstruction of the Pharos and (10) photographs of Kait Bey Fort, where the Pharos stood (p. 18). (8) Cleopatra's Needle in situ (p. 175). At the entrance of Room 6 (left) is a cast of the Rosetta Stone (p. 199) which contains a tri-lingual decree (Hieroglyph, which was the script of the Ancient Egyptian priests, Demotic, a running hand-writing evolved from it, and Greek); the decree was passed by the priests of Memphis, B.C. 196, in honour of Ptolemy V Epiphanes. The original stone was discovered by the French in 1799 in the Fort of St. Julien, Rosetta—water-colour of it hangs close by. General Menou had to surrender it to the English in 1801, and it is now in the British Museum. Carducci's fine poem on Alexandria hangs framed on the adjacent wall.

In the case are stone-age tools from the Fayoum.

From the Vestibule are: right, Room 1 (Christianity);

left, Room 6 (Inscriptions); straight ahead, the Verandah
leads between the Garden Courts to Room 17.

ROOM 1:   CHRISTIAN REMAINS.

RIGHT WALL: Inscriptions. 106 shows a cross with a
looped top, directly derived from the symbol of life (ankh)
that the ancient Egyptian gods carry (p. 74). In the middle
of the wall *Case A:* terra cotta dolls, etc., from St. Menas.

CENTRE OF ROOM, facing door:—magnificent Byzantine
capital, supposed to have been in the church of St. Mark
(p. 50). Found in the Rue Ramleh. *Case K:* Carved ivories
and bones, mostly from Alexandrian rubbish heaps—1979,
2012, 2021, 2025 are good examples. *Case I:* Interlaced
cushion from the Christian necropolis of Antinoe, Upper
Egypt. Middle of room: fine porphyry cover to a sarcophagus, decorated on each side by a charming head. From the
Lebban quarter. Beyond: Christian mummies from Antinoe, still wearing their fine embroideries. At the end: another Byzantine capital, found near the Mahmoudieh
Canal.

LEFT WALL, centre: *Cases La* and *M:* Flasks from St.
Menas. They were filled with water, which must soon have
evaporated, and exported all over the Christian world:
usual design—the Saint between camels. Between the vases
interesting fragments from a church to St. Menas at
Dekhela (p. 185); the bas-relief of the Saint is a clumsy
copy of the one that stood in his shrine in the desert (p.
210). *Cases P, Q, R, S:* Coptic tapestries from Akhmin
and Antinoe—beautiful. Date 3rd cent. onward. Near *Case
N,* two absurd reliefs (Christian era) of Leda and the swan
—in one of them she holds an egg.

ROOM 2:   COINS.

Chronological continuation of the Ptolemaic coins in
Room 3, which should be visited first. Illustrate history of
Alexandria, and also her religion, under Rome and afterwards under Constantinople. Series begins in *Case A*
(further right-hand corner) with Octavian (Augustus)
675; *Case B,* No. 675 (of Domitian) shows the Pharos (*see*

p. 18). 750 (of Trajan)—a temple to Isis in Alexandria, with pylons between which the goddess stands. 771 shows Serapis on his throne. 890–892, the sacred basket that he sometimes carries on his head. *Case C*, 1363–1366—interviews, very friendly, between the Emperor Hadrian and Alexandria. 1409—interviews between him and the god Serapis. 1450, Isis as guardian of the Pharos.

ROUND THE ROOM: Four marble capitals from St. Menas.

ROOM 3:   COINS.

The collection of Ptolemaic coins begins in *Case Ab* (right of room) and continues through *Case C–D* (left) and *Case E–F* (entrance). The coins are numbered consecutively. They are of great historical and artistic interest, but must not be taken seriously as portraits, since the ruler is generally approximated to some god (*i.e.* numeral "one" 1). Silver four-drachma of Alexander the Great, struck by his Viceroy Cleomenes. 2–45. Ptolemy I as Viceroy. On the obverse is always the head of Alexander the Great, with horns of the God Ammon. 46–274. Ptolemy I as King (Soter). A new type gradually appears; on the obverse the head of the King, on the reverse an eagle (note 14 gold coins—four-drachma pieces). 275–510. Ptolemy II (Philadelphus) instructive for the domestic history of his reign (p. 16). At first the King appears alone—*e.g.* on gold five-drachma. 275–280. Then his formidable sister and wife Arsinoe is alone—gold coin 342. Then the couple appear together—gold 428–434, while on the other side of the coins are their predecessors, Ptolemy I and his wife, to show that the dynasty emanated in pairs. 551–619. Ptolemy III (Euergetes). 620. Magnificent gold eight-drachma, representing Euergetes, but struck by Philopator his son; the most gorgeous coin in the collection. 621. Silver four-drachma, with heads of Serapis and Isis. Ptolemaic coinage now deteriorates; the eagle in the later issues (*Case D*) becomes formalised and ridiculous. 1059 (*Case E*) features —what disillusionment!—Cleopatra!

ROUND THE ROOM: Casts.

ROOM 4:   COINS: AKHMIN TAPESTRY.

The coins are coppers of the later Roman Emperors. Not beautiful. Of historical interest to Alexandria. In *Case A–B* (right) 3884—Aurelian and Vabatathe. 3896—Zenobia. In *Case C–D* (left) 4024—Diocletian.

ROUND THE WALLS: 1–8. Tapestries from the Christian cemetery at Akhmin.

BACK WALL: Large and impressive statue of a mourning woman with her child. Hellenistic. Perhaps represents Berenice wife of Ptolemy III Euergetes, mourning for her little daughter—the daughter whom the priests deified in the Decree of Canopus, B.C. 239 (p. 46).

ENTRANCE OF ROOM: Large Christian Jar.

ROOM 5:   COINS.

Beautiful Byzantine gold coins. Note especially the Emperor Phocas and his conqueror Heraclius (p. 58); the latter displays the Exaltation of the Cross, recovered by him from the Persians.

BACK WALL: Pilaster from the Hospice at St. Menas. The cross has been erased, probably at the Arab conquest. At each end of it, more St. Menas flasks.

Case A: Painted masks, from the (pagan) Necropolis of Antinoe. *Case B;* Christian potteries from Kom es Chogafa.

Return to Vestibule.

ROOM 6:   INSCRIPTIONS, ETC.

This room contains nothing of beauty, but is interesting historically. The exhibits are not in numerical order.

RIGHT WALL, close to entrance: 42—Inscription on a statue of Antony (p. 28), dedicated on December 24th, B.C. 50 (Found near Ramleh Station, *i.e.* the site of the Caesareum). 2. Dedication to Ptolemy II Philadelphus. 1. Dedication to Ptolemy I. 37. Doorway with inscription to Ptolemy VI; in it is a case containing (59) two bronze plaques belonging to a Roman soldier, (Julius Saturninus), inscribed with a certificate of his good services and privileges. 61*a*, also in the case, is another military document,

a wooden tablet written at Alexandria, but found in the
Fayoum, and also conferring benefits on a veteran. 94.
Base of a statue of the Emperor Valentinian (4th cent.
A.D.); found in Rue Rosette. 88*b*. Tombstone with the
figures of Isidore and Artemisia, two ladies of Pisidia,
found at Hadra. 87*b*. Tombstone of a lady with her servant.

Then come some painted tombstones protected by glass;
they are inferior to some in the rooms further on. 119 (in
corner of room); Tombstone of a woman expiring between two friends.

LEFT WALL: Inscriptions and tombstones of the Roman
period (p. 48). 480. On a pedestal: Memorial of Aurelius
Alexander, a Roman soldier of Macedonian birth who died
aged 31. 252. Another of Aurelius Sabius, a Syrian soldier,
aged 35.

EACH SIDE OF THE ROOM, near entrance door: Two *Cases*
of papyri—the left hand one containing two interesting inscriptions. 119. Incantation to the Nile and to the great
spirit Sabaoth shewing mixture of Egyptian and Jewish
faiths. 122. Demand of Aurelia, priestess of the crocodile
god, Petesouchos, for a certificate of having worshipped the
gods. It was made during the Decian persecution, (p. 50),
and suggests that, despite her position, she had been accused of Christianity. 352*b*. On a pedestal: Colossal scarab.
35*b*. Fine headless sphinx. 351. Great Apis bull (restored);
period of Hadrian. 350. Sphinx, rather sentimental, with
crossed paws. All these last four were found near "Pompey's Pillar" (p. 157).

ROOM 7: ANCIENT EGYPT: CANOPUS.

These monuments, though mostly found in the Aboukir
sites (p. 190), may have been imported there at some unknown date from Heliopolis or Sais.

1. Statue of a Hyksos Pharaoh (Shepherd King, about
B.C. 1800) which has been appropriated by Rameses II
(B.C. 1300); on the shoulder appears Rameses' daughter
Hout-Ma-Ra, traditionally the princess who found Moses
in the bullrushes.

18. Part of a statue of Rameses II.

Case C (left of room). Two statues of a Ptolemaic official; from the Temple of Serapis, Alexandria (p. 161).

ROOM 8: ANCIENT EGYPT.

Five mummy cases.

Case B (right): The interior is painted—an eerie receptacle. By the head, a winged serpent; along the sides, a serpent with the sign of Life (cf. the Coptic Cross, Room 1, No. 106, also p. 74), and genii, mostly serpent-headed. The mummy lay on the sun-goddess Neith, on a serpent entwined round a lotus, and on the soul as a bird. The outside of the case is also painted. From Deir el Bahri, Upper Egypt.

Case E (centre): Richly painted mummy with the goddess Neith on its breast. Very effective. Date—about B.C. 600.

3 (back wall): Relief from over the door of a tomb. Left, the deceased, enthroned between two bouquets of lotus; to one of them a couple of ducks are tied. Then comes an old harpist, who is singing, accompanied by a girl on a drum, and by two others who clap their hands. To the right, a man preparing drink; then two dancing girls. Beautiful work. From Heliopolis.

ROOM 9: ANCIENT EGYPT: CROCODILE WORSHIP.

The contents of this room, though not Alexandrian, are Ptolemaic, and well illustrate that dynasty in its Egyptian aspect. They come from the Temple of Petesouchos, the crocodile god of the Fayoum. The temple was adorned by Agathodorus, a Greek official there B.C. 137, in honour of Ptolemy VII (Physkon) and of his two wives, one his sister, one his niece, and both called Cleopatra. (For the marriage arrangements of this unattractive monarch, *see* tree, p. 14). The temple itself has been in part brought to the Museum, and well set up in the North Garden, (*see* below).

CENTRE OF ROOM: Wooden stretcher on which is mummied crocodile. It was carried thus in procession by the priests, as the water colour below (copy of a fresco) shows. The stretcher rests on a wooden chest, also found in the shrine.

BACK WALL: Wooden door of the outer gateway (*see* North Garden). Greek inscription. Here are some photographs by which the temple can be reconstructed.

39 (right of the chest): An offering table to the god, ornate and unpleasing. He lies in a little tank.

LEFT OF THE ENTRANCE DOOR: Relief of a priest adoring the god, who crawls upon lotus flowers.

ROOM 10: ANCIENT EGYPT: SMALL EXHIBITS.

IN THE ENTRANCE: Offering table, with basins for the libations.

RIGHT WALL: *Case C;* Statuettes of gods, all named. The most interesting for the history of Alexandria are 3–25 Osiris, and 26–40 the bull Apis, with whom he was compounded to make Serapis (p. 21).

Case D: Mummies of a baby, of an eagle, of an ibis.

Case Aa–Shelf b (at the top): Winged scarabs in blue enamel. *Shelf k* (No. 1): statuette of Sekhet, goddess of the heat of the sun—she has the head of a lioness and holds a gold flower. *Shelf f:* Bast, the cat-god. No. 39 has a kitten between the paws. 51. Gold earrings. *Shelf 1* has more statues of Bast. 55. Very good.

LEFT WALL: *Case H;* "Canopic" vases of alabaster. Used to hold those parts of the dead that could not be embalmed. Each dedicated to a son of Horus. Amset held the stomach; Hapi the intestines; Douamoutef the lungs; Kebehsenouf the liver. For their connection with the town of Canopus, *see* p. 190.

Case Bb:—More statuettes—especially *Shelf i.*—Harpocrates and Horus; and *Shelf k,* Isis nursing Horus—the artistic origin for the Christian design of the Madonna and Child (p. 74). There are some rattles and vases of the Isis cult.

Case L: Little serving figures (Ushabti), which were put in the grave with the mummy to do the work for it in the underworld.

Also round the wall of the room: six painted mummy cases.

Down the middle: two big tables of scarabs, amulets, gold trinkets, etc.

ROOM 11: GRECO-EGYPTIAN.

Objects in which the Greek and Egyptian influences mingle. They are few in number, and not as interesting as one might expect. No living art was born from the union.

RIGHT WALL: 18. Dedication to the Egyptian god Anubis with a Greek inscription. 20. Profile of a Ptolemy—rather charming. 33–40. Serpent worship—very repulsive. 40 is a curious mixture. The male snake has the basket of Serapis and the club of Hercules; the female, the disc of Isis and the sheaf of Ceres. 41. Bad painting, Greek style, of a girl with Egyptian gods round her. From Gabbari.

END WALL (both sides): 43–53. Clumsy statues from the Fayoum, in which Greek influence appears.

LEFT WALL (centre): 61. Large fragment of a relief from a temple at Benha; left, Horus with a falcon's head; right, a human figure, by whose side is a Greek inscription. 62. Model of a shrine, mixed style: in the sanctuary Isis nurses Horus. 69. (in *Case A*)—beautiful statue (headless) of a woman, Egyptian style, but Greek feeling.

Archway between Rooms 11 and 12. ON RIGHT: Portrait of a youth in white marble (from Kom es Chogafa). LEFT: Pleasing portrait of a child of two or three years of age.

ROOM 12: PORTRAITS: MOSTLY GRECO-ROMAN IN STYLE.

CENTRE: 30. Dull colossal statue of Marcus Aurelius. The Emperor, looking bored but benignant, appears as a general: his right arm rests on a cornucopia. A cross has in Christian times been scratched on the stomach of the cuirass.—From Rue Rosette.

RIGHT WALL: 8. Exquisite bust of Venus; 16a and 17. Heads, in marble and granite, of Alexander the Great (p. 8); of no artistic merit; but found in Alexandria. 18. Head of a young soldier. 20. Marble head of a goddess; beautiful hair. Found near "Pompey's Pillar." 21. Head, perhaps of

Berenice, wife of Euergetes; found in same place.—*Cabinet A:* Small portraits: note as especially fine 15 and 15*a* Ptolemy Euergetes (?) and 12 Berenice his wife (?) with elaborate curls; they stand in the centre of the case on the second shelf. *Cabinet D:* Alleged portrait in marble of Cleopatra in her declining years. Thin, firmly compressed lips and general expression of severity discredit the theory. 60. Colossal granite head of Ptolemy IV Philopator; from Aboukir.

LEFT WALL: 51. Bust of Emperor Hadrian. 52. Head in white marble—noble features, supposed to be those of Marcus Aurelius in youth. *Cabinet B:* Heads and torsos: No. 27 (centre shelf), Head of a child with radiant smile—found in Alexandria. 36. Head of Zeus, hirsute countenance—thick lips. Has been scalped. *Cabinet F:* Various small bronzes; 44. Life-sized head of woman in marble: has Rosetti-like neck and mouth.

ROOM 13: MISCELLANEOUS.

CENTRE: 1. Statue of an Emperor, on which a head of Septimus Severus has been fixed.

In *Case F* (right): 2. Smiling face of a Faun. On the top of the case, a queer relief of a winged griffin and a woman on two wheels. (Nemesiṣ ?).

In *Case H* (left): 2. Caricature of a Roman senator with a rat's head.

ROOM 14: MISCELLANEOUS.

CENTRE: Mosaic from Gabbari, once displaying a Medusa's head.

BACK WALL: 1. Marble statue of a Roman orator. The head does not belong.

LEFT CORNER: 2–4. Delicate architectural details. From Rue Sultan Hussein.

LEFT WALL: 6. Door of a tomb-niche, blending Greek and Egyptian styles. The table in front is from the same tomb and was used for funeral offering. From the Western Necropolis.

ROOM 15: ARCHITECTURAL.

Small fragments, etc., many of them very dainty and showing traces of paint.

RIGHT WALL: 9. Sacrificial altar, imitating a building, with doors realistically ajar.

On a column in the right-hand corner: 2. Capital, well illustrating mixture of styles; the general form and the acanthus leaves are Greek, the lotus, papyrus, and serpents are Egyptian.

MIDDLE WALL, behind a curtain: 20. Painted side of a sarcophagus; a shallow and pretty design of two gamecocks about to fight across a festoon of flowers. 2nd cent. A.D.

LEFT WALL: 50. Other side of same sarcophagus; buildings in perspective.

ROOM 16: STATUES, MOSTLY GRECO-ROMAN IN STYLE.

RIGHT WALL: 4. Marble torso of a young hero or god; the head and arms, which were worked separately, are lost, good work. From Alexandria—probably on a temple. 7–8. *On a shelf*—Statuettes, headless and insignificant, but interesting for their subject:—Alexander the Great as a god with the aegis. From Alexandria. 12. On a column—Bust of the composite-goddess Demeter-Selene, showing headdress of Demeter and horns of the moon. 21–23: Priestesses of Isis, recognisable by the sacred knots into which their shawls are tied in front. 28. Large Ionic capital; another stands opposite, four others in the garden court. From Silsileh, and is probably part of the Ptolemaic Palace (p. 18). 27. Greek funeral relief, as old as 3rd cent. B.C. Found at Alexandria, but probably imported from Athens.

CENTRE OF ROOM: 31. Fine bath of black stone, decorated with heads of lions and of a lynx, through whom the water escaped. Further on (37) is another. Both from the Western Necropolis, where they were used as tombs. 33. Colossal votive foot, merging above the ankle into a bust of Serapis. On the head a Greek dedication to Serapis from two of his worshippers; two serpents above with a child (Horus ?) between them. From Alexandria. 34. An immense eagle, rather cumbersome, and presented by the late

Khedive; from the island of Thasos. 39. Gigantic forearm, holding a sphere. From Benha.

LEFT WALL: 40. Big limestone Corinthian capital. 3rd cent. B.C. 47, 48, 49, 51, and (*on shelf*) 53 and 52*a*: Statues and Heads of Serapis. Important (p. 21). 47 is probably a Roman copy of the original—ascribed to Bryaxis —in the Temple, and well renders the type—half terrible half benign. On its head are the marks where the sacred basket was attached. From the Rue Adib. 48 shows Cerberus. 52 and 52*a* were found near the actual Serapeum; the blue-black colour of the latter recalls the original statue. 50. Priest of Serapis (?) headless; robe with seven-rayed stars, scarabs, the crescent moon. Apis Bulls and a great serpent. From the Temple. 53. Realistic Portrait head. 54. Apollo seated on the Omphalos, or Navel of the World at Delphi; a rare subject; probably imported from Antioch, Asia Minor. 59. Headless statues, Roman, some with rolls of papyrus by them. From Sidi Gaber. 62. Entrance of Room 17: Genius of Death asleep.

ROOM 17: MISCELLANEOUS.

An interesting room.

CENTRE: Delightful mosaic of a water party in Upper Egypt; birds, frogs, eels, fish, hippopotami and pigmies; in the middle a lady and gentleman with their offspring and an attendant recline beneath an awning that sways in the wind. Caesar and Cleopatra may have disported themselves thus (p. 27). Greek inscription and ornamental border.

BACK WALL: Colossal headless porphyry statue of Diocletian (?) on a throne. From Rue Attarine.

IN FRONT OF STATUE: Marble sarcophagus; Dionysus and Ariadne. From the Western Necropolis. The type is rare in Alexandria, the decorations being generally fruit or flowers.

PLACED ABOUT THE ROOM: Mummies from the Fayoum (*see* preliminary note); the best (*Case U*) stands against a pillar; it has a realistic portrait of the deceased, painted on wood.

ROUND THE WALLS: *Case A:* Lovely iridescent glass; the

Alexandrian glass was famous. *Case D,* terra cotta dish for
serving poached eggs. *Table Rr:* Funerary objects from the
Western Necropolis; 2506, &c., Gnostic Amulets (p. 75).
Case G and adjoining *Table S:* Fragments of "Egyptian
Queen" pottery, a commercial product of Ptolemaic times.
The type was a green enamel vase on which was a relief of a
princess sacrificing at an altar with some such inscription as
"Good luck to Queen Berenice." These vases were bought
as ornaments by loyal citizens and tourists. *Case G:*
Funerary furniture; in the centre a skull, wreathed with
artificial laurel. 3rd cent. B.C. (From the Chatby Necropo-
lis, p. 178). *Case K:* Fine cinerary urns, dated—earliest,
281 B.C.—Right and left of the door into the gardens;
Marble sarcophagi of the usual Alexandrian design. *Case
P:* Glass vases of exquisite hue and design; there is more
beauty in this little case than in tons of statues.

ROOM 18:   TERRA COTTA STATUETTES.

The statuettes, of which the best are Hellenistic and
Alexandrian, were at first connected with funeral rites and
later placed in the tomb from the sentiment that prompts
us to drop flowers, especially when the dead person is
young. They have mostly been found in the tombs of children and women. They are the loveliest things in the
Museum.

FACING ENTRANCE, and to right (*Cases HH* and *A*): Cinerary urns from Alexandria.

LEFT WALL: *Case F* (covered with curtain): Here are
the masterpieces—27 statuettes of women. 1, 4, 7, 8, 12, 13,
are the most beautiful perhaps—so delicate but so dignified.
1 is crowned with ivy and wears tiny earrings; the shape
of her arm shown through the wrap that covers it. 7 carries
her child. 12 with her little draped head is curiously impressive. *Case G:* 1. Child on his mother's shoulder. *Case
H:* 1. Child on a toy chariot, full of grapes and drawn by
dogs. *Case I:* Caricatures. *Case L:* Moulds for terra cotta.
Case in corner, also *FF:* Fragments from Naucratis, the
Greek predecessor of Alexandria in Egypt.

RIGHT WALL: Terra cottas from the Fayoum—stupid and vulgar.

DOWN THE CENTRE OF ROOM: Four mosaics from Canopus (p. 190); they probably decorated the Temple of Serapis there.

ROOM 19: MISCELLANEOUS.

IN ENTRANCE: Funerary urn still garlanded with artificial flowers. From Chatby. 3rd cent. B.C.

CENTRE: Mosaic—the best geometrical mosaic in the Museum. From Chatby.

IN ANGLES OF ROOM: *Cases A, B, C, D:* Terra cottas from Kom es Chogafa. Note in *Case C, Shelf b,* 1. Model of seven pots and a big jar—like doll's furniture; and in *Case D* some unamusing grotesques.

Also in the angles of the octagon: *Cases I, II, III, IV.* Funerary furniture from Hadra (p. 172). In *Case I* are two beautiful objects; a blue enamel vase decorated with faces of Bes, Egyptian god of luck; and (*Shelf b,* 2): Terra cotta statuette of a boy, who clings, laughing, to a term of Dionysus, and holds an apple in his hand.

ROOM 20: CHATBY NECROPOLIS (p. 178).

Several painted tombstones. The best are protected by tinted glass, and better studied in the water-colour copies hanging above.

LEFT OF ENTRANCE: 1. Isodora, a lady of Cyrene, with her child. 2. A young Macedonian officer, riding; his orderly runs behind holding the horse's tail. Date 4th cent. B.C.—*i.e.* shortly after Alexander had founded the city. 10231: Boy and child.

Cases A and *B:* Funerary furniture. In *Case B* are some pretty terra cottas: 1, 2. Ladies sitting. 7, 8, 9. Schoolgirls at lessons.

Pedestal V (right wall): Tombstone of young man with a foot-stool and pet dog.

CENTRE OF ROOM: Fine marble group, mutilated, of Dionysus and the Faun. Found near the demolished Porte Rosette.

ROOM 21: IBRAHIMIEH NECROPOLIS (p. 179).

Case in entrance: Wreaths of artificial flowers. Ugly really, but one is impressed by their being so old. Double flute of ivory.

Case in centre: Mummied birds from Aboukir (p. 188).

Cases D and *F:* From Ibrahimieh. *Case D.* Inscription in Aramaic—one of the few relics of the early Jewish settlement at Alexandria (p. 65); some more are on the floor. Date 3rd cent. B.C. *Case F* (right wall): Cinerary urns. Groups in painted plaster of the phallic Min (whom the Greeks identified with Pan), Hercules, Horus, etc.

ROOM 22: CANOPUS. (p. 190).

Disappointing; better work than this tenth rate Hellenistic stuff must have existed at the great shrine.

LEFT WALL: 1–3: Inscriptions of historical interest: they mention Serapis and Isis, the deities of the place, and the Ptolemies Philadelphus and Euergetes.

BACK WALL: In cases, sculptures and terra cottas.

RIGHT WALL: Stucco-coated columns from the Temple of Serapis; others have been left in place.

CENTRE: Mosaic from Alexandria.

ROOM 22A: FRESCOES.

RIGHT OF DOOR: Three pagan frescoes, connected with crocodile worship (*see* Room 7 and North Garden). From Temple of Petesouchos, Fayoum. Date 2nd cent. A.D. Thank offerings to the god from Heron Soubathos, an officer: 1. He stands. 2. He rides.

REST OF ROOM: Christian frescoes of great interest, from crypt discovered in the desert beyond Lake Mariout. Date 5th cent. A.D. A staircase led down to a square room. 1 and 2 are from the ceiling of this room; from its walls come— 3, St. Menas standing between camels—4 and 5, the Annunciation. A passage led to a smaller room; on its vault was 6, Head of Christ. In this smaller room were 7 and 8. Out of it opened a little niche at the end of which was 9, a saint in prayer among the scenery of paradise.

VERANDAH AND GARDENS. Large Exhibits.

In the middle of the verandah: Colossal headless statue of Hercules.

North Garden: Left—Gateways and shrine of the *Temple of Petesouchos,* crocodile god of the Fayoum (*see* Room 9 for further details). The first gateway is the entrance Pylon, over which is a Greek inscription dating the temple to B.C. 137. The wooden door in Room 9 belonged here. On each side of the gateway are lions. It led to a brick courtyard, in which was a Nilometer. The court was closed by the second gateway, which is flanked by sphinxes, and led to a second and similar court. Then comes the third gate, and, closing the perspective, the shrine. The shrine has three cavities, in each of which lurked a mummied crocodile upon a wooden stretcher (*see* Room 9). In the left cavity is the fresco of a crocodile; in the central the fresco of a god with a crocodile's head between two other deities. Over the cavities are several decorative friezes—one of snakes. The outside of the shrine is also frescoed to imitate marble. In front of it was found a wooden chest (Room 9).

At back of garden: Granite group of Rameses II and his daughter—headless. From Aboukir. Against the wall behind: colossal green granite head of Antony as Osiris. From near Nouzha (p. 172). The companion head of Cleopatra as Isis is in Belgium.

South garden: Two reconstructed tombs from the Chatby Necropolis (p. 178). The first (in the corner) is remarkable. The sarcophagus imitates a bed with cushions each end. The chamber where it stands was once preceded by a long vestibule for the mourners (as in the Anfouchi tombs, p. 137). The date 3rd. cent. B.C. The second tomb has a shell vault niche (like Kom es Chogafa, p. 163).

The Rue Rosette continues and at last issues from between houses. Here, ever since its foundation, the city has ended; in Ptolemaic times the Gate of the Sun or Canopic Gate stood here, in Arab times the Rosetta

Gate. The Public Gardens (left and right) follow the line of the Arab walls (see p. 86 and Section IV). The tramway to Nouzha crosses the route. The road continues under another name to Sidi Gaber (Section V), thence to Ramleh, and to Aboukir (Section VII). It is a good road and well planted; but terribly straight, like all roads that the Ancients have planned.

SECTION II

From the Square to Ras-el-Tin

ROUTE:—By the Rue de France and Rue Ras-el-Tin to Ras-el-Tin promontory; returning to the Square by Anfouchi Bay and the Eastern Harbour—the "Circular" Tram (Green Triangle) runs along the Quays.

CHIEF POINTS OF INTEREST:—Terbana and Chorbagi Mosques; Mosque of Abou-el-Abbas; Anfouchi Catacombs; Ras-el-Tin Palace; Prehistoric Harbour; Fort Kait Bey; New Quays.

We start from the northwest corner of the Square. The Rue de France traverses the "Turkish Town" (p. 90), which was built in the 17th and 18th cents. on the spit of land that had accreted round the ruined Ptolemaic dyke (p. 11). Its bazaars and Mosques are on a small scale, for the city was then at her feeblest. But the district is picturesque and, especially at evening, full of gentle charm. The best way of seeing it is to wander aimlessly about.†

In the Rue de France:—Right: Rue Pirona. Built into the wall at its entrance are fragments of Egyptian sculpture, the lion-headed goddess Sekhet, &c. The road opens into a picturesque little square which contains a former Native Tribunal, and a building (No. 4) that has a carved gateway and a tranquil courtyard with antique columns.

In the roads to the left of the Rue de France are
some Mosques:—

Mosque of Sheikh Ibrahim Pacha, off the southwest
corner of the Square; big ugly building with red and yellow
minaret.

Chorbagi Mosque, in the Rue el Midan. Well worth a
visit. Date—1757. Plan—similar to the Terbana (*see* below).
Exterior spoilt by restoration, but the door from the vestibule into the Mosque proper has over it a trefoil arch full
of brilliant tiles; in the centre of the arch is a miniature
praying niche (mihrab).—The Interior, though mean architecturally, retains its magnificent Tile Decoration almost intact. The tiles are grouped round the walls in great
panels, the design being sometimes geometrical and sometimes a pot of flowers. Between the panels are bands of
contrasting tiles. Colours:—in the panels, yellow, green, and
a deep cornflower-blue predominate; in the bands, china-
blue and white. A few of the panels are of polished con-
glomerate stone. The Prayer Niche—flanked by two bizarre
twisted columns—has the pot of flowers design. The door
of the pulpit is handsome; it has duplicated Cufic inscriptions, which on the right read from right to left, as is
usual, and on the left are reversed for the sake of symmetry:
a good instance of the decorative tendency of Arab Art. Ex-
ternally the Mosque is flanked by arcades; one overlooks the
street and is used by the Muezzin, since there is no
minaret; the other looks into a courtyard of stilted arches.

Mosque of Abou Ali. (Go nearly to the end of the long
Rue Bab-el-Akdar; thence, right, into Rue Masguid Ali Bey
Guenénah; thence, right again). There is nothing to see in
this humble little Mosque, but it is said to be the oldest
in the city. In it are the figures 677, which, if they record
the date A.H., would mean 1278 A.D. The natives say that
it once stood at the edge of the sea, so that the faithful
made their ablutions with salt water before praying. The
tradition may be correct, for the old line of the coast lay
here (*see* map p. 106). The building in its present appear-

ance cannot be earlier than the 18th cent.; in it, perched on the summit of the pulpit, is the model of a boat.

Continuing from the Rue de France we see ahead the white mass of the *Terbana Mosque.*

Well worth visiting, in spite of modern plaster and paint. Date—1684. The little doorway on the street is in the "Delta" style—bricks painted black and red, with occasional courses of wood between them and Cufic inscriptions above: "There is no God but God," and "Mohammed is the Prophet of God"; better examples of the style at Rosetta (p. 199). The rest of the ground floor is occupied by shops. At the top of the stairs an interesting scene unfolds. To the left are two great antique granite columns with Corinthian capitals, and through them an open air terrace with an iron trellis and barred windows. To the right is the Vestibule of the Mosque, once very beautiful; two thirds of the entrance wall are still covered with tiles, designed like those in the Chorbagi, and over the door is the inscription "Built in 1097 A.H. by Haj Ibrahim Terbana," surmounted by a trefoil arch. More antique columns. The Interior is a rectangle, divided up by eight columns, disfigured but antique. Good painted ceiling, best seen from the western gallery. The Prayer Niche is finely tiled, as is the wall to its right; the large tiles with white daisies on them are inferior modern work. Lamentable chandeliers.—There is an external gallery with antique columns. The Minaret rises above the entrance landing; its topmost gallery is tiled.

The main route now takes the name Rue Ras-el-Tin. Here once began the southern shore of the Island of Pharos. Consequently ancient remains occur in situ.

Right: Rue Sidi Abou el Abbas leads to the square of that name—the most considerable in the Turkish Town; here, by evening light, one sometimes has the illusion of oriental romance; here (1922) is the rallying point of the Nationalist demonstrations. The road, just before it enters the square, crosses the site of a temple to Isis Pharia who watched over the lighthouse. (*see* coin in Museum, Room 2).

Dominating the square is the great white *Mosque of Abou el Abbas Moursi,* built 1767 by Algerians, some of whom still live in the neighbourhood; the tomb of the saint (d. 1288) is under a low dome; the other side of the Mosque (reached by a winding passage to the right) has an unrestored brick entrance in the "Delta" style, with pendentives, tiles, and a Cufic inscription.— At the end of the Square:—little *Mosque of Sidi Daoud,* with tomb of the saint, from whose precinct two tall palm trees rise.—Just off south side of square is a typical street tomb (Sidi Abou el Fath), enclosed in its green lattice; of the houses close to it No. 31 has good carved "Mashrabieh" work, No. 33 a carved lintel, with door posts of alternate courses of limestone and wood. All this tangle of lanes preserves the atmosphere of the 18th cent. East. Between the Abou el Abbas Mosque and the sea is a large modern Mosque—the Bouseiri— where the Sultan usually makes his Friday prayer; a little up the street is a stone fragment, covered with hieroglyphs, and now used upside down as a seat.

The Rue Ras-el-Tin is now joined by the "Circular" tram line. To the right is a large piece of waste ground. In the corner of this, close to the road, are some dilapidated glass roofs; these protect the Anfouchi Tombs; the custodian lives close by.

THE ANFOUCHI TOMBS

Though inferior to the Kom es Chogafa Catacombs, (p. 163), these tomb groups are interesting for their decoration scheme. Their entrances adjoin, their plan

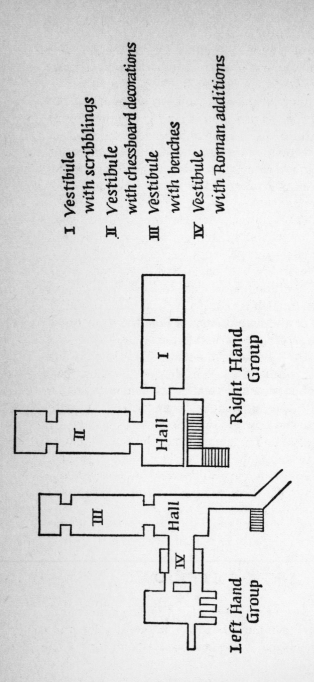

I Vestibule
with scribblings

II Vestibule
with chessboard decorations

III Vestibule
with benches

IV Vestibule
with Roman additions

II

Hall

I

Right Hand
Group

III

IV

Hall

Left Hand
Group

THE ANFOUCHI TOMBS

is similar:—a staircase, cut through the limestone, leads down to a square hall out of which the tomb chambers open. The decoration is of stucco painted to imitate marble blocks and tiles. It is shoddy, and sometimes recalls the imitation wall papers of Victorian England. Archaeologists know it as the First Pompeian style. Date:—Ptolemaic with Roman additions. Name of occupants: unknown.

RIGHT HAND TOMB GROUP (*see* Plan opposite).

At the first turn of the stairs, protected by a cloth, is a good picture. Subject:—Purification of the Dead by water (?); Horus, with a falcon's head, points with one hand to the land of death, and with the other tries to draw the dead man towards it; Osiris holds out a lustral vase; Isis is behind.—At the second turn of the stairs is another picture, half destroyed;—Osiris sits on a throne as king of the Dead with the dog-god Anubis behind him; before him, just discernible, stands Horus introducing the dead man.

Thus the staircase reminded visitors of the difficulties through which the dead must pass, and honoured Osiris, Isis, and their son Horus—a trinity whose worship was popular in Ptolemaic times and often connected with the worship of Serapis. The walls imitate alabaster &c.; on the vault, geometric designs.

The Hall is open to the air. It gives access to two tomb chambers, each of which has a vestibule for mourners. That to the right (i) is undecorated, but the scribblings on the vestibule walls are most amusing; they were made over 2,000 years ago by a visitor or workman, and help us to reconstruct the life of the Greco-Egyptian city. The inscriptions are in Greek. On the left wall Diodorus has immortalised Antiphiles, his friend. Further on is a sailing ship. Right wall, a battle ship with a turret for fighting, such as might have accompanied Cleopatra to Actium.

The vestibule in front (ii) is quite charming. It was decorated in the same style as the staircase—traces of this remains on the inside of its entrance wall—but soon after a fresh coat of stucco was applied, and painted like the first to imitate marble, but in better taste. Below, is a dado of "alabaster," above it an effective design of black and white squares arranged chess board fashion and divided by alabaster bands. In the chess board are mythological scenes, now defaced. The ceiling, being purely geometric, probably belongs to the earlier scheme.

At the end of the vestibule is the entrance to the tomb chamber, with the disc of the Sun (Ra) carved above it, and, on either side, little sleeping sphinxes upon pedestals. A door once closed it; holes for the bolt remain. The tomb chamber itself is decorated in the same pretty style. An altar once stood in the middle. In the back wall is a tiny shrine, closing the vista. The general effect is good, but dainty rather than solemn; the terrors of ancient Egypt are on the wane.

LEFT HAND TOMB GROUP.

The vestibule in front, as one enters the Hall, is very long, and low benches on which the mourners sat run up it on each side. (iii). In the tomb chamber is an enormous sarcophagus of rose coloured granite from Assouan.

The vestibule and tomb chamber to the left (iv) were excavated and decorated on the usual plan. But in the Roman period they were much pulled about, and brick work introduced, together with three new sarcophagi.

There are traces of other tombs over the waste ground, which covers the cemetery of the ancient Island of Pharos. We are now in the centre of the Island, and about to visit its western extremity.

Straight ahead, up a rise, is *Ras-el-Tin Palace*, the summer residence of the Sultan, who makes his state entry every June. It was built by Mohammed Ali (p. 94), who had here the stormy interview with Sir Charles Napier, that ended his loftier ambitions (p. 95); Ismail restored it; Tewfik was here during some of the troubles of 1882 (p. 101). It is not ugly, as palaces go; the grandiose classical portico is rather impressive. To the right are the barracks.†

The peninsula narrows. The road leads on to the Yacht Club (left), and terminates at the Military Hospital which is beautifully situated on the rocky point of Ras-el-Tin (the "Cape of Figs"); splendid views of the Western Harbour and the sea; a Temple of Neptune once stood here, and there are ruins of tombs all along the northern shore. A modern lighthouse stands in the Hospital enclosure, and marks the entrance to the harbour. The Breakwater (constructed 1870–74) starts below, makes towards the isolated rock of Abou Bakr, then bends to the left. Over the water are the island of Marabout and the headland of Agame, which are part of the same limestone chain as Ras-el-Tin, and connected with it by submarine reefs.

The sea west and north of the point is full of remains of the Prehistoric Harbour.

PREHISTORIC HARBOUR

For details of this important and mysterious work see "Les Ports submergés de l'ancienne Isle de Pharos" by M. Jondet, the discoverer. Possibly it may be the harbour alluded to in the Odyssey (see p. 6), but no historian mentions it. Theosophists, with more zeal than probability, have annexed it to the vanished civilisation of Atlantis; M. Jondet inclines to the theory that it may be Minoan—built by the maritime power of Crete. If Egyptian in origin, perhaps the work of Rameses II (B.C. 1300); statues of his reign have been found on Rhakotis (p. 7), and we know that he was attacked by "peoples of the West," and built defences against them. It cannot be as late as Alexander the Great or we should have records. It is the oldest work in the district and also the most romantic, for to its antiquity is added the mystery of the sea.

Long and narrow, the Harbour stretched from the rock

of Abou Bakr on the west to an eastern barrier that
touched the shore beyond the Tour de la Mission d'Egypt.
These two points are joined up by a series of breakwaters
on the north. The entrance was from an unexpected direction, the south. Having rounded Abou Bakr, ships turned
north under the Ras-el-Tin promontory, where there is
deep water. To their left were solid quays, stretching to
Abou Bakr, and recently utilised in the foundation of the
modern breakwater. To their right was another quay. Having entered, they were well in the middle of the main harbour, with a subsidiary harbour to the north.

The visit to the Harbour is best made by boat, since
most of the remains now lie from 4 to 25 feet under the
sea. They have, like all the coast line, subsided, because
the Nile deposits on which they stand are apt to com-
press, and even to slide towards deeper water. They
are built of limestone blocks from the quarries of Mex
and Dekhela, but the construction, necessarily simple,
gives no hint as to nationality or date. The modern
breakwater, being built across the entrance, makes the
scheme rather difficult to follow. (See Plan).

The Small Quay (a) is in perfect condition, and not
four feet under water. Length: 70 yards, breadth, 15;
the surface curves slightly towards the south. The
blocks, measuring about a yard each, are cut to fit one
another roughly, small stones filling up the joints. The
Ras-el-Tin jetty crosses the end of this Quay; the point
of intersection is near the red hut on the jetty.—At the
north end of the Quay is an extension (b) that protected the harbour entrance.

Further north, well inside the harbour, is an islet (c)
covered with remains. Some are tombs, and of later
date; submerged, are the foundations of a rectangular
building (30 yds. by 15) reached on the south by steps,
and connected by little channels with the sea on the

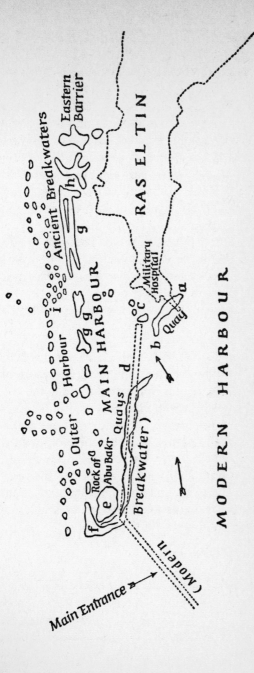

THE PREHISTORIC HARBOUR

Modern work shown thus ----------
Ancient work shown thus ————

Main Entrance (Modern)

Breakwater)

Quays

Rock of
Abu Bakr

Outer Harbour

MAIN HARBOUR

Ancient Breakwaters

Eastern
Barrier

Military
Hospital

Quay

RAS EL TIN

MODERN HARBOUR

north. This islet may have contained the harbour offices.

From the modern breakwater the Great Quays (d) show here and there as ochreous lines below the waves. They are 700 yds. long, and constructed like the Small Quay, but from larger stones. They connect with the rock of Abou Bakr (e), the western bastion of the Prehistoric Harbour; it is a solid mass over 200 yds. square; most is on the sea level, but a part juts up; it is marked all over with foundation cuts and the remains of masonry. West of Abou Bakr is a double breakwater (f) further protecting the works from the sea and the prevalent wind; and on it hinges the huge northern breakwater (g) also double in parts, which runs with interruptions till it reaches the eastern barrier (h). The rock is named after the first Caliph of Islam.

The outer harbour (i) has not yet been fully explored.

Having returned as far as Ras-el-Tin Palace, we bear to the left, and follow the tram line along the shore of Anfouchi Bay. The Bay is very shallow and the entrance is protected by reefs. Pirates used it once. Native boat builders work along its beach and are pleasant to watch. In the corner is Anfouchi Pier, with a bathing establishment; beyond, on a small promontory, stands all that is left of Fort Adda; Arabi had his powder stored here in 1882, and the English blew it up (p. 100). Now the tram turns a sharp corner, and a second Fort swings into view—Fort Kait Bey.

FORT KAIT BEY (THE "PHAROS")

This battered and neglected little peninsula is perhaps the most interesting spot in Alexandria, for here, rising to an incredible height, once stood the Pharos Lighthouse, the wonder of the world. Contrary to general belief, some fragments of the Pharos still remain. But before visiting them and the Arab fort in which they are embedded, some knowledge of history is desirable. The fortunes of the peninsula were complicated, and the labours of scholars have only lately made them clear.

HISTORY.

(1) THE ORIGINAL BUILDING (*see* also p. 17).

The lighthouse took its name from Pharos Island (hence the French "phare" and the Italian "faro"). No doubt it entered into Alexander the Great's scheme for his maritime capital, but the work was not done till the reign of Ptolemy Philadelphus. Probable date of dedication: B.C. 279, when the king held a festival to commemorate his parents. Architect: Sostratus, an Asiatic Greek. The sensation it caused was tremendous. It appealed both to the sense of beauty and to the taste for science—an appeal typical of the age. Poets and engineers combined to praise it. Just as the Parthenon had been identified with Athens and St. Peter's was to be identified with Rome, so, to the imagination of contemporaries, the Pharos became Alexandria and Alexandria became the Pharos. Never, in the history of architecture, has a secular building been thus worshipped and taken on a spiritual life of its own. It beaconed to the imagination, not only to ships at sea, and long after its light was extinguished memories of it glowed in the minds of men.

It stood in a colonnaded court. (Plan II, p. 149.) There were four stories. (Plan I, Fig. i.) The square bottom storey was pierced with many windows and contained the rooms, estimated at 300, where the mechanics and attendants were housed. There was a spiral ascent—probably a double spiral —and in the centre there may have been hydraulic machinery for raising fuel to the top; otherwise we must imagine a procession of donkeys who cease not night and day to go up and down the spirals with loads of wood on their backs.

The storey ended in a square platform and a cornice and figures of Tritons. Here too, in great letters of lead, was the Greek inscription; "Sostratus of Cnidos, son of Dexiphanes: to the Saviour Gods: for sailors"—an inscription which, despite its simplicity, bore a double meaning. The "Saviour Gods" are of course Castor and Pollux who protect mariners, but a courtly observer could refer them to Ptolemy Soter and Berenice, whose worship their son was promoting.

The second storey was octagonal and entirely filled by the spiral ascent. Above that was the circular third storey, and above that the lantern. The lighting arrangements are uncertain. Visitors speak of a mysterious "mirror" on the summit, which was even more wonderful than the building itself. What was this "mirror"? Was it a polished steel reflector for the fire at night or for heliography by day? Some accounts describe it as made of finely wrought glass or transparent stone, and declare that a man sitting under it could see ships at sea that were invisible to the naked eye. A telescope? Is it possible that the great Alexandrian school of mathematics discovered the lens, and that their discovery was lost and forgotten when the Pharos fell? It is possible. It is certain that the lighthouse was fitted with every scientific improvement known to the age, that the antique world never surpassed it, and that the mediaeval world regarded it as the work of Jinns.

Standing on the lantern was a statue of Poseidon. This terminated the tower, whose complete height certainly exceeded 400 feet and possibly touched 500.

(2) HISTORY OF THE BUILDING.

We must now follow this masterpiece of engineering into ages of myth and oblivion. It retained its form and functions unimpaired up to the Arab Conquest (A.D. 641). The first, and irreparable, disaster was the fall of the lantern (about 700), entailing the loss of scientific apparatus that could not be replaced. There is a legend that the disaster was planned by the Byzantine Emperor, who could not attack Egypt owing to the magic "mirror," which detected or destroyed his ships. He sent an agent who gained the

Caliph's confidence and told him that beneath the Pharos the treasure of Alexander the Great lay buried. The Caliph commenced demolition, and before the inhabitants of Alexandria, who knew better, could intervene, the two upper stories had fallen into the sea. Henceforth the Pharos is only a stump with a bonfire on the top.

There were restorations under Ibn Touloun (880), and also about 980, but they were unsubstantial additions to the Octagon, which the wind could blow away. Structural repairs were neglected, and about 1100 the second disaster occurred—the fall of the Octagon itself through an earthquake. The square bottom storey survived, but only as a watchtower on the top of which was run up a small square Mosque. (*See* Plan I, Fig. ii, which illustrates this state of the Pharos. The level of the ground has risen owing to the debris from the octagon, and the lower storey has been buttressed.) Then came the final earthquake (14th cent.), and the slow dissolution was over.

Though unable to preserve the Pharos the Arabs admired it, and speak, with their love of the marvellous, of a statue on it whose finger followed the diurnal course of the sun, of a second statue who gave out with varying and melodious voices the various hours of the day, and of a third who shouted an alarm as soon as a hostile flotilla set sail. The first two statues may have existed; the Alexandrians loved such toys. And there is an element of truth in another Arab legend—that the building rested upon a "glass crab." Some vitreous composition probably did form the foundation, and we know that "Cleopatra's Needles" actually did rest on crabs of metal (p. 176); the oriental mind has confused the two monuments. The legend culminates in the visit to the Pharos of a cavalcade of horsemen who lose their way in the 300 rooms, and inadvertently riding into a crack in the glass crab's back fall into the sea! But sometimes the lighthouse sheltered pleasanter adventures. The poet El Deraoui, for example, writes:

A lofty platform guides the voyager by night, guides him with its light when the darkness of evening falls.

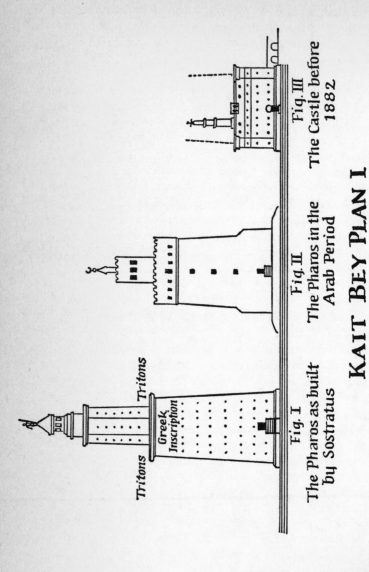

Tritons   Tritons

Tritons

Greek
Inscription

Fig. I
The Pharos as built
by Sostratus

Fig. II
The Pharos in the
Arab Period

Fig. III
The Castle before
1882

KAIT BEY PLAN I

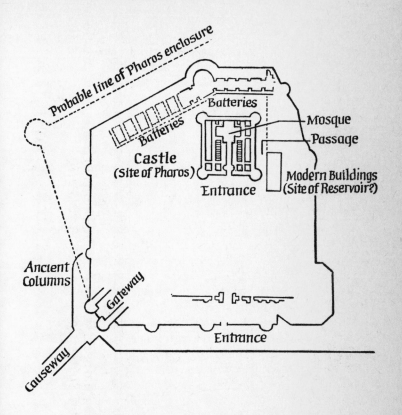

KAIT BEY PLAN II

Thither have I borne a garment of perfect pleasure among my friends, a garment adorned with the memory of beloved companions.

On its height a dome enshadowed me, and thence I saw my friends like stars.

I thought that the sea below me was a cloud, and that I had set up my tent in the midst of the heavens.

Moreover "El Manarah," as the Arabs called it, gave the name to, and became the model for, the "minaret." There is no minaret in Alexandria that closely follows the Pharos, but at Cairo (e.g. at the Tombs of the Mamelukes) one can still see the square bottom storey, the Octagon, the Round and the Summit that exactly reproduce the four-stage design of Sostratus.

(3) FORT KAIT BEY.

For a hundred years ruins cumbered the peninsula. Then (1480) the Mameluke Sultan Kait Bey fortified it as part of his coast defence against the Turks, who had taken Constantinople and were threatening Egypt (p. 87). Kait Bey is a great figure at Cairo, where mosques commemorate his glorious reign. Here he only builds a fort, but like all his work it is architecturally fine, and even in decay its outlines are harmonious. The scheme was a pentagon (Plan II) and in the enclosed area, on the exact site of the Pharos, stood a square castle or keep with a mosque embedded in it. (Plan I, Fig. iii, which shows the castle before it was ruined, the minaret sticking up inside it.) The Turks effected their conquest in 1517, and when their power in its turn declined, Mohammed Ali (1805–1848) modernised the defences. No visitors were admitted, and the Fort gained the reputation of an impregnable and mysterious place. Its career ended with the English bombardment of 1882. Though it did not suffer as much as its neighbour Fort Adda, damage enough was done. The castle was shattered, the minaret snapped, and the desolation and squalor re-established that brood there to-day.†

We can now examine the existing remains. (*See* Plans I & II pp. 148, 149.)

The connecting spit of land only formed in the 9th cent. Previously there was shallow water, spanned by a bridge. Right, as we approach, is anchorage for an Italian fishing fleet; the men come from Bari in the Adriatic.—The road leads by the side of the fort to the new breakwater, built to protect the Eastern Harbour and the sea wall. The Breakwater is a noble work, and it is a pity it is approached through a gateway that suggests an English provincial Jail; the embellishments of modern Alexandria are unduly lugubrious.

The blocked up *Gateway* to the Fort is flanked by round towers; inside it are several rooms with 15th cent. vaulting.—To its left, built into the masonry of Kait Bey's wall or lying on the beach, are about thirty *broken columns* of red Assouan granite; also two or three pieces of fine speckled granite and one piece of marble. These are survivals from the Pharos, and may have stood in the colonnade of its surrounding court; the sea wall of that court probably diverged here from the line of Kait Bey's wall; there are traces of cutting among the rocks.†

The interior of the Fort (best entered from the right) is now a bare enclosure with a few coast-guard huts. The isolated lump of building at the end is the remains of Kait Bey's *Castle*, occupying the ground plan of the Pharos and utilising in part its foundations. Some of these foundations can be seen in the passage immediately to the right of the Castle. The orientation of the Castle and the Pharos was not exactly the same, since the Castle had to be adjusted to the points of the compass on account of the mosque that it contained.— The modern buildings to the right of the passage also rest on old foundations; it is thought that here stood the reservoir, filled with fresh water from the mainland and that on the other side (left of present Castle) stood another edifice with the mechanical statues to balance the design. But this is all conjecture.

The *Mosque* in the Castle is notable for two reasons: architecturally it is the oldest in the city, and in style it is essentially Cairene. It was built by the central government in the course of their coast defence scheme, and so does not resemble the ordinary mosque of the Delta. The entrance, with its five monoliths of Assouan granite, taken from the Pharos, is almost druidical in effect, but the arch above them and the flanking towers faintly recall the glories of Kait Bey's work at Cairo. In the vestibule are remains of stucco on the ceiling and marble on the floor.—The actual Mosque is of the "school" type—a square with an arched recess opening out of each side, each recess being assigned to one of the four orthodox sects of Islam; the Mosque of Sultan Hassan at Cairo is a famous example of this type. The square, and the step leading up to each recess are inlaid with marble. Light enters through carved woodwork above.

Over the Mosque are vaulted rooms. From the summit of the mass is a *View* of Alexandria, not beautiful but instructive.† From right to left are:—Fort Adda, Ras-el-Tin lighthouse (background); minarets of Abou el Abbas and Bouseiri Mosques (foreground); Kom-el-Nadur Fort; Terbana Mosque (foreground); "Pompey's Pillar" (back); Kom-el-Dik Fort; the long line of Eastern suburbs; beyond them the distant minaret of Sidi Bishr; the coast ends in the wooded promontory of Montazah. Close beneath is the modern Breakwater stretching towards the opposing promontory of Silsileh; and left, awash with waves, the Diamond Rock.—And now let the visitor (if the effort is not beyond him) elevate himself 400 feet higher into the air. Let him replace the Ras-el-Tin lighthouse by a Temple to Poseidon; let him delete the mosques and the ground they stand on, and imagine in their place an expanse of water crossed by a Dyke; let him add to "Pompey's Pillar" the Temple of Serapis and Isis and the vast buttressed walls of the Library; let him turn Kom-el-Dik into a gorgeous and fantastic park, with the Tomb of Alexander at its feet; and the Eastern suburbs into gardens; and finally let him suppose that it is not Silsileh that stretches towards him but the peak of the Ptolemaic Palace, sheltering to its right the ships of the royal fleet and flanked on the landward side by the tiers of the theatre and the groves of the Mouseion.— Then he may have some conception of what Ancient Alexandria looked like from the summit of the Pharos —what she looked like when the Arabs entered in the autumn of 641.

Beneath the Batteries on the north of the Fort, and almost level with the beach, is a long gallery in which lie some shells that were fired by the English in 1882.

The tram now follows the curve of the *Eastern Harbour,* a beautifully shaped basin. It was the main harbour of the ancients, but Mohammed Ali when he planned the modern city, developed the Western instead (p. 97). There is a sea wall in two stages, to break the waves which dash right on to the road in rough weather; and there is a very fine promenade—the New Quays—which stretches all the way from Kait Bey to Silsileh. A walk along it can be delightful, though occasionally marred by bad smells.—We pass, right, the Bouseiri Mosque (*see* above) and finally come to the French Gardens, that connect with the Square, whence we started.

Left of the French Gardens are: the French Consulate—an isolated building; the General Post Office—entered from the road behind; and the Church of St. Andrew's—Church of Scotland. To the right, down Rue de l'Eglise Maronite, is the Maronite Church, an inoffensive building; (for the Maronites *see* pp. 82, 229).

SECTION III

From the Square to
the Southern Quarters

ROUTE:—By the Place St. Catherine and "Pompey's Pillar" to the Mahmoudieh Canal, taking the Karmous Tram (Green Lozenge). The Ragheb Pasha Tram (Red Crescent) and the Moharrem Bey Tram (Red Circle) also go from the Square to the Canal. There is also the "Circular" Tram (Green Triangle) which crosses the three lines just mentioned, on its course from Cairo Railway Station to the Docks. There is a carriage road along the Canal.

CHIEF POINTS OF INTEREST:—"Pompey's Pillar," Kom-es-Chogafa Catacombs, the Canal.

The Southern Quarters are neither smart nor picturesque. But they include the site of Rhakotis, the nucleus of ancient Alexandria, and preserve some remarkable antiquities (*see* pp. 7, 21). Here too are the churches and schools of the various religious and political bodies (*see* p. 227).

We start from the south side of the Square, and immediately reach the *Place St. Catherine,* a triangular green. Here is the traditional site of St. Catherine's martyrdom, whence she was transported to Mount Sinai by angels. But the legend only dates from the 9th cent. and it is unlikely that the saint ever existed (*see* p. 51). Franciscans settled here in the 15th cent. and built a church that has disappeared. In 1832 Mo-

hammed Ali granted land to the Roman Catholics, and
the present *Cathedral Church of St. Catherine* was begun. It fell down while it was being put up, but un-
deterred by the omen the builders persisted, and here
is the result. Gaunt without and tawdry within, the
Cathedral makes no attempt to commemorate the exquisite legend round which so much that is beautiful
has gathered in the West; St. Catherine of Alexandria
is without grace in her own city. The approach to the
church has however a certain ecclesiastic calm.—Behind (entered from Rue Sidi el Metwalli) is the Catholic Archbishop's Palace; the wayside tomb of the Mohammedan Saint Sidi el Metwalli, a prior arrival, abuts
into his Grace's garden.

Left of the Cathedral is another in equally bad taste
—the Cathedral of the Greek Community (Greek Orthodox) dedicated to the Annunciation. The Schools of
the Community are close to it.

Left, after leaving the Place St. Catherine:—Rue Sidi
el Metwalli, following the line of the ancient Canopic
Way; it leads past the *Attarine Mosque,* which is worth
looking at. In the past, buildings of greater importance
stood on this commanding site. Here was a church to
St. Athanasius, dedicated soon after his death (4th
cent.). In the Arab Conquest (7th cent.) the church
was adapted into a great mosque, square in shape like
the Mosque of Ibn Touloun at Cairo, and stretching
some way to the north of the present building; travellers mistook it for the tomb or the palace of Alexander
the Great. In it stood an ancient sarcophagus, weighing
nearly seven tons. The English, informed that Alexander had once lain here, took the sarcophagus away
when they occupied Alexandria in 1801 (*see* p. 93).
The French protested, and the sheikhs of the Mosque,
deeply moved, came down to the boat to bid the relic
farewell. The sarcophagus is now in the British Mu-

seum, and has proved to belong to the native Pharaoh
Nekht Heru Hebt, B.C. 378.—The present Mosque is
wedge shaped with a minaret at the point; a good little
specimen of modern Mohammedan architecture. It has
a second façade in the Rue Attarine,† (Scent Bazaar)
whence its name. Inside is the Tomb of Said Mohammed (13th cent.), a friend of Abou el Abbas (p. 137).
—Beyond it the road becomes the Rue Rosette (see
Section I); right is the American Mission Church and
the Cairo Station.

Right after leaving the Place:—district inhabited by
the Armenian community (see p. 229). Their church
is simple and rather attractive, and has the projecting
western vestibule characteristic of Armenian architecture, e.g. of the Metropolitan Cathedral of Etchmiad-
zine. In the graveyard are monuments of Nubar Pasha
by Puech (see p. 170), and of Takvor Pasha. In the
grounds of the school, a black basalt sphinx.

Straight ahead after leaving the Place: is the Rue
Abou el Dardaa. In a turning out of it to the right (Rue
Prince Moneim) in the grounds of a florist named
Mousny, are some remains of the Old Protestant Cemetery.—The burials are of a later date than those at St.
Saba (p. 114). The most interesting is the Tomb of
Henry Salt. Salt, a vigorous but rather shady Englishman with an artistic temperament, first came to these
parts in 1809, when he was sent on a mission to Abyssinia. Six years later he became Consul General and fell
in with the financial plans of Mohammed Ali (p. 95)
and acquiesced in his illegal monopolies. He was an
ardent archaeologist of the commercial type and got
concessions for excavating in Upper Egypt, offering
the results, at exorbitant rates, to the British Museum.
After much haggling the Museum bought his collection
in 1823. He died near Alexandria in 1827. The quaint
inscription on his tomb says:—

His ready genius explored and elucidated the Hiero-
glypics (sic) and other antiquities of this country. His
faithful and rapid pencil and the nervous originality of
his untutored senses conveyed to the world vivid ideas
of the scenes that had delighted himself.

Some of the tombs are hidden among plants and ferns.
The Cemetery was once much larger; the road has cut
through it.

At the end of the Rue Abou el Dardaa, where the
tram turns, is the *Mosque of Amr.* Here probably stood
the Mosque of Mercy which the conqueror Amr ordered to be built where he had sheathed his sword
after the recapture of the city in 643 (*see* p. 62).

We turn right for a few yards, along a road that follows the line of the vanished Arab Walls (p. 86). Then
to the left by the big Italian schools. The tram has now
entered the ancient district of Rhakotis.

"POMPEY'S PILLAR" and the TEMPLE
OF SERAPIS

As often happens in Alexandria, history and archaeology fail to support one another. Ancient writers do
not mention "Pompey's Pillar," but they tell us a great
deal about the buildings that stood in its neighbourhood and have now disappeared. This shapeless hill
was from early times covered with temples and houses.
Long before Alexander came it was the citadel of
Rhakotis (p. 7). Osiris was worshipped here. Then
with Ptolemy Soter it leaps into fame. Osiris is modified
into Serapis (p. 20), and the hill, encased in great bas-
tions of masonry was built up into an acropolis on
whose summit rose the God's temple. Under Cleopatra
it gained additional splendour. The great Library of

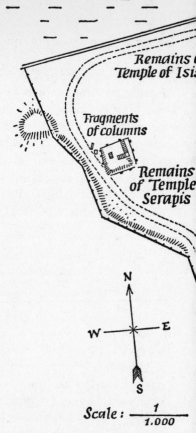

Mohammedan

Remains of Temple of Isis

Fragments of columns

Remains of Temple of Serapis

N
W — E
S

Scale: $\frac{1}{1.000}$

POMPEY'S PILLAR, ETC.

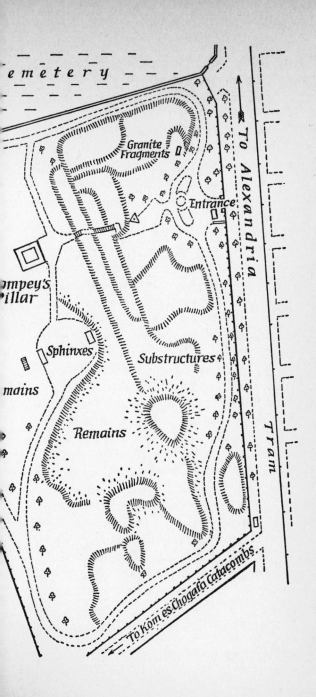

Alexandria had been burnt† in the Caesarian war, and the queen began a new collection which she attached to the Serapeum. Here for four hundred years was the most learned spot on the earth. The Christians wiped it out. In 391 the Patriarch Theophilus (p. 55) led a mob against the temple, sacked it, and broke the statue of the God. It is impossible that the books should not have perished at the same time: they were arranged in the cloisters that surrounded the temple (*see* below) so that the mob had to pass them to reach its central prey. The monks now swarmed over the hill and built a church to St. John the Baptist in the gutted shrine. Here were the headquarters of Theophilus' nephew, Cyril (p. 56) and hence his supporters issued to murder Hypatia at the other end of the town (415). With the invasion of the Arabs the darkness increases. The Library had already disappeared (the legend accusing them of burning it has the flimsiest foundations), but they did plenty of harm in other ways: one of the Arab governors threw a quantity of columns into the sea in the hope of obstructing a hostile fleet. When the Crusaders visited Egypt (15th cent.) the original scheme of the Acropolis had vanished, and their attention was caught by this solitary pillar. The Crusaders were no scholars but they had heard of Pompey, so they called the pillar after him, and said that his head was enclosed in a ball on the top (*see* Belon's View p. 89). The error has been perpetuated and the visitor must remember, firstly that the pillar has nothing to do with Pompey and secondly that it is a subordinate monument that the accident of time has preserved: it is a part and a small one of the splendours of the Temple of Serapis.

The following remains can be visited (*see* Plan p. 158).

(i). *"Pompey's Pillar."* 84 feet high and about 7

thick; made of red granite from Assouan. An imposing but ungraceful object. Architecture has evolved nothing more absurd than the monumental column; there is no reason that it should ever stop nor much that it should begin, and this specimen is not even well proportioned. The substructure is interesting. It is made up of blocks that have been taken from older buildings. On the eastern face (nearest turnstile) is a block of green granite with an inscription in Greek in honour of Arsinoe, the sister and wife of Ptolemy Philadelphus (p. 16). On the opposite face (upside down in a recess) is the figure and hieroglyph of Seti I (B.C. 1350), suggesting the great age of the settlement on Rhakotis.

Why and when was the pillar put up?

Probably to the Emperor Diocletian, about A.D. 297. There is a four line Greek inscription to him on the granite base on the western side, about 10 feet up. It is illegible and indeed invisible from the ground. Generations of scholars have worked at it with the following result:—

"To the most just Emperor, the tutelary God of Alexandria, Diocletian the invincible: Postumus, prefect of Egypt."

The formidable Emperor (p. 51) had crushed a rebellion here and was a god to be propitiated; the Pillar, erected in the precincts of Serapis, would celebrate his power and clemency and presumably bore his statue on the top.—There is another theory: that the column was dedicated after the triumph of the Christians in 391 and glorifies the new religion; if this is so it must itself have previously been pagan, for by this date the Alexandrians had not the means or the power to erect a new monument of such a size.

(ii). *The Temple of Serapis.* West of the Pillar, reached by a staircase, are long subterranean galleries, excavated in the rock and lined with limestone. These were probably part of the Serapeum—basements of some sort—and enthusiastic visitors have even identified them with the library where the books were kept; in them are some small semicircular niches of unknown use. Some marble columns stand on the ground above. —South of the Pillar, near the Sphinxes, are more passages, lined with cement; these too may have been part of the temple. All is conjectural, and the plan of the Serapeum, as we gather it from classical writers, can in no way be fitted in with existing remains. According to them, it was rectangular, and stood in the middle of a cloister, with each of whose sides it was connected by a cross-colonnade. The temple consisted of a great hall and an inner shrine. The architecture was probably Greek; certainly the statue was—made of blue-black marble (p. 21), the work of Bryaxis.

(iii). *The Temple of Isis.* Isis, wife of Osiris, was equally united to his successor Serapis, and had in Ptolemaic times her temple on the plateau. North of the Pillar are some excavations that have been identified with it.

(iv). *Two Sphinxes.* Found in the enclosure and set up south of the Pillar. Of Assouan granite.

(v). *Fragments of a Frieze.* These, magnificently worked in granite, lie on the slope east of the Pillar; we pass them on the way up. Date:—about 1st cent. A.D. They may have belonged to the great entrance gate of the temple enclosure. He who meditates on them for a little may recapture some idea of the shrine. Not the Pillar itself so suggests vanished glory and solidity.

This concludes the remains. They are disappointing for so famous a site, but there is one satisfaction: this is the actual spot. Long in doubt, it has been identified by the statues and inscriptions that have been found here; they are now in the Museum (*see* Rooms 6, 12, and 16).

Just beyond the enclosure of "Pompey's Pillar" we leave the tram route and turn to the right, reaching in ten minutes the Kom es Chogafa Catacombs.

CATACOMBS OF KOM ES CHOGAFA

Through the turnstile (5 piastres) is modern asphalt laid down to preserve the subterraneans from wet. Left, four fine sarcophagi of purplish granite. Above, the original level of the hill, which has been cut down by quarrying and excavations; in its slopes are some cemented passages, antique but uninteresting. On the top of the hill, a mosaic of black and white stones, much broken away. The entrance to the catacombs is down the larger of the two glassed well-shafts.

The Catacombs of Kom es Chogafa ("Hill of Tiles") are the most important in the city and unique anywhere: nothing quite like them has been discovered. They are unique both for their plan and for their decorations which so curiously blend classical and Egyptian designs; only in Alexandria could such a blend occur. Their size, their picturesque vistas, their eerie sculptures, are most impressive, especially on a first visit. Afterwards their spell fades for they are odd rather than beautiful, and they express religiosity rather than religion. Date—about the 2nd cent. A.D. when the old faiths began to merge and melt. Name of occupants— unknown. There is a theory that they began as a family vault which was developed by a burial syndicate. They were only discovered in 1900.

The scheme should be grasped before descending;

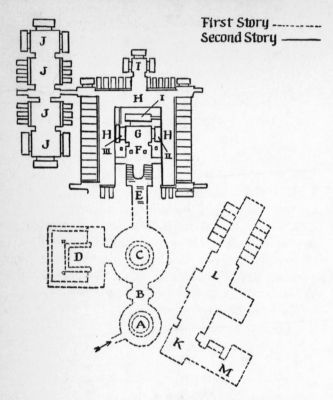

KOM ES CHOGAFA
PLAN OF CHIEF CHAMBERS

First Story ----------
Second Story ————

A   Well Staircase
B   Vestibule
C   Rotunda
D   Banquet Hall
E   Staircase
F   Vestibule
G   I II III Central Tomb

H   Passage
I   Tomb Chamber
J   Gallery
K   Square Well
L   Hall of Caracalla
M   Gallery of Painted Tomb

there are three stories, the lowest is under water. (*See* Plan opposite.)

The Staircase (A) is lit from a well, down which the dead bodies were lowered by ropes.—It ends at the Vestibule (B). Here are two semicircular niches, each fitted with a bench and elegantly vaulted with a shell—a classical motive unknown to the art of ancient Egypt. Close by is the Rotunda (C): in its centre is a well, upon whose parapet stand 8 pillars, supporting a domed roof. A circular passage runs round the well.—Left from the Rotunda is the Banquet Hall (D), where the friends and relatives ate ceremonially in memory of the dead. It is a gloomy scene. Here, cut out of the limestone, are the three couches where they reclined upon mattresses; the table in the middle has disappeared; it was probably of wood. Pillars support the roof.—From the Rotunda a Staircase (E) goes down to the second storey; the amazing Central Tomb is now revealed; weird effects can be got by adjusting the electric lights. The Staircase is roofed by a shell ornament; half-way down, it divides on each side a thing that looks like a prompter's box; this masks yet another staircase that descends to the third storey, now under water.

THE CENTRAL TOMB.

In the Vestibule (F) the Egyptian note predominates. In front, two fine columns with ornate capitals and two pilasters with square papyrus capitals—the four supporting a cornice adorned with the winged Sun (Ra), and guardian falcons. Inside the Vestibule, to right and left, are white limestone statues of a man and woman—the proprietor and his wife, perhaps. On the further wall the religious and artistic confusion increases. Two terrific bearded serpents guard the entrance to the Tomb Chamber, and each not only enfolds the pine-cone of Dionysus and the serpent-wand of Hermes, but also wears the double crown of Upper and Lower Egypt. Above each serpent is a Medusa in a round shield. Over the lintel of the inner door is the winged Sun and a frieze of snakes.

The Tomb Chamber (G) contains three large sarcoph-

agi, all cut out of the rock. They are classical in style—
decorated with festoons of fruit or flowers, Medusa heads,
Ox skulls, &c. The lids do not take off; the mummies
would have been pushed in from the passage behind (*see*
below). But as a matter of fact none of the three sarcophagi
have ever been occupied; it is part of the queerness of
Kom-es-Chogafa that its vast and elaborate apparatus for
mourning should culminate in a void.

In the niche over each sarcophagus are bas reliefs,
Egyptian in style but executed with imperfect understanding.

Centre niche (G.i). A mummy on a lion shaped bier:
the lion wears the crown of Osiris and has at its feet the
feather of Maat, goddess of truth. Behind the bier, Anubis
as the god of embalming; at its head Thoth with the symbol
of immortality; at its foot, Horus; beneath it three "Canopic" deities—vases for the intestines—there ought to be four.
—Lateral relief: Left, a man with a priest, right, a woman
with a priest.

Right hand niche (G.ii). Graceful design of a prince,
who wears the double crown of Egypt, offering a collar
to the Apis Bull, who, with the Sun between his horns
stands on a pedestal. Behind Apis, Isis, holding the feather
of truth and stretching out her protective wings with good
decorative effect.—Lateral reliefs: Left, a king before a god
(Chons ?); right, two "Canopic" deities, one ape headed,
one a mummy.

Left hand niche (G.iii). Similar to right hand, except
that on the right lateral wall one of the "Canopic" deities
has the head of a hawk.

On either side of the entrance door stands an uncanny
figure. Right, (as one goes out) is Anubis, with a dog's
head, but dressed up as a Roman soldier, with cuirass, short
sword, lance and shield complete. Left, the god Sebek, who
though mainly a crocodile is also crushed into military cos-
tume with cloak and spear. Perhaps the queer couple were
meant to guard the tomb, but one must not read too much
into them or into anything here; the workmen employed
were only concerned to turn out a room that should look

suitable for death, and judged by this standard they have succeeded.

Surrounding the central tomb is a broad Passage (HHH) lined with cavities in two rows that provided accommodation for nearly 300 mummies. Where the passage passes behind the central tomb one can see the apertures through which the three grand sarcophagi were hollowed out, and through which the mummies would have been introduced. Leading out of this passage is another tomb-chamber (I) and, to the left, a big Gallery (JJJJ), fitted up with receptacles in the usual style.

All the above chambers form part of a single scheme. We now return to the Rotunda (C), and enter, through a breach in the rock, an entirely distinct set of tombs. They are lighted by a square Well (K) and were reached by a separate staircase now ruinous. The Hall (L) is fancifully called the Hall of Caracalla because that emperor massacred many Alexandrian youths whom he had summoned to a review, and because many bones of men and horses have been found intermingled on its floors; it is lined with tomb cavities on the usual plan.—The Gallery (M) contains rather a charming tomb: it was once covered with white stucco and delicately painted. In the niche above the sarcophagus are Isis and her sister Nephtys, spreading their wings over the mummy of Osiris. More figures on the lateral walls. Above, on the inner wall, the soul as a bird. Above the entrance, the Sun and golden Vase on either side of which is a sphinx with her paw on a wheel.

We now ascend the staircase (A). View of Mariout. Those who are not tired of empty tombs will find plenty more to the right, down a stairway cut in the rock.

Immediately below Kom es Chogafa flows the *Mahmoudieh Canal,* made by Mohammed Ali (for the circumstances *see* p. 97). There is a road along it which leads, right, into the region of cotton warehouses. (Section VI).—To the left one can walk or drive all the way to Nouzha (Section IV). The route is partly pleasant

partly not. It crosses, at Moharrem Bey, the Farkha
Canal, which leaves the Mahmoudieh Canal at right
angles and which went all the way to the sea.—Fur-
ther on, there is a shady tract called the "Champs
Elysées"; it resembles, neither for good or evil, its
Parisian original.†

SECTION IV

From the Square to Nouzha

ROUTE:—Take Nouzha Tram (Green Trefoil) at the lower end of the Boulevard Ramleh, just off the Square. The Rond Point Tram (White Star) passes through the Square, but does not go further than the Water Works—about half-way to Nouzha.

CHIEF POINTS OF INTEREST:—Municipal Gardens; Nouzha and Antoniadis Gardens.

For the Boulevard Ramleh *see* Section V. Having traversed it, the tram bears to the right and passes the Alhambra Theatre, the only one in the town—not a bad building.—Just beyond the Theatre a road leads left, to the Cathedral of the *Coptic Catholic Patriarchate* (p. 229), or Church of the Resurrection. The building is not remarkable, but of interest to all who would explore the ecclesiastical ramifications of Alexandria. It was dedicated in 1902 by the Patriarch Cyril II and endowed by the Emperor Francis Joseph of Austria, as an inscription by the entrance (shortly to be removed) states; the alternative date—1618—reckons by the Coptic Calendar, which begins not with the birth of Christ but with the persecutions of the 3rd cent. (p. 51). The façade of the church imitates that of St. John Lateran, Rome. Beyond the church are the British Consulate and the Egyptian Government Hospital (Section V).

The tram turns left, along the Rue Sultan Hussein, still popularly known as the Rue d'Allemagne, and passes between the Menasce Schools (Jewish) and Cromer Park, a small fenced garden reserved for ladies and babies.—*Place Said,* a round space in the midst of which is a large Ptolemaic Column, erected in memory of the retaking of Khartoum, Sept. 2, 1898; on each side of the column, statues of the lion headed goddess, Sekhet. The native women who sometimes sit in masses in the Place are professional mourners and await a funeral out of the Egyptian Government Hospital behind. Roads go from the Place: left, to Mazarita Station on the Ramleh tram line (Section V); right, to the Rue Rosette (Section I).

Left, the *Municipal Gardens,* small but admirably planned; the designer, M. Monfront, has shown real genius in his treatment of the area. The gardens follow the line of the Arab Walls (p. 86) and also cross the course of the old Farkha Canal that once connected the Mahmoudieh Canal and the sea (p. 168). Both these features have been utilised; the fortifications have turned into picturesque hillocks or survive as masses of masonry, which, though of little merit in themselves, have been cleverly grouped and look mediaeval by moonlight; while the water of the canal has been preserved in an artificial pool, the abode of ducks. The gardens should be thoroughly explored.† In them— visible from tram—is a *Statue of Nubar Pasha,* by Puech; the tarboosh is too large but the general effect dignified; the left hand rests on a tablet inscribed "La justice est la base de tout Gouvernment," and the same maxim appears on the pedestal. Nubar was an Armenian—a politician whose honesty is variously estimated, though there is no question as to his ability. He became minister under the Khedive Ismail (1878) and tried to regulate his finance, also serving under

Tewfik. He was, as his favourite motto suggests, cautious in temperament. He is buried outside the Armenian Church (p. 156).

The tram touches the end of the Rue Rosette (Section I) and passes through the belt of the gardens: they continue on the right, still following the course of the vanished Arab Walls and utilising the acclivities, and are to be continued still further, as far as the railway station; they will then form a great horseshoe.— Left are the Roman Catholic Cemeteries, and in the second of these, at the end of the main walk, is a fine *Antique Tomb*, which should be seen. It lies in a hole; great walls of alabaster have fallen and exposed their shining surfaces. The shrine (Heroon) of Pompey stood near here, and it has been suggested that this was the actual place where his head was deposited after his murderers had brought it to Julius Caesar; this is pure conjecture, but the tomb may well date from the period (B.C. 48) for the work is very good.—To the right, in the new part of the Cemetery are other ancient tombs, also a cemented shaft with foot holds cut on its interior.

Almost opposite the entrance to the Cemetery is the War Memorial to French Soldiers, a truncated obelisk of Carrara marble, designed as a labour of love in memory of his fallen comrades by Mons. V. Erlanger, the French architect of Alexandria and unveiled April 23, 1921 by Lord Allenby.

The scroll facing the main thoroughfare bears the following inscription:

"In memory of French Soldiers fallen during the Great War and offered by members of the British Community to the French Colony to Commemorate the glorious deeds of arms, performed by the French Armies 1914–1918."

Now the tram turns, right, by the Rosetta Gate Police Station, surmounted by a turret clock in com-

memoration of King Edward VII, and comes to the
Rond Point, where are the Waterworks, and up the rise
Hadra Prison; then crosses the railway, the ancient
Hadra Cemetery (*see* Museum Room 19) and Hadra
village, and reaches its terminus at Nouzha, close to
Nouzha railway station and to the Mahmoudieh
Canal.

Nouzha was in Ptolemaic times the suburb of Eleusis.
Here lived Callimachus the poet (p. 33); here (B.C.
168) Popillius the Roman general checked the King of
Syria who was about to seize Alexandria, and, drawing
a circle round him in the sand, obliged him to decide
forthwith between peace and war. Here (A.D. 640),
were quartered the cavalry of Amr (p. 60), before he
entered the town.—The Gardens are across the railway.
They have been developed by the Municipality out of
a small park of Ismail's, and are most beautiful; if one
could judge Alexandria by her gardens one would do
nothing but praise. Some are formalised, others free;
those who like pelicans will find them in a pond to the
right; the zoological garden, a bandstand, and a restau-
rant, are straight ahead; view from over the top over
Lake Hadra towards Abou el Nawatir (Section V).—
Right of the bandstand is an enclosure entered by payment; this too should be visited as the trees and flowers
are fine; glasshouses also.†

Above the pelican pond a small gate leads from the
Nouzha Gardens into the *Antoniadis Gardens* (entrance charge; varying according to the day of week).
These too belong to the Municipality of Alexandria.
They are full of modern statues, which, though of no
merit, make a pleasant formal effect. The trees and
creepers are fine, and there is a beautiful lawn at the
back of the house. Here, until recently, lived the Antoniadis family, wealthy Greeks.

In the field behind the Antoniadis Gardens is an
Antique Tomb. It is easiest reached through the back
gate, which a gardener will sometimes unlock; otherwise one must return to the Nouzha Gardens, pass out,
and follow the canal for a little way, finally turning to
the left. The tomb is behind an absurd spiral of rock-
work. It is reached down a flight of steps and the hall
is often under water. Same plan as at Anfouchi (p.
137); a sunken hall, out of which three tomb chambers
open.

The road beyond the Gardens, along the edge of the
Canal, is pretty, and probably follows the course of the
ancient Canal to Canopus, whither the Alexandrians
used to go out in barges, to enjoy themselves and to
worship Serapis. In one place it skirts the waters of
Hadra.

The other way (west) the Canal flows into the city
(Section II) finally entering the Harbour.—(For history of the Canal *see* p. 97.)

There is a road direct from Nouzha to Sidi Gaber
(Section V) by the side of the lake. It passes, left, the
place where two colossal statues were discovered: Antony as Osiris, and Cleopatra as Isis: Antony is in the
Museum (Garden Court, p. 132).

SECTION V

From the Square to Ramleh

ROUTE:—By the Boulevard Ramleh to the Tram Line terminus—10 min. walk. Then take tram with red label to Bulkeley, San Stefano, and Victoria. Tram with blue label goes to San Stefano only, *via* Bacos. The service is fair.

CHIEF POINTS OF INTEREST:—The Sea; the view from Abou el Nawatir; private gardens; the Spouting Rocks.

We start at the northeast corner of the Square, and take the Rue de l'Ancienne Bourse, in which are, right, the Union Club frequented by British, and, left, the former Bourse—the latter not a bad building, with a portico of marble columns and a vaulted interior; it is now the offices of the Lloyd Triestino. The street leads into the Boulevard Ramleh—turn to right.

The Boulevard (officially Rue de la Gare de Ramleh) is a busy shabby thoroughfare, full of people who are escaping to or from the tram terminus.†

Right from Boulevard, in Rue Debbane, is a Greek and Syrian Catholic Church, dedicated to St. Peter (p. 229). It was built by Count Debbane, a Syrian under Brazilian protection who received his title from the Pope. His family vault extends along the whole length of the Chancel. The scene is of no interest, but typical of the complexities of religion and race at Alexandria.

Left from Boulevard, at end of Rue Averoff, is the
Church of the Armenian Catholics (p. 228).

Right from Boulevard, in Rue de l'Eglise Copte, is
the *Cathedral of the Coptic Orthodox Patriarchate*
(p. 228) dedicated to St. Mark. Those who have never
seen a Coptic Church should look in. It is fatuously
ugly. On the screen that divides nave from sanctuary
are several pictures—among them St. Damiana with
her wheel; she is the native Egyptian Saint who was
probably the origin of St. Catherine of Alexandria:
round her are the forty maidens who shared her martyrdom. In the sanctuary are some pictures of St.
Mark, whose primitive church is wrongly supposed to
have stood on this site (p. 50); he is shown writing
his Gospel or standing between Cleopatra's Needle
and "Pompey's Pillar." Outside the Church are the
Schools, ineptly adorned with a Lion of St. Mark of the
Venetian type.

Right from Boulevard, the Rue Nebi Daniel leads
past the chief Jewish Synagogue to the Rue Rosette
(Section I).

The Boulevard reaches the tram terminus. To the
right is the road to Nouzha (Section IV), to the left
the sea and the New Quays (Section II).

On this featureless spot once arose a stupendous
temple, the *Caesareum,* and a pair of obelisks, *Cleopatra's Needles.*†

(i) HISTORY OF THE CAESAREUM. Cleopatra began it in
honour of Antony (p. 28). After their suicide Octavian finished it in honour of himself (B.C. 13). He was worshipped
there as Caesar Augustus, and the temple remained an Imperial possession until Christian times. Constantius II
(A.D. 354) intended to present it to the Church, but before
the transference could be effected St. Athanasius, who was
always energetic, had held an Easter Service inside it. The

Emperor was offended. Two years later his troops nearly killed Athanasius inside the building, and gave it to the Arians. Arians and Orthodox continued to fight for and in it and smashed it to pieces (p. 54). Athanasius, just back from his final exile, built on the ruins a church which was dedicated to St. Michael but usually retained the famous title Caesareum. It became the Cathedral of Alexandria, superseding St. Theonas (p. 50). Here in 415 Hypatia was torn to pieces by tiles (p. 56). Here in 640 the Patriarch Cyrus held a solemn service before betraying the city to the Arabs (p. 60). Date of final destruction—912.

(ii). APPEARANCE. Nothing is known of the architecture of the temple, but the Jewish philosopher Philo (p. 66) thus writes of it in the day of its glory:

"It is a piece incomparably above all others. It stands by a most commodious harbour: wonderful high and large in proportion; an eminent sea-mark; full of choice paintings and statues with donatives and oblatives in abundance; and then it is beautiful all over with gold and silver; the model curious and regular in the disposition of the parts, as galleries, libraries, porches, courts, halls, walks, and consecrated groves, as glorious as expense and art could make them, and everything in the proper place; besides that, the hope and comfort of seafaring men, either coming in or going out."

(iii). THE OBELISKS. In front of the Caesareum (between present tram terminus and sea) stood Cleopatra's Needles of which one is now in the Central Park, New York, and the other on the Embankment, London. They had nothing to do with Cleopatra till after her death. They were cut in the granite quarries of Assouan for Thothmes III (B.C. 1500), and set up by him at Heliopolis near Cairo, before the temple of the Rising Sun. In B.C. 13 they were transferred here by the engineer Pontius. They rested not directly on their bases but each on four huge metal crabs, one of which has been recovered. Statues of Hermes or of Victory tipped them. In the Arab period, when all around decayed, they became the chief marvel of the city. One

fell. They remained in situ until the 19th cent., when they
were parted and took their last journey, the fallen one to
England in 1877, the other to the United States two years
later.

The walls of the Arab city used to reach the sea at
this point (cf. Belon's View, p. 89); they ended in a
tower that was swept away for the New Quays. We
now take the tram.†

The first half mile of the tram lines traverses ground
of immense historical fame. Every inch was once sacred or royal. On the football fields to the left were the
Ptolemaic Palaces (p. 18) stretching down to the sea
and projecting into it at the Promontory of Lochias
(present Silsileh). There was also an island palace on
a rock that has disappeared. The walls of the Mouseion, too, are said to have extended into the area, but
we know no details and can only be certain that the
Ancient World never surpassed the splendour of the
scene. On the right, from the higher ground, the Theatre overlooked it, and the dramas of Aeschylus and
Euripides could be performed against the background
of a newer and a greater Greece. No eye will see that
achievement again, no mind can imagine it. Grit and
gravel have taken its place to-day.

Right of the line on leaving:—The British Consulate,
an imposing pile. Next to it, the *Egyptian Government
Hospital* probably on the site of the Ancient Theatre,
so a visit should be made.‡ In the garden is the tomb
of Dr. Schiess a former Director; an early Christian
sarcophagus has been used, and on each side of it
are impressive Christian columns, probably from the
church of St. Theonas (p. 50) and each carved with a
cross in a little shrine. In the spiral ascent above the
tomb are other antiquities and a howitzer of Arabi's:

on the summit, an antique marble column, erected in memory of Queen Victoria's Jubilee.

MAZARITA STA.—A road leads, right, to the Public Gardens (Section IV) and, left, to the Promontory of Silsileh (*see* above). The promontory, like the rest of the coast, has subsided; in classical times it was broader and longer than now, and extended in break-waters towards the Pharos (Fort Kait Bey), thus al-most closing the entrance to the Eastern Harbour. The private port of the Ptolemies lay immediately to its left. A beacon, the Pharillon, was at its point in Arab times.†
The original Church of St. Mark, where the evangelist was buried, must have stood on the shore to its right. There is nothing to see to-day except a coast-guard station and the exit of the main drain.

CHATBY STA.—The tram has now pierced the ancient royal city and enters the region of the dead, where ow-ing to the dryness of the ground the cemeteries both ancient and modern have been dug. Right, the modern cemeteries, Jewish nearest the tram line, behind them English, then Greek and Armenian, then Catholic, opening into the Aboukir road (Section I). Close to the sta. are the spacious schools of the Greek Commu-nity, and the Orwa el Woska schools. Left of the sta-tion, is the Sultanian Institute of Hydrobiology, con-taining a small but interesting aquarium and an extensive and valuable technical library, also models of fishing craft, nets and marine instruments. Visit by arrangement with the Director, Prof. Pachundaki. In the enclosure in front of the Institute some ancient Mosaics have been recently (1921) discovered; they are said to be of fine period and in good condition, but are not on exhibition yet; it is to be hoped that they will be accessible shortly. Traces of ancient roads and drains have also been found here.

CHATBY-LES-BAINS STA.—Turn left, as far as the fire station, then turn right. Here, in the waste to the left of the road, is the great Chatby Necropolis, the oldest in the Ptolemaic city (*see* Museum, particularly Room 20 and Garden Court). Little remains. There is a tomb-group close to the road of the Anfouchi type (p. 137) *i.e.* a sunken court out of which the burial places open; at the end of the tombs is a double sarcophagus of the shape of a bed, with cushions of stone. —Right of the tram line, other burial places, Ptolemaic and Roman, can be found all the way to the canal.— The tram goes through a cutting; right is the fine French Lycée, subsidized by the French Government.

CAMP DE CÉSAR STA.—Caesar never camped here. An unattractive suburb, anciently Eleusis by the Sea.

IBRAHAMIEH STA.—Then to the right, flat fertile land appears. This, geologically, is delta deposit, which has been silted up against the narrow spur of limestone on which Alexandria stands (p. 5). In the foreground, the green turf of the Sporting Club; further, the trees of Nouzha and the waters of Hadra. Traces of ancient Cemeteries continue on the dry ground on the left.

SPORTING CLUB STA.—Close to the Grand Stand of the Race Course. Bathing beach left.

CLEOPATRA STA.—Cleopatra never lived here. Right begin the famous fig trees of Sidi Gaber, reputed the best in Egypt. Also broad leaved bananas, maize, &c. A pleasant road leads across the railway and by the side of the lake to Nouzha Gardens (Section IV); it

can be beautiful here in the evening.—Left from the
sta., at the base of a cliff by the edge of the sea, is a
Ptolemaic tomb with painted walls, but even while one
describes such things they are being destroyed. The
reefs by this tomb form the pretty little "Friars' pool."

Sidi Gaber Sta.—Close to the main-line railway sta.
where all the Cairo expresses stop.—Left, a road leads
between fine trees to the *Abercrombie Monument,* a
poor affair, but interesting to Englishmen, as it commemorates our exploits in 1801 (p. 93). It is a three-
sided column of white marble, surmounted by a flam-
ing urn. Inscription:

> "To the memory of Sir Ralph Abercrombie K.B.&C.
> and the Officers and Men who fell at the battle of Alex-
> andria, March 21st, 1801 . . . . . As his life was hon-
> ourable so was his death glorious. His memory will be
> recorded in the annals of his country—will be sacred to
> every British soldier—and embalmed in the recollection
> of a grateful posterity."

Close to the Monument is the modern Mosque of Sidi
Gaber, a beneficent local saint, who flies about at night,
looks after children, &c.

Mustapha Pacha Sta.—Right, up the road, is the hill
of Abou el Nawatir, the highest near Alexandria, overlooking the lakes of Hadra and Mariout; exquisite view,
especially by evening light. The square enclosure at
the top belongs to the reservoir; to its S.E. half-way
between it and the railway, a *Gun* lies in the sand. This
is a relic of the fighting of July 1882. General Alison
placed most of his artillery up here (p. 102), and the
gun still points to the Mahmoudieh Canal, in the direction of Arabi's camp.—Left of Mustapha Pacha Sta.
on the rise, are the British Barracks, occupying the site
of the Roman; history repeats herself, just as she has

done in the Cemeteries. Octavian's town of Nicopolis, which he founded in B.C. 30 to overawe Alexandria (p. 48), began here. Among the Roman Units here quartered were the 2nd Trajana Fortis and the 3rd Cyrenaic; the British are too numerous to record.

CARLTON STA.—The big Villa up the hill to the right was built by a German in the Greek style, regardless of expense or taste.

BUCKELEY STA.—We are now in the heart of Ramleh ("Sand") the straggling suburb where the British and other foreigners reside. Lovely private gardens, the best in Egypt. Left of the sta. is Stanley Bay, a fine bit of coast scenery and a favourite bathing place: also the Anglican Church of All Saints (p. 230).

The tram line here divides into two branches that re-unite at San Stefano. The left branch—more direct—goes by Saba Pacha (pretty cove in coast), Glymeno-poulo, Mazloum, Zizinia—all bathing places. The right branch, through pretty palm groves, via Fleming, Bacos,† Seffer, Schutz, Gianaclis (left is the fine new Mosque of Ahmed Pacha Yehia, the statesman, with provision for his tomb).

SAN STEFANO STA.—Close to the Casino, a fashiona-ble summer hotel, by the side of a sea that seems es-pecially fresh and blue. There are Symphony concerts here in the season. The audience however comes not to listen but to talk; their noise is so great that from a little distance the orchestra appears to be performing in dumb show.

The tram goes on by St. George, Laurens and Palais stations to Sidi Bishr, on the edge of a desert coast. Fine walk or ride past Sidi Bishr Mosque to the *Spout-ing Rocks*. These are most remarkable. Masses of limestone project into the sea, which penetrates beneath them and spouts up through blow holes and cracks. Some of the vents have been artificially squared, and the Ancient Alexandrians, who loved scientific toys, may have fitted them up with musical horns or mechanical mills.—The expedition may be continued along the coast to the woods of Montazah (Section VII).

VICTORIA STA.—The terminus. Here is a Ry. sta. for the Aboukir and Rosetta lines (Section VII), also Victoria College, a huge building. It offers an education on English Public School lines to residents in Egypt, whatever their creed or race, and was much approved by Lord Cromer, who founded a scholarship here.

The coast walk from Alexandria to Ramleh is rarely taken but is charming—low crumbly cliffs, sandy beaches, flat rocks, and vestiges of ancient houses and tombs that help one to realise how the whole site of the city has sunk. There is no road east of Silsileh. The scheme for a grandiose "Corniche" drive has fortunately failed, and the scenery has escaped the standardised dulness that environs most big towns.†

Ramleh can also be reached by the Aboukir Road, an extension of the Rue Rosette (Section I).

SECTION VI

From the Square to Mex

ROUTE:—By the Rue des Soeurs and Gabbari, taking the Mex Tram (White Star). The journey is uncomfortable and uninspiring, but Mex is pleasant.

We start from the south side of the Square, down the long Rue des Soeurs, which takes its name from the Roman Catholic Convent and School near its entrance. The surroundings become squalid.

Right of Rue des Soeurs:—Rue Behari Bey leads to the mound of *Kom-el-Nadoura*, which rises abruptly out of mean streets. Its history before the arrival of Napoleon (1798 p. 91) is unknown. His engineer Cafarelli fortified it for him, and it held back the British advance in 1801, (p. 93). The entrance is on the south side, through a doorway by a winding path fringed with prickly pear and pepper trees. The summit—104 feet above the sea—is now used as a signalling station and observatory under the Ports and Lights Administration. Interesting set of instruments, and fine view of harbour and city. At the N.N.W. corner are some remains of Cafarelli's masonry.—Outside the Fort, in the Rue Bab-el-Akhdar (Section II) is the Gold and Silver Bazaar.

Left of Rue des Soeurs is the Genenah, a curious rabbit warren.

The tram passes down Rue Ibrahim Premier. To the right, close to the docks, in the Rue Karam, is a Franciscan church and school. They are modern and of no interest, but stand on a site that was important historically. Here was the *Church of St. Theonas* (p. 50) and the early palace of the bishops. Here St. Athanasius was brought up. The Arabs (641) incorporated what they found into a fine Mosque, called the Mosque of the Seventy (from some fallacious connection with the Septuagint) or the Mosque of the 1,000 Columns. It was on the lines of the Mosque of Ibn Touloun at Cairo; the Rue Karam bisects its area; its prayer niche faced southwest. It was standing in a ruined condition when the French came, and was turned into artillery barracks.

Just before the tram reaches the Canal we pass, right, the cotton exchange of Minet-el-Bassal. A visit—introduction necessary—is interesting. The Exchange is round a pleasant courtyard, with a fountain in the midst. Samples are exhibited. The whole neighbourhood is given up to this, the main industry, of Alexandria; warehouses; picturesque wooden machinery for cleaning the cotton and pressing it into bales; in the season, the streets are slippery with greasy fluff.

The Mahmoudieh Canal (p. 97) is now crossed. The banks have here their original stone casings and double descents, recalling the commercial enterprise of Mohammed Ali. A walk along the banks to the left is dirty but attractive; it can terminate at the Kom-es-Chogafa Catacombs (Section III). Right, the Canal enters the Western Harbour.

Then comes the district of Gabbari, called after a sheikh of that name. Here was the Western Cemetery of the Ancient City; the finds have been taken to the Museum (Room 14). Nothing interesting until Mex.

Mex, once a fishing village, might have become a

prosperous suburb of Alexandria, like Ramleh. But the intervening slums have choked access to it. It lies midway on the big curve of the Western Harbour, the waters of Lake Mariout being close behind. There is a good pier, with a wooden causeway that leads on to a distant rock. The little sea front has rather a Neapolitan air.

Beyond Mex are the limestone quarries that provided the stone for the ancient and the modern towns. They are cut in the ridge that here separates lake and sea.

The village of Dekhela lies further along the beach. Fine walk from it to Amrieh (Section VIII). Beyond it the desert begins, strewn with fragments of antique pottery.

Beyond Dekhela, at the western point of the Harbour: *Fort Agame.*† A strategic point in Napoleonic times (p. 91) and in the Bombardment of Alexandria (p. 100). Magnificent bathing. Just off the Fort is *Marabout Island,* so called from the tomb of a local saint which stands here, adorned with votive models of boats. Makrizi (writing in the 14th cent.) says that men lived longer on Marabout Island than anywhere else in the world, but no one at all lives here now. From it extends the chain of reefs that close the entrance of the Western Harbour (p. 6).—It is easy to visit this district from Alexandria by sailing boat, but not easy to get back again in the evening when the wind drops.

SECTION VII

Aboukir and Rosetta

ROUTE:—By train from the Main (Cairo) sta., or from Sidi-Gaber, where all trains stop, and which is also a sta. for the Ramleh Tram (Section VI).

CHIEF POINTS OF INTEREST:—Montazah; Canopus; Aboukir Bay; Rosetta.

At Sidi Gaber sta. is a view of Lake Hadra on the right.—Five stations on:—Victoria, close to the College and tram terminus.—The train passes over sand and through a palm oasis, which is carpeted with flowers in spring.

MANDARAH STA.—One of the houses in the village is painted outside in commemoration of the inmate's pilgrimage to Mecca—pictures of things that he saw or would like to have seen, such as a railway train, a tiger, a siren, and a very large melon.†

MONTAZAH STA.—Close to the station is the *Summer Resort* of the ex-Khedive Abbas II, now (1922) being restored and refurnished by King Fouad. Permission to enter should be obtained if possible, for the scenery is unique in Egypt and of the greatest beauty. The road leads by roses, oleanders and pepper trees. From it a road turns, right, up the hill to the Selamlik (men's

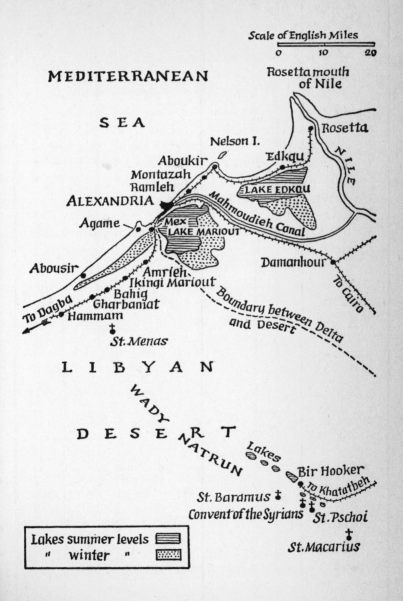

COUNTRY ROUND ALEXANDRIA

Scale of English Miles

0   10   20

MEDITERRANEAN

SEA

Rosetta mouth of Nile

Rosetta

NILE

Nelson I.

Edkqu

Aboukir

Montazah

Ramleh

LAKE EDKQU

ALEXANDRIA

Mahmoudieh Canal

Agame

Mex

LAKE MARIOUT

Abousir

Damanhour

To Cairo

Amrieh

Ikingi Mariout

Bahig

Gharbaniat

Boundary between Delta and Desert

To Dagba

Hammam

St. Menas

LIBYAN

WADY

DESERT

NATRUN

Lakes

Bir Hooker

To Khatatbeh

St. Baramus

Convent of the Syrians

St. Pschoi

St. Macarius

Lakes summer levels

" winter "

quarters), built by the Khedive in a style that was likely to please his Austrian mistress; on the terrace in front is a sun dial and some guns.† From the terrace, *View* of the circular bay with its fantastic promontories and breakwaters; the coast to the right is visible as far as Aboukir, whose minaret peeps over a distant headland; to the left are the Montazah woods; beneath, down precipitous steps, a curved parade. Beautiful walks in every direction, and perfect bathing. On the promontory to the right is a kiosk, and at its point are some remains of buildings or baths—fragments of the ancient Taposiris Parva that once stood here; some of them form natural fishponds. The woods are Pines Maritimes, imported by the Khedive from Europe, and in the western section, beyond the Pigeon House, the trees have grown high. Various buildings are in the estate; in one corner are the foundations of an enormous mosque. During the recent war (1914–1919) Montazah became a Red Cross Hospital; thousands of convalescent soldiers passed through it and will never forget the beauty and the comfort that they found there.‡

MAMOURAH STA.—The low ground to the right is on the site of the Aboukir Lake (p. 92), drained in the 19th cent. Here the Aboukir and Rosetta railways part.

ABOUKIR

ROUTE:—Aboukir Station is the terminus. Walk or take donkey. Turn sharply to the left to Canopus, 1 mile, then follow coast all the way round by Fort Kait Bey to Fort Ramleh; return to Aboukir Village.

Aboukir, though intimately connected with Alexandria, has a history of its own. Three main periods.

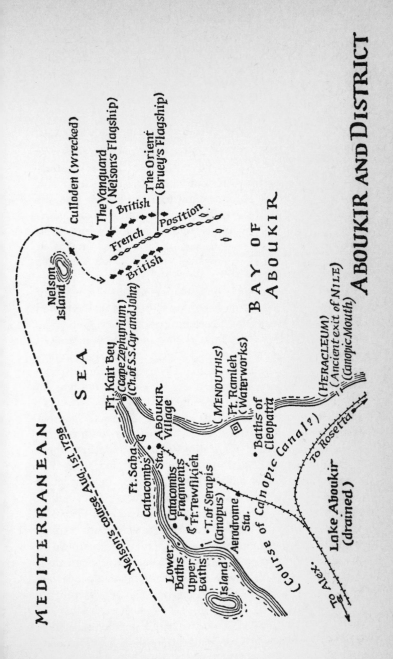

ABOUKIR AND DISTRICT

(i). ANCIENT (*see* also p. 7).

Geologically, this is the end of the long limestone spur that projects from the Libyan desert (p. 5). The Nile had to round it to reach the sea, and it is to the Nile that its early fame is due. The river poured out just to the east, through the "Canopic" Mouth, which has now dried up, and there were settlements here centuries before Alexandria was founded. On the left bank of the Nile (south of the present Fort Ramleh) Herodotus (B.C. 450) saw a temple to Heracles, and was told that Paris and Helen had sought shelter here on their flight to Troy—shelter that was refused by the local authorities, who disapproved of their irregular union. There was a second settlement at Menouthis (Fort Ramleh itself), and a third and most famous at *Canopus* (present Fort Tewfikieh), from which the whole district took its name.

Canopus, according to Greek legend, was a pilot of Menelaus who was bitten here by a serpent as they returned from Troy, and, dying, became the tutelary God. The legend, like that of Paris and Helen, shows how interested were the Greeks in the district, but has no further importance. There is also a legend that Canopus was an Egyptian God whose body was an earthenware jar: this too may be discredited. With the foundation of Alexandria (B.C. 331) the district lost much of its trade, but became a great fashionable and religious resort. There was a canal from Alexandria, probably connecting with the Nile just where it entered the sea, and the Alexandrians glided along it in barges, singing and crowned with flowers. In connection with his new cult of Serapis (p. 20) Ptolemy Soter built a temple here (*see* below) whose fame spread over the world and whose rites made the Romans blush with shame or pale with envy; here originated the idea, still so widely held in the west, that Egypt is a land of licentiousness and mystery. The district decayed as soon as Christianity was established; it had not, like Alexandria, a solid basis for its existence in trade. But Paganism lingered here, and as late as the end of the 5th century twenty camel-loads of idols were found secreted in a house and were carried away to make a bonfire at Alexandria. Demons gave trouble even in later times.

(ii). CHRISTIAN.

The Patriarch Cyril (p. 56) having destroyed the cults of Serapis and Isis in the district (A.D. 389) sent out the relics of St. Cyr to take their place. The relics were so intermingled with those of another martyr, St. John, that St. John had to be brought too, and a church to them both arose just to the south of the present Fort Kait Bey. The two Saints remained quiet for 200 years, but then began to disentangle themselves and work miracles, and recovered for the district some of its ancient popularity; indeed many of their cures are exactly parallel to those effected in the Temple of Serapis. With the Arab invasion their church vanishes, but St. Cyr has given his name to modern Aboukir ("Father Cyr"). In the 9th century the Canopic branch of the Nile dried up. The Turks built some forts here for coastal defence, but history does not recommence until the arrival of Nelson.

(iii). MODERN.

In Napoleonic times Aboukir saw two great battles.

(a). "Battle of the Nile."

For the event that led to this engagement *see* p. 91. Brueys, Napoleon's admiral, brought his fleet into the bay for safety, and anchored them in a long line, about two miles from the coast. He had 13 Men-of-War, 4 Frigates, 1,182 cannons, and 8,000 men. To the north was "Nelson's Island," as it is now called, which he had fortified and upon which his line was supposed to rest. His flagship, the *Orient*, was midway in the line. He took up this position on July 7th, 1798.

On August 1st Nelson arrived in pursuit, with 14 Men-of-War, 1,012 cannons and 8,068 men. The wind was N.W., a usual direction in summer. Half his fleet, including his flagship the *Vanguard*, attacked Brueys from the expected quarter, the east. The other half, led by the *Goliath*, executed the brilliant manœuvre that brought us victory. It gave Brueys a double surprise: in the first place it passed between the head of his line and "Nelson's Island" where he thought there was no room; in the second place it took up a position to his west, between him and the shore, where he thought the water was too shallow. Thus he was caught between two fires—attacked by the whole British Fleet with the exception of the *Culloden*, which, sailing too near "Nelson's Island", stranded.

The engagement began at 6.0 p.m. At 7.0 Brueys was killed, at 9.30 the *Orient* caught fire and blew up shortly afterwards; the explosion was tremendous and terminated the first act of the battle; an interval of appalled silence ensued. Casabianca was sailing the *Orient*, and it was on her "burning deck" that the boy of Mrs. Hemans' poem stood. The fighting recommenced, continuing through the night, and ending at midday on the 2nd with the complete victory of Nelson. The French fleet had been annihilated; only two Men-of-War and two Frigates escaped, and Napoleon had lost for ever his command of the Mediterranean. Nelson accordingly signalled the following message:—

> Almighty God having blessed His Majesty's arms with victory, the Admiral intends returning public thanksgiving for the same at two o'clock this day, and he recommends every ship doing the same as soon as convenient.

The French expected an attack on Alexandria, but Nelson had suffered too much himself to attempt this; having rested for a little, he dispersed his fleet, leaving only a few ships behind to watch the coast. In his despatches home he stated that the engagement had taken place not far from the (Rosetta) mouth of the Nile; hence the official "Battle of the Nile" instead of the more accurate "Naval Battle of Aboukir."

(*b*). *Land Battle of Aboukir.*

Less important than its predecessor, but the strategy is interesting, and Napoleon himself was present. For the events that led up to it *see* p. 92; Turkey, at the instigation of England, had declared war on France, and in July 1799 the Turks occupied Aboukir Bay and landed 15,000 men.

Their left rested on the present Fort Ramleh, their right on the present Fort Tewfikieh, their camp was in the narrow extremity of the peninsula, between the redoubt and the Fort at the very tip. They were supported on three sides by their fleet, which was stationed in the Mediterranean, in the Bay of Aboukir, and in the (vanished) Lake of Aboukir. From this stronghold they proposed to overrun Egypt.

On receiving the news, Napoleon hurried down from Cairo and arrived (July 25th) with only 10,000 men, mostly cavalry. Murat and Kléber accompanied him. He began by clearing the Turkish gunboats out of Lake Aboukir; then his force attacked Forts Ramleh and Tewfikieh, while his cavalry under Murat, advancing over the level ground between them, drove the flying defenders of each into the Mediterranean and the Bay respectively. 5,400 Turks were drowned. The tip of the peninsula remained and resisted vigorously, but Napoleon managed to mount some of his guns on the hard spit of sand that still extends along the shore of the Bay, and thus to cannonade the Turkish Camp, which was finally taken by storm.

RUINS OF CANOPUS.

The ruins (*see* above) lie round Fort Tewfikieh which is seen to the left as the train runs into the station. They were once of interest, but have been almost entirely destroyed by the military authorities, who use the limestone blocks for road making, and allow treasure hunting to go on. The remains are not easy to find, as the area is pitted with excavations. Consult map.

(*a*). About 50 yds. from the gateway of the fort, in a hollow to the left of the road, are two huge *Fragments* of a granite temple. Here were found the busts of Rameses II in the Museum (Room 7) and the colossi of the same King and his daughter (Museum, Court). Date of statues:—B.C. 1300.

(*b*). Further to the left, round the Fort, is the site

of the *Temple of Serapis*, the most famous building on
the peninsula, and celebrated throughout the antique
world. It was dedicated by Ptolemy III Euergetes (p.
17) and his wife Berenice. A few years later (B.C. 238)
their baby daughter died, and the priests met here in
conclave to make her a goddess, and incidentally to
endorse some reforms in the Calendar that the King,
who had a scientific mind, was pressing. The pro-
nouncement has been preserved in the "Decree of
Canopus," now one of the chief documents for Ptolemaic history. As for miracles, the temple even out-
stripped the original Temple of Serapis at Alexandria:
invalids who slept here even by proxy discovered next
day that they were well. It was also the abode of magic
and licentiousness according to its enemies, and of philosophy according to its friends. Christianity attacked
it. Just before its destruction (A.D. 289) Antoninus, an
able pagan reactionary, settled here, and tried to re-
vive the cult. "Often he told his disciples that after his
time there would be no temple, and that the great and
venerable sanctuary would remain only as an unmeaning mass of ruins, forgotten by all." (Eunapius, life of
Edesius). Antoninus was right.

In ancient time the Temple probably stood on the
highest ground, but with the general rising of level the
site is now in a deep depression and must be hunted
for patiently. An oblong space has been cleared and
some columns and capitals from the excavations have
been ranged round it, but it is impossible to reconstruct the original plan, and much has yet to be unearthed. Indeed it is not quite certain that this is the
right temple; an inscription has been discovered dedi-
cating it not to Serapis but to Osiris—with whom however Serapis was often identified. The columns are of
granite or of stucco-coated limestone. Beneath the
broken tin shelter was once a pretty mosaic. The finest

object is a stupendous fluted column of red granite that lies in a pit close by; no use for it has yet occurred to the military authorities. To the south and east of the Temple were the houses of the priests, showing fine cemented passages; these have been destroyed.

The canal by which revellers and worshippers approached this shrine ran to the south, through the low land by the railway; its course is uncertain; its exit was either into the (vanished) Nile, or into Aboukir Bay.

(c). *The Upper Baths.*—These lie about 100 yds. nearer the sea, on the slope just above the corner of the great bay that stretches to Montazah (p. 186). When excavated a few years ago they were almost perfect. The swimming bath—lined with the hard pink cement that indicates Ptolemaic or Roman work—had at the top a double step for the bathers. All round its sides were inserted large earthenware pots, their mouths level with the surface. Of this unique building a small fragment now survives. The brick central cistern and the hot baths can also still be traced.

(d). *The Lower Baths and Broken Colossus.*—Continuing to round Fort Tewfikieh we reach the coast and follow it N.E. Awash with the sea are the foundations of some large baths, showing the entrance channels which were probably closed with sluices, also some grooves of unknown use. On the shore above are the hot baths of the same establishment, retaining traces of pink cement. In the surf to the left lie blocks of granite: closely inspected, they resolve into fragments of a Colossus (Rameses II ?) and a sphinx.

(e). *Catacombs.*—Fifty yards on, at a point about halfway between the coast and the fort are a couple of catacombs, lying each of them in a hollow. One has a subterranean room, the other a sarcophagus slide. Traces of tombs and tunnels all over the area and along the low cliff by the shore.

This completes our survey of Canopus, once so enchanting a spot. Of its ancient delights only the air and the sea remain.

Continue to follow the coast. Perfect bathing. To the right, halfway between the coast and the railway sta. in some rising ground, are catacombs that have been filled in. Then comes the end of the promontory, which is fine. There are two forts:—Fort Saba, closing the neck, where the French resisted when the Turks landed in 1799 (*see* above); and Fort Kait Bey, on the extremity, founded in the 15th cent. by the Sultan of that name as part of his defence scheme against the Turks (cf. Fort Kait Bey at Alexandria, p. 87). The views are good, with the Mediterranean on one side and the tranquil semicircle of Aboukir Bay on the other, and from here or from Fort Ramleh the scene of the "Battle of the Nile" can be surveyed, and Nelson's great manœuvre appreciated; "Nelson's Island" from which the French line depended and where the Culloden was wrecked lies straight ahead (*see* above). The promontory was anciently called Zephyrium, because it caught the cool zephyr winds; here stood a little temple to Aphrodite and when the great queen Arsinoe died in B.C. 270, one of the court admirals had the happy idea of associating her with the elder goddess so that mariners might render thanks to both. The shrine then became fashionable and Queen Berenice hung up her hair here in 244 as a thank-offering for her husband's safe return; in the following year the hair was snatched up to heaven, where it may still be observed on any fine night as the constellation of Coma Berenice. The temple was less fortunate, and all that remains of it is the base of a column, down among the rocks.—In Christian times the Church of St.

Cyr and St. John (*see* above) stood here, on the side of Aboukir Bay.

Aboukir Bay.—The shore is airless and there are palm trees, the waters shallow. From a boat one can look down on the mud in which the Orient, Brueys' flagship, has disappeared with all her treasure; attempts have been made to locate her, but in vain. Good sailing. Turtle fishing. On the projecting spit to which Napoleon dragged his guns (*see* above) is the landing enclosure for the fishing boats; many of the fishermen are Sicilians; they have lived at Aboukir for generations and form a community by themselves. Here (site uncertain) once stood Menouthis.

Fort Ramleh.—Topped by the waterworks. Magnificent view. The flat ground to the south marks the Canopic Mouth of the Nile, through which Herodotus entered Egypt; here Heracleum stood (*see* above).

About quarter mile S.W. of Fort Ramleh, and close to a small modern pumping tower, are the so-called *Baths of Cleopatra*. She had nothing to do with them, but they are worth seeing. The western outer wall, of limestone blocks, is well preserved. Steps lead up through it. Within are pavements of pebble mosaic, fragments of stucco, a stone with a drain groove, &c. In a chamber to the left, is an oblong bath nearly six feet deep; steps lead down to it and in the centre of its pebbled floor is a little depression; in the edge of the brim and on the wall opposite are niches, as if to support beams, and provision for the entrance and exit of the water can also be seen. Further on, past a small stucco cistern, is an entrance to a small room which contains an oblong bath to lie down in, quite modern and suburban in appearance; close to it, under a niche, is a footbath—the bather sat on a seat which has disappeared but whose supports can be seen.—These baths are all in the western part of the enclosure; the rest contains other and larger chambers but is in worse preservation. It is much to be wished that these baths, which have been recently excavated, could be protected properly; otherwise they will share the fate of the other antiquities within the military zone.

Aboukir Village, to which we return through palm trees, contains nothing of note.

On leaving Mamourah Junction (p. 188) the railway to Rosetta bears to the right, and crosses the salt marshy ground over which the Canopic branch of the Nile once flowed to the sea. Rural Egypt can be seen at last. Beyond El Tarh station the train crosses a bit of Lake Edku; view of the village to the left.

Edku (no hotel or café) stands on a high mound between the lake and the Mediterranean. The houses in its steep streets are of red brick strengthened with courses of palm and other woods; they anticipate the more complicated architecture of Rosetta; there are some carved doors, Italianate in style. Mosques, unimportant. On the top of the ridge are some eight sailed windmills; they grind corn. Fine date palms grow on the sand dunes towards the sea, for there is fresh water just beneath the surface. There is an interesting local weaving industry, chiefly of silk, imported in its rough state from China. The work rooms are generally on the upper floors of the houses, and reached by an outside staircase. Quiet pleasant places; on the walls of some are Cufic inscriptions, inlaid in brick. The weavers sit to their looms in small oval pits; they have the hands of craftsmen and produce on their simple wooden machinery fabrics that are both durable and beautiful.

Fish are caught in Lake Edku. Some of the fishermen wade far into shallow waters; there is also a fleet of boats which moor to the long wooden jetty by the station. Occasional flamingoes.

The railway continues between lake and sea, finally bending northward and curving round great groves of palm trees, behind which lie the town of Rosetta and the river Nile.

ROSETTA†

Rosetta and Alexandria are rivals; when one rises the other declines. Rosetta, situated on the Nile, would have dominated but for an overwhelming drawback; she has, and can have, no sea-harbour, because the coast in this part of Egypt is mere delta; the limestone ridges that created the two harbours of Alexandria do not continue eastward of Aboukir. Alexandria required organising by human science, but once organised she was irresistible. It is only in an unscientific age that Rosetta has been important. Let us briefly examine the birth and death, rebirth and decay, of civilisation here.

(i). In Pharaonic times the town and river-port of *Bolbitiné* were built hereabouts—probably a little up stream, beyond the present mosque of Abou Mandour. Nothing is known of the history of Bolbitiné. When Alexandria was founded (B.C. 331) traffic deserted the "Bolbitiné" mouth of the Nile for the "Canopic" and for the Alexandrian harbours, and the town decayed consequently. Its chief memorial is the so-called "Rosetta Stone," a basalt inscription now in the British Museum. The inscription enumerates the merits of King Ptolemy V Epiphanes (B.C. 196; *see* genealogical tree p. 14). It is a dull document, a copy of the original decree which was set up at Memphis and reproduced broadcast over the country. But it is important because it is written in three scripts—Hieroglyphic, Demotic and Greek—and thus led to the deciphering of the ancient Egyptian language. The antique columns &c., that may be seen in Rosetta to-day also probably came from

Bolbitiné. But it was never important, and the sands have now covered it.

(ii). *Rosetta* itself was founded in A.D. 870 by El Motaouakel, one of the Abbaside Caliphs of Egypt. The date is most significant. By 870 the Canopic mouth of the Nile had dried up, and isolated Alexandria from the Egyptian water system. Shipping passed back to the Bolbitiné mouth, and frequented it again for nearly a thousand years. "El Raschid" as the Arabs named the new settlement, became the western port of Egypt, Damietta being the eastern. It was important in the Crusades; St. Louis of France (1049) knew it as "Rexi." In the 17th and 18th centuries it was practically rebuilt in its present form; the mosques, dwelling houses, cisterns, the great warehouses for grain that line the river bank, all date from this period. It evolved an architectural style, suitable to the locality. The chief material is brick, made from the Nile mud, and coloured red or black, there was no limestone to hand, such as supplied Alexandria: with the bricks are introduced courses of palm wood, antique columns &c., and a certain amount of mashrabiyeh work and faience. The style is picturesque rather than noble and may be compared with the brick style of the North German Hansa towns. Examples of it are to be found throughout the Delta and even in Alexandria herself (p. 136), but Rosetta is its headquarters. In architecture, as in other matters, the town kept in touch with Cairo; an Oriental town, scarcely westernised even to-day. So long as Alexandria lay dormant, it flourished; at the beginning of the 19th century its population was 35,-000, that of Alexandria 5,000.

In 1798 Napoleon's troops took Rosetta, in 1801 the British and Turks retook it, in 1807 the reconnoitering expedition of General Frazer (p. 94) was here repulsed. These events, unimportant in themselves, were the prelude to an irreparable disaster: the revival of Alexandria, on scientific lines, by Mohammed Ali. As soon as he developed the harbours there and restored the connection with the Nile water systems by cutting the Mahmoudieh Canal, (p. 97), Rosetta began to decay exactly as Bolbitiné had decayed two thousand years before. The population now is 14,000 as against Alexandria's 400,000, and it has become wizen and puny through inbreeding. The warehouses and mosques are falling down, the costly private dwellings of the merchants have been gutted, and the sand, advancing from the south and from the west, invades a little farther every year through the palm groves and into the streets. One can wander aimlessly for hours (it is best thus to wander) and can see nothing that is modern, nor anything more exciting than the arrival of the fishing fleet with sardines. It is the East at last, but the East outwitted by science, and in the last stages of exhaustion.

The main street of Rosetta starts from the Railway Station and runs due south, parallel to the river, so it is easy to find one's way. In it is the only hotel, kept by a Greek; those who are not fastidious can sleep here: the rest must manage to see the sights between trains. The hotel has a pleasant garden, overlooked by the minaret of a mosque.

In the main street, to the right;—*Mosque of Ali-el-Mehalli*, built 1721, but containing the tomb of the Saint, who died in the 16th century. A large but uninteresting building, with an entrance porch in the "Delta" style—bricks arranged in patterns, pendentives, &c.

Further down, to the left, by the covered bazaars: Entrance with old doors to a large ruined building, probably once an "okel" or courtyard for travellers and their animals; one can walk through it and come out the other side through a fine portal, in the direction of the river. All this part of the town is most picturesque. The houses are four or five stories high, and have antique columns fantastically disposed among their brickwork. The best and oldest example of this domestic architecture is the *House of Ali-el-Fatairi*, in the Haret-el-Ghazl, with inscriptions above its lintels that date it 1620; its external staircase leads to two doors, those of the men's and women's apartments respectively. Other fine houses are those of:—Cheikh Hassan el Khabbaz in Rue Dahliz el Molk; Osman Agha, at some cross roads,—carved wood inside, date 1808; Ahmed Agha in the Chareh el Ghabachi to the west of the town, invaded by sand.

At the end of the main street is the most important building in the town, the *Mosque of Zagloul*. It really consists of two mosques: the western was founded about 1600 by Zagloul, the Mameluke or body-servant of Said Hassan; the other and more ruinous section is the Mosque of El Diouai. There is a courtyard with fountain in centre. The entire mass measures about 80 by 100 yds. All is brick except the two stone minarets; the ruined one was "cut with scissors" according to local opinion, but according to archaeology fell in the early 19th cent. The sanctuary of the Mosque of Zagloul proper is a stupendous hall; over 300 columns, many of them antique, are arranged in six parallel rows, there are four praying niches, three of them elaborately decorated, there is the tomb of the ex-body-servant himself, now worshipped as a saint and wooed by votive offerings of boats, and, in the tomb, his former master, the Said Hassan, lies with him, and shares his honours. The sanctuary is ruinous and carelessly built, but its perspective effects, especially from the south wall, near the tomb, are very fine and rival those of the Mosque of El Azhar at Cairo. Light enters through openings in the roof.

East of the Mosque of Zagloul and close to the river is the Mosque of *Mohammed el Abbas*, date 1809, of superior construction but on the same style; it has, unlike the other mosques of Rosetta, a fine dome, covering the tomb of the saint.

Other Mosques:—Toumaksis Mosque, built by Saleh Agha Toumaksis in 1694; it is reached up steps; fine iron work round the key holes; there is a good pulpit inside, also tiles, and the prayer niche retains its original geometrical decoration of hexagons and "Solomon's seals."—Mosque of Cheikh Toka, which stands in an angle of the Chareh Souk el Samak el Kadim; portal in "Delta" style with rosace over its arches; inside, pulpit dated 1727.

About a mile to the south of the town, best reached by boat, is the *Mosque of Abou Mandour*, a showy modern building, well placed on the bend of the river bank, and backed by huge sand hills that threaten to bury it, as they have buried Bolbitiné.

North of the town, and halfway between it and the sea, is the site of Fort St. Julien, which Napoleon's soldiers built, and where they discovered the Rosetta Stone. The Fort has disappeared; there is a sketch of it in the Alexandria Museum (Vestibule).

Sailing on the Nile: delightful.

SECTION VIII

The Libyan Desert

Routes:—By the Mariout Railway to Bahig for Abousir and for St. Menas; each expedition takes a day.

By Railway *via* Tel el Baroud and Khatatbeh to the Wady Natrun; 2 or 3 days.†

Alexandria, though so cosmopolitan, lies on the verge of civilisation. Westward begins an enormous desert of limestone that stretches into the heart of Africa. The very existence of this desert is forgotten by most of the dwellers in the city, but it has played a great part in her history, especially in Christian times, and no one who would understand her career can ignore it.

The Mariout Railway was originally the property of the ex-Khedive. The line starts from the central station and diverges from the main line at Hadra. Having passed Nouzha Station (Section IV) it crosses the Mahmoudieh Canal (p. 97), then bends westward along the edge of Lake Mariout. Just before Gabbari Garden Station is a fishing village built on a tiny creek and quite Japanese in appearance. It is worth going down here when there has been a catch: the lake fish are uncanny monsters. The neighbourhood is very fertile—palms, bananas and vegetable gardens. But it does not make pleasant walking owing to the smells.‡

MEX STATION (Section VI). The train crosses the western or Mellaha arm of Mariout. Right, are the salt pans that turn dull purple and red in the summer; beyond them the white spur of limestone that divides lake from sea.

ABD EL KADER STATION. Now we approach the Libyan Desert. The scenery and the people change. From the hill to the right, by the tomb, is a fine view, and wonderful colour effects in the evening.

AMRIEH STATION. This large village was formerly head of the Eastern district of the Western Desert Province, but the Administration is transferring to Burg el Arab. Bedouins come to the train, bigger and wirier than the Egyptians, and more graceful; they wear rough white robes and soft dark red tarbooshes.—There is a fine walk from Amrieh to Mex—the best day's tramp near Alexandria. The path leads north from the station, by the communal gardens, then makes for a ridge where limestone is quarried. View from the top over the western arm of Mariout. Take the causeway that crosses the lake and on the further bank turn to the right, finally crossing the coastal ridge to Dekhela (Section VI) and so to Mex by the sea shore.

IKINGI MARIOUT STATION. (Ikingi is Turkish for "second.")—A good centre for the wild flowers of February and March. Go northward towards the lake, and keep to the lower ground; the local flora is one of the finest in the world.

BAHIG STATION. Centre for two fine expeditions—Abousir on the coast, and St. Menas inland.

ABOUSIR†

The ruins of Abousir lie 5½ miles N.W. from Bahig station. They can be found without a guide (*see* map). There is a good road as far as Bahig village (¾ mile). Just above the village is a big quarry, worked in ancient times and very picturesque. A path crosses the ridge rather to the left of this quarry, after which the ruins are in sight all the way. The end of Mariout has to be crossed, so the expedition should not be made in winter on account of the mud. The last half hour of the journey is magnificent. The Temple and the Tower stand out on the height, which is golden with marigolds in spring time; and near the top of the ascent the sea appears through a gap, deep blue, and beating against a beach of snowy sand. The flowers can be amazing, colouring the earth in every direction. The ruins are supposed by the Bedouins to be the palace of Abou Zeit; they really mark the Ptolemaic city of Taposiris, whose name is preserved in the modern Abousir.

Taposiris must have been built soon after Alexandria (about 300 B.C.), and it is instructive to compare the two towns. They stand on the same spur—Taposiris at its base, where it has emerged from the mass of the desert. The lake is to their south, the sea to their north, so each commanded two harbours, to the advantage of their trade. Each has a lighthouse, each worshipped Osiris. Little is known of the history of Taposiris—called the "Great" to distinguish it from "Little" Taposiris at Montazah (p. 186). Its immediate trade was with the lake, its sea harbour being ½ mile below, at the vanished port of Plinthinus. The Arabs turned the Temple of Osiris into a fortress, and in modern times coast guards have been installed here.

The chief remains are:—

(i). *Temple of Osiris.* The eastern, and main, entrance adjoins the coast-guard station. At first sight it looks no more than a hole in a ruined wall, but it can easily be reconstructed. Each side of the entrance were Gate-towers (Pylons) like those of Edfu or Kom Ombo in Upper Egypt. Their bases project from the main wall, and up the face of each are two grooves for flag staffs, from whose tops crimson streamers floated. Staircases, reached from the inside, ascend each tower, and there are also two square rooms in the base of each.

The enclosure—about 100 yards square—is in a terrible mess. The actual temple has disappeared. There must have been a colonnaded court with an altar in the middle, and beyond it the temple façade: on north and south of temple would have been other courts. The arrangements were Egyptian, but some of the workmen were Greek; mason marks with Greek letters (*e.g.* Alpha Kappa Rho) have been found on the stone in the boundary wall.

The north boundary wall of the enclosure is very fine; it projects over the slope of the hill and rests on substructures: in it is a gate for the descent to the sea. Note the projections in the masonry. In the northwest corner are some architectural fragments, piled up by the Arabs.

(ii). *Lighthouse.* The ruined tower on the hill to the east of the temple was once mistaken for a tomb, since it stands in the ancient cemetery. It is really the Ptolemaic lighthouse of Taposiris, first of a chain that stretched from the Pharos at Alexandria all down the North African coast to Cyrene. It has, like the Pharos, three stages: a square basement, an octagonal central stage and a cylindrical top. On the north, where the

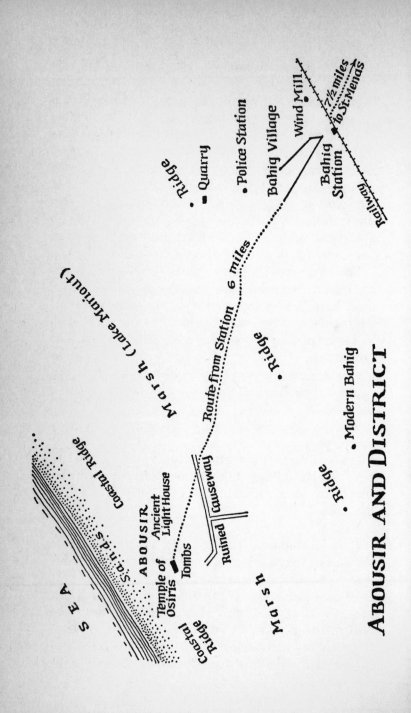

ABOUSIR AND DISTRICT

SEA

Coastal Ridge

Sand springs

Coastal Ridge

ABOUSIR

Ancient Light House

Temple of Osiris

Tombs

Ruined Causeway

Marsh (Lake Mariout)

Marsh

Ridge

Ridge

Route from Station 6 miles

Ridge

Quarry

Police Station

Bahig Village

Wind Mill

Bahig Station

7½ miles to St-Menas

Modern Bahig

Railway

outer wall of the octagon has fallen, one can see the
marks of the staircase by which the wood was carried
to the top—a simpler version of the double spiral that
ascended the huge Alexandrian building. There can be
no doubt that the Taposiris lighthouse was modelled
on its gigantic contemporary—scale about $\frac{1}{10}$th—and it
is thus of great importance to archaeologists and historians (*see* p. 144 ff.).

There are tombs close to the lighthouse, and tombs
and houses all along the slope to the south of the
temple.

(iii). *Causeway.* South of the town, in the bed of
the lake, are traces of the embankment that connected
with the desert. It was doubtless pierced with arches
like the Heptastadion at Alexandria, to allow boats to
go through.

The other point of interest in the district is *Burg el
Arab* (Modern Bahig). It lies some miles west of Bahig
village (*see* above) but is easily located by the tower
of the new carpet factory. Here is to be the capital of
the Eastern District of the Western Desert Province
Frontier Districts Administration; it is being planned
and executed with great taste, thanks mainly to the
genius of the Officer Commanding, W. E. Jennings
Bramly, M.C. The factory consists of a great cloister
and of two halls, one each side of the big tower. Fragments of antique sculpture and architecture have been
cleverly introduced. The carpets are woven from camels' and goats' hair by Bedouin and Senussi women—
the industry was started at Amrieh, during the late
war. Specimens can be had in the Alexandrian shops.
Further to the west other buildings are rising, including a small walled town. It is all most interesting, and

one of the few pieces of modern creative work to be seen in these parts.

ST. MENAS†

Seven and a half miles south of Bahig Station, in the loneliness of the desert, lie the ruins of a great Christian city. They can be visited between trains on a good horse, but it is better to camp out. The track passes over gently undulating expanses of limestone. The scenery grows less interesting, the flora scarcer, as the coast is left behind. At last the monotony is broken by the square hut where the excavators used to live. The ancient name of the place is preserved in the modern —Abumna.

Menas, a young Egyptian officer, was martyred during his service in Asia Minor because he would not abandon Christ (A.D. 296). When the army moved back into Egypt his friends brought his ashes with them, and at the entrance of the Libyan Desert a miracle took place: the camel that was carrying the burden refused to go further. The saint was buried and forgotten. But a shepherd observed that a sick lamb that crossed the spot became well. He tried successfully with another lamb. Then a sick princess was healed. The remains were exhumed, and a church built over the grave.

This church can still be traced. It is the Basilica of the Crypt (Plan I, p. 212) date 350, to which, at the end of the century, an immense extension was added by the Emperor Arcadius. What caused so rapid a growth? Water. There were springs in the limestone that have since dried up, and that must have had curative powers. Baths were built, some of them opening out of a church (Plan II). Little flasks, stamped with the saint's image, were filled from the sacred source by his tomb. The environs were irrigated, houses, walls, cemeteries built, until in the pure air a sacred city sprang up, where religion was combined with hygiene. Nor did the saint only protect invalids. He was also the patron of the caravans that passed by him from Alexandria to the Wady Natrun, the Siwan Oasis, and Tripoli, and so he is always seen between two camels, who crouch in adoration because he guides them aright. By the 6th century he had become god of the Libyan Desert, then less deserted than now, and his fame, like that of his predecessor Serapis, had travelled all round the Mediterranean, and procured him worshippers as far as Rome and France.

Islam checked the cult. But as late as the year 1,000, an Arab traveller saw the great double basilica still standing. Lights burned in the shrine night and day, and there was still left a little trickle of "the beautiful water of St. Menas that drives away pain."

The site, entirely forgotten, was discovered in 1905. It has been carefully excavated. Little more than the ground plans of the buildings remain, but they are most interesting, and the marble decorations delightful.

The Sanctuary Group. This lies a little to the south of the excavators' huts. Combined length, nearly 400 ft. In the centre is the original church covering the tomb. To its east is the impressive addition of Arcadius; to its west a baptistery. On its north side a monastery. The best view of the group is from a mound outside the baptistery. The general arrangement is quite clear (Plan I, p. 212). Taken in detail:—

(i). *Church of Arcadius.* Length nearly 200 feet. A cruciform basilica with a nave and two aisles, and aisled transepts. Over the intersection was a dome, beneath which, now much ruined by its fall, is the High Altar. Behind the altar are curved steps that supported the ecclesiastical throne. Both altar and throne are in a square enclosure where the priests and singers stood; a narrow alley connects it with the nave. The eastern apse has been used for burials.

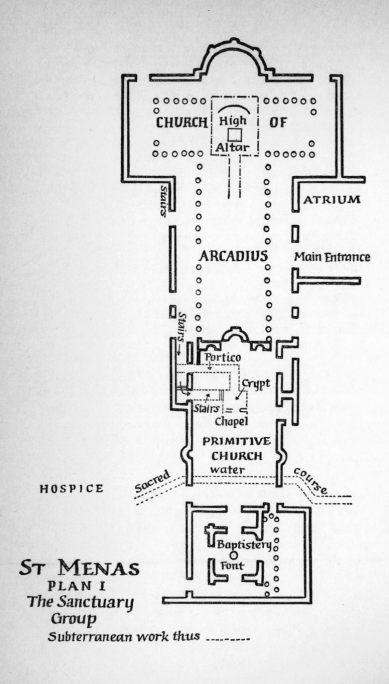

CHURCH | High | OF

Altar

Stairs

ATRIUM

ARCADIUS

Main Entrance

Stairs

Portico

Crypt

Stairs

Chapel

PRIMITIVE

CHURCH

water

HOSPICE

Sacred

course

Baptistery

Font

ST MENAS

PLAN I

The Sanctuary

Group

Subterranean work thus ----------

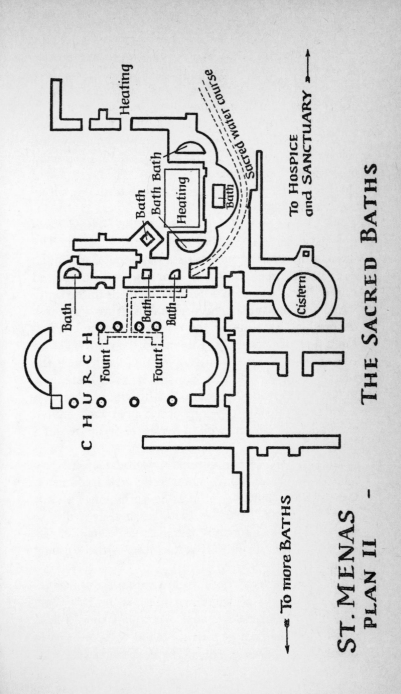

ST. MENAS — THE SACRED BATHS
PLAN II

The Nave is paved with white marble from the Greek archipelago. Green and purple marbles (verde antico and porphyry) were also used. From its south aisle, three doors open into a fine atrium. This was the principal approach to the church. The north aisle opens—at its east end—on to a staircase that ascended to the roof of the church; the other doors to the monks' apartments and hospice (*see* below). The west end of the nave is irregular, because the apse of the primitive church impinges.

(ii). *Primitive Church.* A small, three-aisled basilica, not well preserved, but with interesting crypt. The descent to this is by a marble staircase that starts in the Arcadian church, passes by a portico with a vaulted roof of brick, and then, after a little, turns to the south into an oblong subterranean chamber. Here, amid rich decorations, the ashes of the young saint once lay, in a tomb that was probably visible from the church above. A bas-relief of him was fixed to the south wall; the place for the marble slab can still be seen there. The ugly bas-relief in the Alexandria Museum (Room I) is a copy. Attached to the crypt is a chapel once vaulted with gold mosaic; the well in it was made by treasure-hunters.

On the west of the church runs the sacred water course from which the sanctuary derived its fame. It is a subterranean cistern, over 80 yards long; a shaft was sunk into it from the nave. Passing, as it did, so near to the saint's remains, it had special sanctity. The water was used to fill flasks, and also in the adjacent Baptistery.

(iii). *The Baptistery* is square without and octagonal within. In its centre, down steps, is the chief font, which had an over-flow canal; we do not know how it was filled. The floor was richly inlaid with serpentine, porphyry and other marbles. There was a dome. On its south side is an atrium. On its western exterior, niches for statues.

A Baptistery of this type—separate from the rest of the church—is common enough in the West. But in the East it is unique. Only at St. Menas, where water was so prominent in the worship, does it occur.

Immediately to the north of the Sanctuary Group are the *Monastery Buildings and Hospice*, a confused labyrinth. Best is a hall paved with marble and one supported by eight columns. It lies 40 yards due north from the gate of the Primitive Church. These buildings, together with the Sanctuary Group that they served, cover an area of over 40,000 square yards.

The Sacred Baths (Plan II). About 80 yards from the Monastery Buildings. Best located by the fine circular cistern of well-cut limestone blocks. The main building has a heating apparatus and three baths. Also a small but finely finished church; basilica type; apses at each end; three aisles. Two baths open straight out of its south aisles, and in its nave are two marble fountains that were probably filled from the source in the central sanctuary (*see* above). Throughout the arrangements are significant. The line between the hygienic and the miraculous is nowhere clearly drawn; heating apparatus and church have each to play their parts. Date of the group, probably 5th century. Another group lies beyond.

Northern Cemetery. This, the most important in the city, is some way from the groups above described. Indeed the visitor from Bahig leaves it to his left on his way to the hut. There is a good view of it from a mound. The main object is a church (150 ft. long), with three aisles, a square apse and numerous mortuary chapels where the more prominent invalids were buried. Others lie outside. Late date—7th–9th cent.

This by no means catalogues the ruins of St. Menas. There is a Southern Cemetery, private houses, wine presses, a kiln where the terra cotta flasks were made. All the desert around shows remains of the curious cult, which in some ways anticipated the methods of Lourdes.

Half a day over the desert southward brings a rider to the Wady Natrun.

THE WADY NATRUN†

The Wady is best visited by arrangement with the Egyptian Salt and Soda Company, who have the concession for developing that section of it where the Lakes and the Monasteries lie. The Company's private railway starts at Khatatbeh, on the branch line between Cairo and Tel-el-Baroud (see Map, p. 187). The train curves up the desert to Bir Victoria, where it waters beneath a solitary tree. Then it leaves civilisation, and for three hours nothing is seen except an occasional gazelle. At the end of that time the ground falls away to the left, and the monastery of St. Macarius appears far off. Then is seen the chain of the lakes, and across them, often in mirage, the monasteries of St. Pschoi and The Syrians. The train descends to the terminus of Bir Hooker, close to the Company's factory and rest house.

The Wady Natrun (i.e. Natron, Soda) is a curious valley that begins near Cairo, and slopes northwestward into the heart of the Libyan Desert. It may have once been an outlet of the Nile, though it is barred now from the sea by coastal hills. Its upper and lower reaches are both barren,

but in the central section—that which the railway taps—
water survives in the form of a chain of mineral lakes.

The deposits were worked from antiquity, but with the
rise of monasticism the Wady took a new importance, owing to its discomfort. As early as A.D. 150 St. Fronto retreated here from Alexandria. St. Ammon followed in 270;
St. Macarius or Mercury a hundred years later. The more
moderate ascetics extracted soda with the assistance of lay-
men; the extremists sought a waterless stretch called Scetis
—probably the southern portion of the valley where the
monastery to St. Macarius still stands. There were soon
5,000 monks. It is natural that so remote a community
should lose touch with the theological niceties of the capital, and in 399 the Patriarch Theophilus was obliged to
rebuke the monks for minimising the divine element in the
Second Person. Their reply was startling. They crossed the
desert, stormed Alexandria, and made the Patriarch apolo-
gise. A few years later he led an army into the Wady to
punish them, but by now, oddly enough, they had veered
to the opposite error; they minimised the human element.
The truth is they represented native Egypt, the Patriarch
the Hellenising coast (*see* p. 56). The quarrel was racial
rather than theological, and when in the 6th century it
came to a head, the Wady became the natural stronghold
of the national or Monophysite party who, under the name
of Copts, worship there to this day.

With the 19th century came a new colony—the industrial. It is the factory chimney of the Salt and Soda Company that now dominates the scene. The lakes are dredged
for their deposits. The chief product is caustic soda which
is poured red hot into metal drums, and exported all over
the east. Ordinary soda (natron) is also produced. The factory is interesting. It, and the surrounding settlement, are
due in their present form to Mr. A. H. Hooker, after whom
the settlement is named.

More than eighty different species of birds have been
identified in the marshes surrounding Bir Hooker.

The Mineral Lakes.

These lie between the factory and the monasteries.

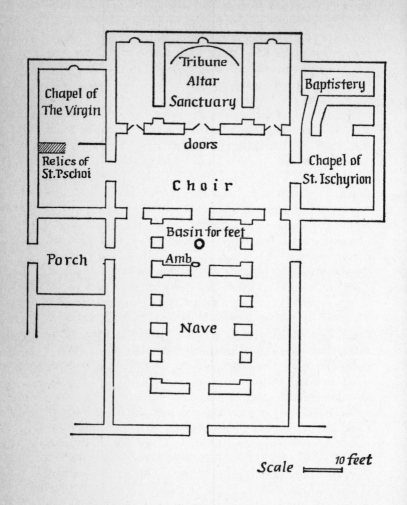

Chapel of The Virgin

Relics of St. Pschoi

Tribune
Altar
Sanctuary

doors

Baptistery

Chapel of St. Ischyrion

Choir

Basin for feet

Porch

Amb.

Nave

Scale ▭ 10 feet

THE NATRUN MONASTERIES
PLAN I – CHURCH OF ST. PSCHOI

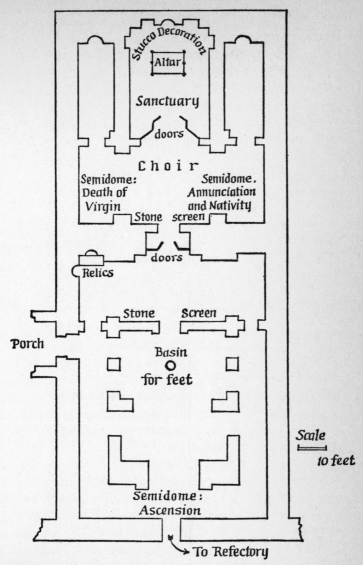

Stucco Decoration

Altar

Sanctuary

doors

Choir

Semidome:
Death of
Virgin

Semidome.
Annunciation
and Nativity

Stone screen

doors

Relics

Stone   Screen

Porch

Basin
○
for feet

Scale
├─┤
10 feet

Semidome:
Ascension

↘ To Refectory

The Natrun Monasteries - Plan II
Convent of the Syrians - Church of the Virgin

Some of them are squalid, others are indescribably beautiful, especially in summer. The deposits form at the bottom. As they reach the top, the lake seems to be covered with white and crimson ice, in the midst of which are pools of blue and green water, and trickling streams of claret, and tracts that blush like a rose. When the scene is in mirage, its strangeness passes belief. A bird looks as big as a man, and the lump of salt it perches on shows like a boat of snow. The finest of these lakes is just to the left of Bir Hooker.

The Monasteries.

Four of these survive, and there are the ruins of many others. They are all of the same type, and to avoid repetitions it may be thus summarised:

Exterior:—an enclosure of stone laid in the middle of the desert, covering about an acre. Palm trees and buildings show over its walls. The walls are blank except for one high arch, which indicates the position of a little door, the only entrance. The black-robed monks, when the bell has been rung, look down from the parapet, then unbar the door, and take the traveller to the Guest House for coffee and lemonade. They are dirty and ignorant, but most courteous and hospitable. All payment is refused.

In the enclosure:—two or three churches, normally consisting of nave, choir, and sanctuary (kaikal). Refectory. Sleeping cells for the monks. Mill for grinding corn. Oven, where is baked the hard brown bread, and also the "isbodikon" (somatikon, sacrament), a cake of fine flour beautifully stamped with a cross and used for the Eucharist. Olive press. Granary. Garden of palm trees, bananas, capsicums, etc. Keep (kasr) for final retreat when attacked; reached only by a drawbridge from the parapet of the wall; contains library, dungeons, chapels; usually dedicated to St. Michael.

Date: general appearance and arrangement are of the 6th century. Most of the details are later.

Extract from the Thanksgiving offered at the arrival of a distinguished visitor:—

> He who visits these mansions with firm faith, fervent desire, true repentance and good works, shall have all his sins forgiven. Then, O my reverend fathers and my beloved brethren, come that we may pray for these our dear and honourable brethren, who are come upon this visit and have reached these habitations, let us pray that Jesus Christ, who was with his servants in every time and every place, may now be with them, and may deliver them from all sins and iniquities. May he grant them the best of gifts and full reward, recompensing them for all that they have endured through toil and peril and the weariness of the journey as they travelled hither; giving them abundance of blessing; bring them back to their homes in safety; and after long life transport them to the brightness of Paradise and the life of bliss, through the intercession of Our Lady the Virgin, and of all our holy fathers. Amen.*

THE FOUR MONASTERIES.

(A). *Convent of St. Pschoi* (Deir Abou Bishoi).— About an hour's ride from Bir Hooker. Dedicated to St. Pschoi or Besa. "B" is the Coptic article, so the saint's name is ultimately "Isa" *i.e.* Isaiah. Little is known about him.

The convent enclosure contains:

(i). *The Church of St. Pschoi* (Plan I, p. 218). 6th–11th cents. with later additions. A spacious entrance

---

* From A. J. Butler's Ancient Coptic Churches.

porch leads to the dark but impressive interior. There
are three divisions: Nave, Choir and Sanctuary.

The Nave has an arched vault; massive piers with
pointed arches divide it from its aisles. In it is an Am-
bon (lectern for reading the Gospel), and a small marble basin level with the floor, where the priest washes
the feet of the people on Maundy Thursday in commemoration of the action of Christ. Many of the Nave
arches have been blocked up to strengthen the building. High and narrow folding doors—recalling a Japanese screen—close the lofty arch that leads from the
Nave into the Choir; they are set with fine carved
panels, enclosed in ivory borders. Other doors lead
from the aisles.

The Choir too has vaulting, but it is at right angles
to that of the Nave. At each side of the Choir are
chapels, probably of later date. Left—Chapel of the
Virgin, with a chest containing the relics of St. Pschoi,
whom the monks state remains intact. Right—Chapel
of St. Ischyrion; off it is the Baptistery. The entrance
into the Sanctuary is through ancient carved doors;
over them is a triumphant arch.

The Sanctuary has, behind the altar, a fine tribune
of six steps—three straight and three curved. In the
centre was the throne of the Abbot. It has gone, and
the marble decorations of the steps are ruined. Above
the throne is a marble mosaic. In the centre of the
eastern dome is a Cross.

(ii). *The Refectory.* This solemn room contains the
immense stone table, narrow and low, at which the
monks break their yearly ·fast. They do not eat here
usually, and use the table as a drying place for onions,
bread, etc., while cakes of salt are stacked against the
wall. At the head of the table is the Abbot's seat. The
place is rough and indescribably untidy. But one could

scarcely find a more striking relic of primitive Christianity.

(B). *Convent of the Syrians* (Deir es Suriani).— Close to the Convent of St. Pschoi. Founded by monks from Syria. Dedicated to the Virgin. Here Robert Curzon (1833) discovered in the oil cellar priceless Syrian, Coptic, and Abyssinian MSS., now in the British Museum. He describes his find in "Monasteries of the Levant": it was facilitated by plying the Abbot with liqueurs. More were brought away by Archdeacon Tattam, and nothing valuable remains now.

The enclosure contains:—

(i). *Church of the Virgin* (Plan II, p. 219). A fine building 40 ft. by 90, probably the model for the church in St. Pschoi—*i.e.* originating in the 6th century.

The Nave has piers with high pointed arches, and lofty vaulting, slightly pointed. In the middle, the basin for the Maundy feet washing, a marble slab with a circular depression. In the western semi-dome, fine fresco of the Ascension. Precious folding doors between nave and choir, inlaid with ivory panels of Christ in the nimbus of the Cross, the Virgin, St. Peter and St. Mark; round their posts and lintels a Syriac inscription, dating them back to the 7th century.

The Choir—North semi-dome; fresco of the Death of the Virgin. South semi-dome; fresco of the Annunciation and Nativity. Admirable work. More ancient doors between Choir and Sanctuary; ivory panel representing Dioscurus (Patriarch of Alexandria 450 and founder of Monophysism, *see* p. 56), Mark, Emmanuel, the Virgin, Ignatius, and Severus (512). Syriac inscriptions of rather later type—8th century.

Sanctuary—Skilful and effective plaster frieze with a border below and panels of conventional trees and vines above. Above the eastern niche a panel of crosses. This unique decoration should be studied closely.

(ii). *Smaller Church of the Virgin.* Over its entrance to the southwest a marble cross in low relief. Inside, another cross in black marble. Probably dedication crosses. Pulpit in the choir.

(iii). *Tamarind tree under the enclosing wall.* St. Ephraim the Syrian (date 373) inadvertently, so they say, laid his staff down, and it took root at once. But it is unlikely that St. Ephraim ever visited Egypt.

(C). *Convent of St. Baramus* (Deir el Baramus).—About two hours ride from Bir Hooker. Dedicated to an unknown saint (Romaios ?).

In the enclosure are:—

(i). *Church of the Virgin.* The piers of the nave are built round antique marble columns. There are ten dedication crosses, marking places signed with holy oil at the consecration of the church—six in the nave and four in the choir. Fine carvings on the sanctuary screen. In the reliquary lie the brothers SS. Maximus and Domitius from whose mouths, when they prayed, fiery ropes ascended to Heaven. Attached to this church are two smaller ones—St. George (Mari Girgis) now used as a granary; it has an ornamented dome— and St. Theodore (Al Amir Tadrus).

(ii). *Church of Baramus.*—Ruined by restoration.

(iii). *The Refectory.*—Similar to that at St. Pschoi. Date 5th or 6th century. At this entrance is a great book-rest of stone.

(iv). *Keep.*—With chapel to St. Michael.

(D). *Convent of St. Macarius* (Deir Abou Makar).—This monastery is the least accessible of the four, being ten miles from Bir Hooker.

St. Macarius, or Mercury, the founder, was an Alex-

andrian who was seen by another saint in a vision killing the apostate Emperor Julian (d. 363). He is also
celebrated for a bunch of grapes that he refused to eat,
and for a mosquito that he killed. Overcome with remorse at its death, he retired naked to the marshes
near, and at the end of six months was so distended
by stings that the brethren could only recognise him
by his voice. He selected this site for his monastery on
account of the badness of the communications and
water supply. It was repaired in 880. Of its later history
nothing is known.

The monastery enclosure is on the usual plan. It
contains:—

(i). *Church of Macarius.* Byzantine in character;
three sanctuaries, a choir, and an irregular western
end. The central sanctuary is roofed by a fine brick
dome, once covered with frescoes, and still showing
traces of its ancient windows, with their stucco parti-
tions and tiny panels of coloured glass. There were also
frescoes in the eastern niche, and paintings upon the
entrance arch. The sanctuary doors are well carved.

Left of Sanctuary: Chapel of St. John, with a double
screen. The outer screen is set with exquisitely carved
panels—probably 8th century. Frame later. The plaster
of the dome has fallen; it too was once coloured. St.
Macarius lies in the Reliquary.

(ii). *Church of the Elders* (Al Shiulah).—Marked by
a detached bell-tower. A small building of similar plan.
One of its columns has a late classical capital.

(iii). *Church of St. Ischyrion* (Abou Iskharun).—One
of the martyrs whom Alexandria, in the past, so freely
produced. A magnificent low-pitched dome almost
covers both choir and nave. It is made of bricks that
must have been carried on camels from the Delta.

(iv). *The Keep* (Kasr).—Reached by a flight of steps

and a drawbridge. On its first floor are three chapels dedicated to:—

St. Michael—Corinthian and Doric capitals in the nave; the Sanctuary Screen has ivory inlay; in the Sanctuary are the bodies of sixteen patriarchs, each in a plain deal box: St. Anthony—three ancient frescoed figures: and St. Suah, with more frescoes. On the ground floor, a chapel to the Virgin, with a triple altar containing depressions of unknown use.

THE MODERN RELIGIOUS COMMUNITIES

The ecclesiastical life of Alexandria is not as intense to-day as in the days of St. Athanasius, but it is even more complicated. The city is the seat of four patriarchates, and many other religious bodies are represented in her. The complications are partly due to the activity of Roman Catholicism, which, in order to win oriental schismatics back to the fold, has in each case created a counter church that shall approximate as nearly as possible to the conditions and ritual that are familiar—e.g. an Armenian Catholic Church for the Armenians, a Coptic Catholic for the Copts. And further complications proceed from the modern commercial communities who tend to regard religion as an expression of nationality rather than of dogma.

The following list of the Churches may indicate the unsuspected vastness of the subject:—

GREEK PATRIARCHATE: "Orthodox Greek," or "Melchite" church (from Melek, Arabic for King). Present Patriarch, Photius I. His position is curious. He is a subject neither to the Kingdom of Greece, nor to the Patriarch of Constantinople, but holds, or rather held, his position from the Sultan of Turkey direct. Thus ecclesiastically he is independent. His title is "Patriarch of Alexandria, Libya, Pentapolis, Ethiopia, and all Egypt," but his patriarchate does not extend beyond Egypt, which he administers through four bishops. Historically he represents the church that kept loyal to Byzantium and to the Emperor at the Council of Chalcedon (A.D. 451) when the rest of Egypt began to drift away over the Monophysite question. After the Arab Conquest the Greek Patriarch resided in Cairo, but came back to Alexandria about sixty years ago to the Convent and Church of St. Saba (p. 114). As for dogma, the Greek Orthodox chiefly differs from the Roman Catholic and the Protestants over the "Filioque" clause in the Nicene creed. It holds that the Holy Ghost proceeded not from the Father and the Son, but through the Son. This is the point over which the East and West split, and failed to reunite in 1449.

CHURCHES OF THE GREEK COMMUNITY: These too are Greek Orthodox in faith. But they do not recognise the Patriarch. Indeed their relations with him during the late war were of the liveliest. They are the churches of a body of business men who only owe allegiance to the Kingdom of Greece. They are self-administering, and choose their own priests. The Patriarch, however, has the right of examining those priests' credentials, and of giving them permission to officiate. The Community has a Cathedral (The Annunciation) near the Place St. Catherine (p. 154); also three churches in Ramleh,—St. Stefano, St. Nicolas, and the Prophet Elias.

SYRIAN GREEK ORTHODOX: The Church of those members of the Syrian Community who hold the Greek Orthodox faith. Independent of the Patriarch. Under an archimandrite. Services in Arabic. Church—"Dormition de la Sainte Vierge" in the Rue el Kaid Gohar.

This completes the Greek Orthodox Churches.

COPTIC PATRIARCHATE: The Copts are Monophysites—*i.e.* believe that after the Incarnation the Divine and the Human in Christ were united into a single nature (p. 81). This severs them from the rest of Christendom. Historically the Patriarchate is the opponent of the Greek Orthodox Patriarchate, from whom it split at the Council of Chalcedon, and it claims to represent Egyptian Christianity. In 960 the Patriarch went to reside at Cairo, and the custom has continued, though the title of "Patriarch of Alexandria" was retained. Besides his powers in Egypt, the Patriarch consecrates the Metropolitan of Abyssinia. Alexandria has a resident archbishop. Cathedral—in the Rue de l'Eglise Copte (p. 175).

ARMENIAN CHURCH: Founded by St. Gregory the Illuminator in the 4th century, and, like the Coptic, Monophysite. Its head is a "Catholicos" at Etchmiadzin, Armenia. The Alexandrian community has a church, SS. Peter and Paul, Rue Abou el Dardaa (p. 156).

We now come to the group of churches that are in communion with Rome. Dogma, identical. Rite, differing.

LATIN PATRIARCHATE: Founded after the Crusades—13th century. The Patriarch does not reside but lives at Rome, and governs through an Apostolic Vicar who lives at Alexandria. Chief Church—Cathedral of St. Catherine (Place St. Catherine, p. 155).

COPTIC PATRIARCHATE: Organised in 1895, with title of "Patriarchate of Alexandria and of all the Preaching of St. Mark." The Patriarch resides at Alexandria, and administers Egypt through the suffragan bishops of Hermopolis Magna and Thebes. Cathedral—Rue de l'Hôpital Indigène (p. 169).

GREEK CATHOLIC CHURCH: Under the Patriarch of Antioch who now lives at Damascus and governs Alexandria through a Vicar General. Church: St. Pierre, Rue Debbane (p. 174). The priests generally officiate in Arabic, though the ecclesiastical language is Greek.

MARONITE CHURCH: Founded in the 5th century by St. Maro, and at one time adhering to the Monothelite heresy.

This was a fainter version of the Monophysite, and asserted that though Christ might have two natures, He only had one will (p. 82). The Catholic view is that Christ had two wills, human and divine, which were exercised in unison, and in the 18th century the Maronite Community subscribed to this, and is consequently in communion with Rome. Patriarch at Antioch. Ecclesiastical language—Syrian. Church at Alexandria in the Rue de l'Eglise Maronite (p. 153).

ARMENIAN CATHOLIC CHURCH: Under the Patriarchate of Cilicia, formed in the 18th century. There is a Bishop of Alexandria, but he lives at Cairo. Church—Rue Averoff (p. 175).

CHALDEAN CATHOLIC CHURCH: Under the Patriarchate of Babylon, formed 1843, to counteract the Nestorian heresy. The Chaldeans of Alexandria, 100 strong, are said to be looking for a plot of ground on which to build a church.

This concludes the Catholic group. As regards the Protestants:

UNITED PRESBYTERIAN CHURCH OF EGYPT: Most, but not all, native Protestants belong to this body. It is attached to the American Mission, which proselytizes mainly among the Copts. Church—Rue Tewfik I.

CHURCH OF ENGLAND: Alexandria is in the diocese of Egypt and the Sudan. The official church of the British community is St. Marks in the Square, built on land given to the community by Mohammed Ali (p. 110). There is another Anglican church at Ramleh (All Saints) built by some residents there. Its living, after some heart-burnings, has been placed in the hands of the Bishop of London (p. 181).

CHURCH OF SCOTLAND: St. Andrew's, in the French Gardens.

APPENDIX II

THE DEATH OF CLEOPATRA
(p. 30)

The death of Cleopatra as described by Plutarch took hold of the imagination of posterity, and was dramatised by Shakespeare and by Dryden.

(i). PLUTARCH (in North's Translation which Shakespeare used).

Her death was very sodain. For those whom Caesar sent unto her ran thither in all haste possible, and found the soldiers standing at the gate, mistrusting nothing, nor understanding of her death. But when they had opened the doors, they found Cleopatra stark dead, laid upon a bed of gold, attired and arrayed in her royal robes, and one of her two women, which was called Iras, dead at her feet: and her other woman called Charmian half dead, and trembling, trimming the diadem which Cleopatra wore upon her head. One of the soldiers seeing her, angrily said to her: Is that well done, Charmian? Very well said she again, and meet for a princess descended of so many royal kings. She said no more, but fell down dead hard by the bed.

(ii). SHAKESPEARE (Antony and Cleopatra, Act V, Scene 2).

Cleopatra. Give me my robe, put on my crown; I have
Immortal longings in me; now no more
The juice of Egypt's grape shall moist this lip.
Yare, yare, good Iras; quick. Methinks I hear
Antony call; I see him rouse himself
To praise my noble act; I hear him mock
The luck of Caesar, which the gods give men
To excuse their after wrath: husband, I come:

Now to that name my courage prove my title!
I am fire and air; my other elements
I give to baser life. So; have you done?
Come then, and take the last warmth of my lips.
Farewell, kind Charmian; Iras, long farewell.

(kisses them. Iras falls and dies).

Have I the aspic in my lips? Dost fall?
If thou and nature can so gently part,
The stroke of death is as a lover's pinch,
Which hurts and is desired. Dost thou lie still?
If thus thou vanishest, thou tell'st the world
It is not worth leave-taking.

   Charmian. Dissolve thick cloud and rain; that I may say
The gods themselves do weep.

   Cleopatra.   This proves me base:
If she meet first the curled Antony
He'll make demand of her, and spend that kiss
Which is my heaven to have. Come thou mortal wretch

(to the asp, which she applies to her breast)

With thy sharp teeth this knot intrinsicate
Of life at once untie; poor venomous fool,
Be angry, and despatch. O! couldst thou speak,
That I might hear thee call great Caesar ass
Unpolicied.

   Charmian.   O eastern star!

   Cleopatra.   Peace, peace!
Dost thou not see my baby at my breast,
That sucks the nurse asleep?

   Charmian.   O, break! O, break!

   Cleopatra. As sweet as balm, as soft as air, as gentle—
O Antony!—Nay, I will take thee too.

(applying another asp to her arm)

What should I stay—   (dies).

   Charmian. In this vile world? So, fare thee well.
Now boast thee, death, in thy possession lies
A lass unparallel'd. Downy windows, close;
And golden Phœbus never be beheld
Of eyes again so royal! Your crown's awry;

I'll mend it, and then play.

(enter the Guard, rushing in)

First Guard. Where is the queen?

Charmian. Speak softly, wake her not.

First Guard. Caesar hath sent—

Charmian. Too slow a messenger.

(applies an asp)

O! come apace, dispatch; I partly feel thee.

First Guard. Approach, ho! All's not well; Caesar's be-
guil'd.

Second Guard. There's Dolabella sent from Caesar; call
him.

First Guard. What work is this? Charmian, is this well
done?

Charmian. It is well done and fitting for a princess
Descended of so many royal kings.
Ah! Soldier.

(dies)

(iii). DRYDEN (All for Love, Act V, Scene I).

Charmian. To what end
These ensigns of your Pomp and Royalty?

Cleopatra. Dull that thou art! why, 'tis to meet my Love;
As when I saw him first, on Cydno's bank,
All sparkling, like a goddess; so adorned,
I'll find him, once again: my second spousals
Shall match my first in glory. Haste; haste, both,
And dress the bride of Antony.

Charmian. 'Tis done.

Cleopatra. Now set me by my lord. I claim this place:
For I must conquer Caesar too, like him,
And win my share o' th' world. Hail, you dear relics
Of my immortal love!
O let no impious hand remove you hence;
But rest for ever here. Let Egypt give
His death that peace, which it denied his life.
Reach me the casket.

Iras. Underneath the fruit
The aspic lies.

Welcome, thou kind deceiver!

Cleopatra.

(putting aside the leaves)

Thou best of thieves; who, with an easy key,
Dost open life, and, unperceived by us,
Ev'n steal us from ourselves; discharging so
Death's dreadful office, better than himself,
Touching our limbs so gently into slumber,
That Death stands by, deceived by his own image,
And thinks himself but sleep.

  Serapion (within).   The Queen, where is she?
The town is yielded, Caesar's at the gates.

  Cleopatra. He comes too late t'invade the rights of death.
Haste, bare my arm, and rouse the serpent's fury.

(holds out her arm, and draws it back)

Coward flesh—
Would'st thou conspire with Caesar to betray me,
As thou wert none of mine? I'll force thee to it
And not be sent by him,
But bring myself my soul to Antony.

(turns aside, and then shows her arm bloody)

Take hence; the work is done.

  Serapion (within)   Break ope the door
And guard the traitor well.

  Charmian.   The next is ours.

  Iras. Now, Charmian, be too worthy
Of our great queen and mistress.

(they apply the aspics)

  Cleopatra. Already, death, I feel thee in my veins;
I go with such a will to find my lord,
That we shall quickly meet.
A heavy numbness creeps through every limb,
And now 'tis at my head: my eyelids fall
And my dear love is vanished in a mist.
Where shall I find him, where? O turn me to him,
And lay me on his breast—Caesar, thy worst;
Now part us if thou canst.

(Dies. Iras sinks down at her feet and dies;
Charmian stands behind her chair as dress-
ing her head. Enter Serapion, two priests,
Alexas bound, Egyptians).

Two Priests. Behold, Serapion, what havoc death hath made.

Serapion. 'Twas what I feared. Charmian, is this well done?

Charmian. Yes, 'tis well done, and like a queen, the last Of her great race: I follow her.

(sinks down; dies).

Appendix III

THE UNCANONICAL GOSPELS OF EGYPT
(p. 77)

(i). From the Gospel according to the Egyptians.

The Lord said unto Salome, who asked how long death would prevail, "As long as ye women bear children. I have come to undo the work of woman." And Salome said "Then have I done well in that I have not borne children." The Lord answered and said "Eat every plant, but that which has bitterness eat not." When Salome asked when would be known the things about which he spake (*i.e.* the Last Judgement) the Lord said "Whenever ye put off the garment of shame, when the two become one, and the male with the female, there being neither male nor female."

(ii). From the Gospel according to the Hebrews.

Jesus saith:—"Let not him who seeks cease until he find and when he finds he shall be astonished; astonished, he shall reach the Kingdom, and having reached the Kingdom he shall rest."

(iii). From uncertain sources (about 200 A.D.)

Jesus saith:—"Except ye fast to the world, ye shall in no wise find the Kingdom of God; and except ye make the sabbath a real sabbath, ye shall not see the Father."

Jesus saith:—"Wherever there are two, they are not

without God, and when ever there is one alone, I say, I am with him. Raise the stone and there thou shalt find me; cleave the wood, and there am I."

APPENDIX IV

THE NICENE CREED
(pp. 53 and 80)

Here is the text as originally passed by the Council, including the paragraph against the Arians; additions to the original texts are enclosed within brackets.

We believe in one God, the Father Almighty, maker of all things, both visible and invisible.

And in one Lord, Jesus Christ, the Son of God, begotten of the Father (only begotten, that is to say of the substance of the Father) God of God and Light of Light, very God of very God, begotten, not made, being of one substance with the Father, by whom all things were made (both things in Heaven and things on Earth); who for us men and for our salvation came down and was made flesh, made man, suffered and rose again on the third day, went up into the heavens and is to come again to judge the quick and the dead;

And in the Holy Ghost;

But the Holy Catholic and Apostolic Church anathematises those who say that there was a time when the Son of God was not, and that he was not before he was begotten, and that he was made from that which did not exist; or who assert that he is of other substance or essence than the Father, or is susceptible of change.

THE CITY OF WORDS
by Michael Haag

I first went to Alexandria in 1973, shortly before the October war, when visitors and guide books were scarce. Instead, in a Cairo bookshop I bought a neglected copy of Lawrence Durrell's *Justine* and began rereading it as the train drove through the widening Delta.

It is strange to explore a city through the pages of a novel. I was not led to Pompey's Pillar or round the Greco-Roman Museum, but to the mirrors and splintered palms of the Cecil Hotel, the café tables at Pastroudis, and along Tatwig Street towards its vanished child bordellos. I was sad to have missed Justine at the Cecil, but then I had not expected to meet Cleopatra either. I knew that Alexandria had changed.

The city was much as Durrell describes her in his Introduction to this edition. The Suez fiasco of 1956 had unhappily though not surprisingly led to a convulsive rejection of the Western presence in Egypt. And even earlier the Second World War tolled the death of an era when "Alexandria was the foremost port of Egypt, and a hive of activity for the country's cotton brokers ... with wide streets flanked by palms and flame trees, large gardens, stylish villas, neat new buildings, and above all, room to breathe. Life was easy. Labour was cheap. Nothing was impossible, especially when it involved one's comfort" (as Jacqueline Carol remembers in *Cocktails and Camels*, New York 1960).

But it was not ease that made Alexandria special, rather her cosmopolitan population: Greeks, Italians, British, French, Armenians, White Russians mixing with one another, though rarely mixing with Egyptians. Cavafy, for example, never visited an Egyptian house and knew hardly any Arabic, and this in a city where 50,000 Greeks (and 80,000 foreigners in all) lived among nearly half a million Egyptians. Still, the families of many of these foreigners had lived in Alexandria for generations, and the Greeks particularly had rooted their culture, as they had long ago, on this distant littoral.

Forster wrote to a friend in 1917: "The Greeks are the only community here that attempt to understand what they are talking about, and to be with them is to re-enter, however imperfectly, the Academic world. They are the only important people east of Ventimiglia – dirty, dishonest, unaristocratic, roving, and warped by Hellenic and Byzantine dreams – but they do effervesce intellectually, they do have creative desires, and one comes round to them in the end."

Forster's great discovery was the poet Constantine Cavafy. Before they met, Forster wrote: "One can't dislike Alex ... because it is impossible to dislike either the sea or stones. But it consists of nothing else as far as I can gather: just a clean cosmopolitan town by some blue water." But later, in his Preface to this book, he writes of another dimension: "The 'sights' of Alexandria are in themselves not interesting, but they fascinate when we approach them through the past." It was Cavafy who supplied the imaginative link between past and present, as Forster acknowledges by placing 'The God Abandons Antony' between his History and his Guide.

But Cavafy did more than resurrect a historical city. As he himself wrote in 1907: "By now I've got used to Alexandria," – he was born and had lived there almost all his life – "and it's very likely that even if I were rich I'd stay here. But in spite of this, how the place disturbs me. What trouble, what a burden small cities are – what a lack of freedom." Yet in 1910 he published 'The City'; these are its last few lines:

> You'll always end up in this city. Don't hope for things
>   elsewhere:
> There's no ship for you, there's no road.
> Now that you've wasted your life here, in this small corner,

you've destroyed it everywhere in the world.

Alexandria has not wasted your life, that you have done yourself. The city is what you make her, as you would make any
city, and so there is no escape in blaming Alexandria for
your misfortunes. In fact he accepted her, as he accepted
himself, and through her he gained command of time and
space. When Nikos Kazantzakis met Cavafy in 1927 he described him as becoming "all memory" – or as Forster observed
in *Two Cheers for Democracy*: "The amours of youth, even when
disreputable, are delightful, thinks Cavafy, but the point of
them is not that: the point is that they create the future,
and may give to an ageing man in a Rue Lepsius perceptions
he would never have known."

> In the loose living of my early years
> the impulses of my poetry were shaped,
> the boundaries of my art were plotted.

>   ('Understanding', 1918)

Also:

> The setting of houses, cafés, the neighbourhood
> that I've seen and walked through years on end:
> I created you while I was happy, while I was sad,
> with so many incidents, so many details.
> And, for me, the whole of you has been transformed
> into feeling.

>   ('In the Same Space', 1929)

– in this way he draws the whole of Alexandria, and her
history, into his personal experience; and it is this that puts
his often erotic and sometimes seemingly demeaning poetry
onto the same plane, within the same universe, as such historical poems as 'The God Abandons Antony'. In Alexandria
the poet created a world in which later Forster and Durrell
would build many possible Alexandrias.

Forster says Alexandria was suspiciously like a funk-hole,
but this was a funk-hole in which he found love, and much
else. He notes the peculiarity of the site's geography, to which
the city owed its founding and the direction of its development,
physically, culturally and historically. On the verge of sea
and land, Greece and Egypt, neither simply one nor the other,

the city mediated between opposites. Reconciling the irreconcilable became the essence of her existence, as when early Christian Alexandria disputed man's relationship with and exact distance from God. She has always been an explosive city, known for her riots and passions, struggling to contain great tensions.

In a 1923 review in *The Times Literary Supplement* of Forster's other books about Alexandria, *Pharos and Pharillon*, Middleton Murry says: "To this dubious race" of people with a strange angle of vision "Mr Forster indisputably belongs. Being a dubious character, he goes off to a dubious city, to that portion of the inhabited world where there is most obviously a bend in the spiritual dimension ... where the atmosphere is preternaturally keen and there is a lucid confusion of the categories. At this point a spinning eddy marks the convergence of two worlds, and in the vortex contradictions are reconciled. It is nothing less than a crack in the human universe. Mr Forster wanders off to put his ear to it. He finds Mr Cavafy already engaged in the enterprise. So they listen together."

Following a novel through the streets of Alexandria may lead you to strange places but, like following Bloom through Dublin, you glimpse the city that really matters. *Alexandria* still works well as a guide, not least because it works like a novel, or like Cavafy's poetry, commanding time and space and intimacies. On another visit I had it with me. Near the Ramleh tram terminus I came to what in Forster's day was a "featureless spot" (now, as it happens, the square which lies before the Cecil Hotel) and discovered that here Cleopatra began the Caesareum in honour of Antony. And then told to look at p.28 of the History I read: "Voluptuous but watchful, she treated her new lover as she had treated her old. She never bored him, and since grossness means monotony she sharpened his mind to those more delicate delights, where sense verges into spirit. Her infinite variety lay in that. She was the last of a secluded and subtle race, she was a flower that Alexandria had taken three hundred years to produce and that eternity cannot wither, and she unfolded herself to a simple but intelligent Roman soldier."

Yes, I had arrived too late at the Cecil Hotel "stripped of all its finery and echoing like a barn with the seawind sweeping under the doors and through the windows," and like Durrell and like Antony before him I reflected on that exile to which we are abandoned by the passage of time.

This is what haunts you in Alexandria. If more of the ancient city survived it would haunt you less. Unlike Rome or Athens with their monuments extant, Alexandria is all intimation: *here* (some spot) is where Alexander lay entombed; *here* Cleopatra committed suicide; *here* the Library, the Serapeum, etc. . . . and there is nothing physically there. "I stepped laughing out into the street once more to make a circuit of the quarter which still hummed with the derisive, concrete life of men and women . . . I began to walk slowly, deeply bemused, and to describe to myself in words this whole quarter of Alexandria for I knew that soon it would be forgotten and revisited only by those whose memories had been appropriated by the fevered city, clinging to the minds of old men like traces of perfume upon a sleeve: Alexandria, the capital of Memory" (*Justine*, p.152).

Forster's *Alexandria*, with time in one section, place in the other, and its many invitations to flip between the two, is a Guide to Memory, as the *Alexandria Quartet* is in a sense the novel of the guide – *Justine*, *Balthazar* and *Mountolive* the spatial dimensions, while *Clea* unleashes time. Nor since the foreign community has been expelled from the city has Alexandria ceased being the capital of memory. Neguib Mahfouz, the outstanding Arab novelist who has made Cairo his literary universe, chose Alexandria as the setting for this criticism of the Nasser regime's excesses and failures, "Alexandria. At last, Alexandria, Lady of the Dew. Bloom of white nimbus. Bosom of radiance, wet with sky-water. Core of nostalgia steeped in honey and tears" (*Miramar*, p.1).

Durrell calls Alexandria "the unburied city" (*Justine*, p.96), as perhaps memories are never wholly buried. In one sense she is literally unburied: the visitor still today can find so much of the city of Durrell, Forster and Cavafy eerily extant down to the seemingly most ephemeral detail. The physical city has been embalmed by events, and lacking sufficient opportunity and prosperity the old has remained in place. But these are the last few years that she can be seen this way: the population now stands at nearly three million and is expected to reach nearly five million within 20 years; the University of Liverpool, funded by Britain's Overseas Development Administration, has drawn up a plan ... I wonder what they have in mind for the Rue Lepsius, the Billiards Palace, Alexander's tomb, or the sparrows in the trees at St Mark's?

Durrell's description of Alexandria in 1977 is now, I think, overly severe – as Alexandria suffered after the Suez invasion, so rapprochement with the West and liberalisation at home have slowly brought some sparkle to the lives of those who once lived only on the edge of foreign consciousness. They do not all bid farewell to her, to Alexandria whom you are losing.

Between the Third Circle of Irrigation and the Rue Lepsius – where "kings, emperors, patriarchs have trodden the ground between [Cavafy's] office and his flat" (*Pharos and Pharillon*) – there are one or two clubs where the city's remaining Greeks still gather, listening to their wailing, amplified *laïká tragoudiá*. All round lies Iskandaria. For someone who knew it as a cosmopolitan city and remembers old haunts and old friends now vanished, the uncomprehended Arabic of its people today may only translate into emptiness.

But there would be nothing new in this alienation: "No, I don't think you would like it," Durrell wrote to Miller in spring 1944, "... this smashed up broken down shabby Neapolitan town, with its Levantine mounds of houses peeling in the sun. A sea flat, dirty brown and waveless rubbing the port. Arabic, Coptic, Greek, Levant French; no music, no art, no real gaiety. A saturated middle European boredom laced with drink and Packards and beach-cabins. NO SUBJECT OF CONVERSATION EXCEPT MONEY. Even love is thought of in money terms ... No, if one could write a single line of anything that had a human smell to it here, one would be a genius."

* * *

The architecture of Alexandria is found in the words written about her, and among her builders are Cavafy, Forster and Durrell. Some of the following notes amend here and there Forster's History and Guide where time has made this necessary. Otherwise they refer to those architects of Alexandria's literary dimension, locating them at one spot or another round the city, locating too the characters they created, and listening to what they have to say. These are glimpses only, and as footnotes necessarily bitty, but they may suggest the ways in which the city of words came to be built, and what, if any, future cities might rise from present-day Alexandria.

I am indebted to these other Histories and Guides:

Constantine Cavafy, born 1863 in Alexandria, died there in 1933. The only biography of him in English is *Cavafy, A Critical Biography*, by Robert Liddell, published by Duckworth, London 1974. *The Mind and Art of C P Cavafy*, published by Denise Harvey and Company, Athens 1983, is an excellent collection of essays on the poet's life and work by E M Forster, Robert Liddell, George Seferis and others. See also E M Forster, below. Cavafy's poetry quoted in these notes is taken from *C P Cavafy, Collected Poems*, translated by Edmund Keeley and Philip Sherrard, published by Chatto & Windus, London 1975.

E M Forster, born 1879 in London, died in Coventry in 1970. His biography is *E M Forster: A Life*, by P N Furbank, published by Oxford University Press, Oxford 1979; unless otherwise indicated, all Forster quotations and biographical details are from this book. His novels include *A Room with a View* and *Howards End*, both published before his stay in Alexandria, and *A Passage to India*, attempted before the Alexandrian sojourn but only completed later and published in 1924. These are available in Penguin editions. *Pharos and Pharillon*, a series of sketches about ancient and modern Alexandria, was first published in London in 1923; it is now published by Michael Haag, London 1983 – both this and Forster's *Two Cheers for Democracy*, published in London in 1951, contain essays on Cavafy.

Lawrence Durrell, born in Jullundur, India ("within sight of the Tibetan Himalayas") in 1912. A biography is in progress, but for the moment biographical details must be gleaned from various works of literary criticism or from published letters. *Lawrence Durrell and Henry Miller: A Private Correspondence*, edited by George Wickes, published by Faber, London 1963, covers the years 1935 through 1959. This is out of print, but a new edition, edited by Ian S MacNiven, is to be published by Michael Haag, London, and will carry the correspondence through to Miller's death in 1980. *Literary Lifelines: The Richard Aldington-Lawrence Durrell Correspondence*, edited by Ian S Mac-Niven and Harry T Moore, published by Faber, London 1981, covers the years 1957 through 1962. Durrell's novels include his Avignon quincunx (touching also on Egypt), *Monsieur*, *Livia*, *Constance*, *Sebastian* and *Quinx*, published by Faber, London 1974 through 1985, and *The Alexandria Quartet*: this comprises *Justine*, *Balthazar*, *Mountolive* and *Clea*, the individual volumes published by Faber, London 1957 through 1960. The edition to which the page numbers in these notes refers is the 1962 one-volume *Quartet*. Among his travel books are *Prospero's Cell* (Corfu), *Reflections on a Marine Venus* (Rhodes) and *Bitter Lemons* (Cyprus). His poetry is published by Faber in editions of *Selected Poems* and *Collected Poems*, some of it dealing with Alexandria. Also his translations of some of Cavafy's poems appear in the *Quartet*: 'The City' and 'The God Abandons Antony' at the end of *Justine*; 'The Afternoon Sun', 'Far Away', 'One of Their Gods' and 'Che Fece ... Il Gran Rifiuto' at the end of *Clea*.

Neguib Mahfouz, born in Cairo in 1912. Two novels set in

Cairo and available in English are *Midaq Alley* and *Children of Gebelawi*. His Alexandrian novel, *Miramar*, translated by Fatma Moussa-Mahmoud and with an Introduction by John Fowles, is published by Heinemann, London and the American University in Cairo Press, Cairo 1978.

For a study of Alexandria's literary dimension, see *Alexandria Still: Forster, Durrell and Cavafy*, by Jane Lagoudis Pinchin, published by Princeton University Press, Princeton, New Jersey 1977.

NOTES

p.xxii† *Rue Chérif Pacha* is now Sharia Salah Salem, named for one of the Free Officers who, under Nasser's leadership, made the 1952 revolution. Salem became Minister for National Guidance. He died in 1961.

A list of street and place names of Forster's time (and Durrell's) with their present equivalents will be found after these notes.

p.xxii‡ Forster does not quite tell the whole story. *Alexandria* was first published in the city in December 1922, but soon afterwards Forster received a regretful letter from Whitehead Morris & Co., informing him that there had been a fire in the warehouse and that the entire edition had been burnt. Fortunately, they said, it had been insured; and they enclosed a substantial cheque in compensation. A few weeks later Forster received a yet more regretful letter from the publishers. The books had been found intact, in a cellar which had escaped the flames. This, in view of the insurance money, his publishers wrote, had created a most awkward situation, and they had taken the only way out: they burnt the books deliberately.

p.xxvi† Since the first edition of this book the pageant has willy-nilly continued, literary celebrants and their creations strolling past with mummers of recent political history. Their appearances, and the present appearance of the city, are noted in both the History and the Guide sections of the text.

p.xxvi‡ The Guide continues to be of practical use to anyone exploring Alexandria and her environs. Where important changes have occurred these have been noted. To avoid getting lost like Forster (see p.xxii) you should know that the *new railway station* (opened in 1927) was built just to the east of the one it replaced: the station square (Midan Mahattat Misr) is at the south end of Sharia Nebi Danyal. The stretch of *Arab walls* nearby (see pp.113–114) vanished in the process.

More recent victims of time are the "bucking, clicking trams of yore", displaying stars, lozenges, crescents, etc., to indicate the routes followed; these have been replaced in the past decade by modern trams which, like the municipal buses, follow prosaically numbered routes. Some of the tram routes Forster describes still exist, some are modified, some have gone. Trams 4 and 5 from Midan Orabi will take you to Anfouchi; tram 5 will also take you to Pompey's Pillar, or take tram 2 from the main railway station square (Midan Mahattat Misr). From the Ramleh tram terminus (Midan Sa'ad Zaghloul) there are trams to Sidi Bishr (see *Victoria College*, p.182, now Al Nasr College), one along the coast via Glymenopoulo (tram 2), the other inland via Bacos (tram 1). A taxi or a gharry are alternatives – though walking is best through the heart of the city.

p.13 † For these and all following members of the Ptolemaic Dynasty, see the following note.

p.14 † Certain details of Forster's identification of the reigning Ptolemies is at variance with those now generally accepted by historians. For example, his Ptolemy VII is now commonly identified as Ptolemy VIII, his Ptolemy VIII as Ptolemy VII; the great Cleopatra he lists as the sixth of that name, while she is now identified as Cleopatra VII. Also, some of the dates he gives for periods of rule need changing. A corrected outline follows.

Ptolemy I Soter (ruled from 323 BC; King 304-282 BC)
Ptolemy II Philadelphus (282-246 BC)
Ptolemy III Euergetes (246-221 BC)
Ptolemy IV Philopator (221-205 BC)
Ptolemy V Epiphanes (205-181 BC)
Ptolemy VI Philometor (181-145 BC)
Ptolemy VII Neos Philopator (145–144 BC)
Ptolemy VIII Euergetes II (145-116 BC)
Ptolemy IX Soter II (116–107, 88-80 BC)
Ptolemy X Alexander I (107-88 BC)
Ptolemy XI Alexander II (80 BC)

NOTES   **247**

Ptolemy XII Neos Dionysos (80-58, 55-51 BC)
Cleopatra VII (51-49, 48-30 BC)
Ptolemy XIII (51-47 BC)
Ptolemy XIV (47-44 BC)

Ptolemy XIII and XIV were brothers of Cleopatra; her son by Caesar would have been Ptolemy XV, but he never reigned.

p.26 † The belief that Caesar caused the burning of the Library is now refuted. The flames that spread from the fleet in the Great Harbour to the quays and dock buildings destroyed a large number of books held there, either awaiting delivery to the Library or export overseas. The Library and Mouseion remained untouched in this action, but the Serapeum, containing Cleopatra's new Library, was burnt by the Christians in AD 391 (see p.55).

p.29 † The story of Cleopatra's cowardice or treachery at Actium (Aktion in Greek), indeed the whole character of the naval engagement, rests on the dramatic licence of Horace's *Odes* and the tales of other Roman propagandists. Forster accepts this version, as did Shakespeare, but it is refuted by present-day historians. For the sake of Cleopatra's and Antony's reputations the account needs to be put right.

The Ambracian Gulf, on the western coast of Greece, narrows to a strait less than a kilometre across where it meets the sea. The ruins of Nikopolis, which Octavian founded after the encounter, and the modern town of Preveza are on the north side of the strait; at its south side is a sandy headland bearing the slight remains of the Temple of Apollo Aktios. Here in 31 BC Antony and Cleopatra camped with their 120,000 infantry and 12,000 cavalry they had massed for their invasion of Italy.

But in spring, Octavian's daring admiral, Marcus Agrippa, had captured Antony's vital supply station at Methoni in the Peloponnese, and in summer had succeeded in blockading Antony and Cleopatra's combined fleet within the Ambracian Gulf. Antony's greatness was as a land commander; in Agrippa he was now facing perhaps the only Roman who ever understood naval strategy. As the blockade wore on throughout the hot month of August, time too turned against Antony; his men became restless, some (including Ahenobarbus) deserted to Octavian's side, while so many rowers died of fever that when finally battle was joined Antony could man only 230 ships to Octavian's 400.

Antony considered abandoning the fleet and striking across Greece with his army where twice before, at Philippi and Farsala, the fate of Rome had been decided. But abandoning the fleet meant abandoning Cleopatra's major contribution to his cause, and abandoning Cleopatra could mean losing Egypt and all its wealth. Antony instead decided to try and break through the blockade and return to Egypt with Cleopatra, leaving instructions for his army to cross Greece under his generals in preparation for a Macedonian campaign under Antony's direction the following spring.

What in fact happened was distorted by Roman propagandists to show Antony, supposedly feckless and un-Roman, deserting his fleet and his army to be with his treacherous Oriental queen. Far from intending to flee, Cleopatra and Antony were carrying out their plan to break through the Roman blockade. True, most of their fleet was captured or destroyed, but as one naval historian has written, "to save even 60 ships out of 230 was a creditable achievement for a man embayed on a lee shore and vastly outnumbered." The real disaster struck when Antony's army began marching towards Macedonia but was intercepted by Octavian's emissaries who offered them favourable terms, including the Roman soldier's traditional plot of land in Italy, if they would surrender.

It was not that Antony lost the world in that one battle, nor that he lost it for a woman, but that over the course of a combined land and sea campaign, Octavian prudently avoided engagement by land, while Antony was checked and checked again by Agrippa at sea. It was morale that finally deserted Antony's waiting, onlooking army that September day – Antony only discovering the awful truth when it followed him to Egypt. (See eg Michael Grant's *Cleopatra*, London 1972)

p.62 † These last two sentences are quoted in the Notes to Lawrence Durrell's *Justine*, to elucidate the reference to Amr (and to Justine) made on p.77 of the novel (see following note).

p.63 † Amr's reply is quoted on p.77 of *Justine*. Darley recalls it after first making love to Justine:

"It was as if the whole city had crashed about my ears; I walked about in it aimlessly as survivors must walk about the streets of their native city after an earthquake, amazed to find how much that had been familiar was changed. I felt in some curious way deafened and remember nothing more except that much later I ran into Pursewarden and Pombal in a bar, and that the former recited some lines from the old poet's famous 'The City' which struck me with a new force – as if the poetry had been newly minted: though I knew them well. And when Pombal said: 'You are abstracted this evening. What is the matter?' I felt like answering him in the words of the dying Amr: 'I feel as if heaven lay close upon the earth and I between them both, breathing through the eye of a needle.' "

p.76 † "In [Justine], as an Alexandrian, licence was in a curious way a form of self-abnegation, a travesty of freedom; and if I saw her as an exemplar of the city it was not of Alexandria, or Plotinus that I was forced to think, but of the sad thirtieth child of Valentinus who fell, 'not like Lucifer by rebelling against God, but by desiring too ardently to be united to him'. Anything pressed too far becomes a sin" (*Justine*, p.39).

Forster's review of Valentinus' cosmogony is quoted at length by Durrell in the Notes to *Justine*.

p.98 † In the decade following Forster's stay in the city, buildings did rise along the *New Quays*, and the *Corniche*, as it is known, became one of Alexandria's most attractive features and a focus of social activity. The creation of *Midan Sa'ad Zaghloul*, which opens onto the Eastern Harbour near the Ramleh tram station, has shifted the centre of the city away from the Place Mohammed Ali (Midan el Tahrir) and has helped turn Alexandria's face to the sea.

p.103 † In a 1920 Fabian pamphlet, Forster said of the bombardment of Alexandria and the defeat of Arabi: "Thus perished a moment which, if treated sympathetically, might have set Egypt upon the path of constitutional liberty." Instead, 1882 marked the beginning of British military occupation and Egypt's *de facto* incorporation into the Empire. The nationalist movement was crushed, while the Khedive's shattered authority permitted him to retain his throne only as a British puppet. Thereafter, Alexandria's history became part of the broader struggle between revived nationalism and foreign imperialism, and between the extremes to which the protagonists went cosmopolitan Alexandria was ground to a husk.

A review of the city's history after 1882 necessarily requires some reference of these broader events.

1918: Gamal Abdul Nasser was born on 15 January 1918 in the *Bacos quarter* of Alexandria (see p.181). Abdul Nasser means Servant of the Victorious One; he was to become the first truly Egyptian ruler of Egypt in 2500 years. Nasser attended the El Attarine and Ras-el-Tin secondary schools; while at the latter he took part in his first political demonstration, getting hit in the face by a police baton and spending the night in jail. He was 11 years old. At 15 he moved to Cairo, though Alexandria was to figure again in his activities.

1919-22: In March 1919 the nationalists, led by Sa'ad Zaghloul (1860-1927), demanded independence. Instead, the British deported Zaghloul to Malta. Immediately the country rose and more than 800 Egyptians were killed before he was released. Three years of negotiations followed, during which Zaghloul was again shipped off, again released. His returns were triumphs, vast crowds lining the railway between Alexandria and Cairo. In Alexandria today a statue of Zaghloul looks out upon the sea of his captivity (see notes for pp.98 and 175).

Though Zaghloul began the modern movement towards independence, he himself did not achieve it. In 1922 the British chose to declare Egypt a sovereign state, but retained control of the Suez Canal, maintained an army in Egypt, and reserved to themselves the protection of minorities and foreign interests.

1936: The Anglo-Egyptian Treaty: foreign interests were made subject to Egyptian jurisdiction (see note for p.109) and the British army withdrew to the Canal Zone, though with the right of reoccupation of the country in the event of war. For the first time since 1882 Egypt gained control over its security forces. These were expanded, new officers were needed, and the Military Academy was opened to young men from a broader social class. Nasser entered the Academy the following year, along with Anwar Sadat and six other leaders of the 1952 revolution.

1941-42: With the Second World War events focus on and around Alexandria. Throughout the spring and summer of 1941 she was bombed by the Germans (see note for p. 175). In summer 1942 Rommel was within a day's dash of the city.

El Alamein, scene of that series of battles which from July to November 1942 halted Rommel's thrust to the Delta and reversed the tide of war in northern Africa, lies 106 kilometres west of Alexandria (see note for p.206). On 1 July as the Afrika Korps arrived at Alamein, the British fleet left Alexandria and withdrew through the Suez Canal into the Red Sea; British sappers prepared to blow up their own ammunition dumps at the western end of the city; Alexandrians were certain that the British were fleeing Egypt; and the outside world believed that Britain had lost the Middle East.

But Rommel was over-extended, his men exhausted, and the majority of his supplies consigned by the Royal Navy to the bottom of the sea. General Auchinleck coolly gauged the situation. "On 17 July 1942, Auchinleck had won a historic battle. It had been as desperate, difficult and gallant as Wellington's repulse of Napoleon at Waterloo ... He saved the Middle East, with all that this implied for the general course of the war. It was the turning point" (*The Decisive Battles of the Western World*, by General J F C Fuller, London 1954).

Later, Montgomery took command of the Eighth Army: "A man of dynamic personality and of supreme self-confidence ... a past-master in showmanship and publicity; audacious in his utterances and cautious in his actions ... He was the right man in the right place at the right moment" (Fuller), and during 23 October-5 November decisively defeated the Germans and put Rommel on the run. Within little more than six months the Germans and Italians were cleared from Africa altogether.

1948-49: In May 1948 Britain withdrew from Palestine and the Egyptian army went to war to prevent the loss of Arab land to the newly-created state of Israel. Like others of his generation, Nasser, who was wounded in the fighting, blamed Egypt's defeat (armistice signed February 1949) on the corruption and criminal incompetence of the King and his ministers. With the war still in progress, Alexandria's neglected slum population rose in near-revolution. Against this and the gathering strength of the Communists and right-wing Moslem Brotherhood, the government offered not reform but only repression. In 1949 Nasser called a secret meeting of fellow radical officers; the Free Officers Movement pledged itself to revolution within five years.

1952: After incidents between extremist guerillas and British troops in the Canal Zone, the British attacked a police barracks in Ismailia suspected of helping the guerillas, killing 41 police and wounding many more. The following day, 26 January, outraged at the British action and their own government's inaction, a Cairo mob, led by the Moslem Brotherhood and abetted by the police, destroyed 700 buildings, shops and restaurants owned by Britons, Italians, Greeks and Jews, while 17 foreigners and 50 Egyptians were killed before the army, fearful of British military intervention, restored order. Alexandria remained quiet throughout.

On the night of 22-23 July Egyptian army units loyal to the Free Officers Movement occupied army headquarters and key communications centres in Cairo. At 7am Anwar Sadat broadcast to the Egyptian people announcing the revolution and crowds filled the streets dancing and cheering. The King was at *Montazah*, his summer palace in Alexandria (see p.186); terrified, Farouk moved to *Ras-el-Tin Palace* on the Western Harbour (see p.140 and note). Nasser, who was directing operations in Cairo, sent a note to General Mohammed Neguib in Alexandria: "Let us spare Farouk and send him into exile. History will sentence him to death." At 7am, 26 July, the army seized Ras-el-Tin Palace without loss of life. Early that afternoon the King abdicated. At 6pm, dressed in admiral's uniform, he sailed for Italy aboard the royal yacht to the accompaniment of a 21-gun salute.

1954: On 19 October Britain signed an agreement ending the 1936 Treaty; her forces would be withdrawn from the Canal Zone within 20 months. Nasser declared: "The ugly page of Anglo-Egyptian relations has been turned and another page is being written ... There is now no reason why Britain and Egypt should not work constructively together." The Moslem Brotherhood resented not being able to pursue their guerilla activities to immediately dislodge the British from the Canal Zone; on 26 October, in Alexandria, one of their number attempted to assassinate Nasser at the *Bourse* from which he was addressing a crowd in Midan el Tahrir. All six shots missed and the Brotherhood was suppressed.

1956: Prime Minister Anthony Eden, however, was soon blaming Nasser for every gesture of Arab nationalism throughout the Middle East. Successor to Churchill and recalling Britain's pre-war appeasement of Germany, Eden now displayed a talent for correcting past mistakes by misinterpreting the present. He began comparing Nasser to Hitler and brought himself to a pitch of anti-Egyptian hysteria bordering on insanity: "But what's all this nonsense about isolating Nasser, of 'neutralising' him, as you call it? I want him destroyed, can't you understand? ... And I don't give a damn if there's anarchy and chaos in Egypt."

In response to an Egyptian arms deal with Czechoslovakia, Britain and the United States refused to aid construction of the Aswan High

Dam. On the fourth anniversary of Farouk's abdication, speaking from the *Bourse* in Alexandria where two years earlier he had escaped the assassin's bullets, Nasser announced to an exultant crowd the nationalisation of the British-owned Suez Canal Company, its £35,000,000 annual revenue to go towards the High Dam project.

In Israel the withdrawal of British troops from the Canal Zone had been seen as the loss of a buffer between itself and Egypt. France feared and resented Nasser's (largely verbal) support for the Algerian liberation struggle which was tying down a quarter of a million French troops. The destruction of Nasser became a shared aim and Israel, France and Britain formed a conspiratorial alliance to invade Egypt.

On 29 October Israeli forces entered Sinai. On the pretence of preventing a clash between Israeli and Egyptian forces, British and French troops landed in the Canal Zone on 5 November – though not before British bombers pounded Egyptian airfields to protect Israel from counter-attack.

The invasion ended in ignominy when outraged world reaction and strong pressure from the United States and the Soviet Union forced its withdrawal. The abortive British, French and Israeli attack immeasurably strengthened Nasser's position at home and throughout the Arab world – and in Egypt created a climate of anger and fear which tragically destroyed the old cosmopolitan Alexandria.

The original invasion plan was for British and French troops to land at Alexandria but was dropped only a month before the attack; a major battle in a large port would not be acceptable to world opinion. But if Alexandria was spared physically, little thought was given to her foreign community. As in 1882, the British Embassy warned its citizens to leave the country. Other foreigners, however, including Maltese, Cypriots and Gibraltarians closely associated with Britain, were not considered, nor were Egypt's Jews.

Until 1956 Nasser's policies had been moderate and necessary, confined mostly to breaking up large feudal estates and redistributing land to relieve rural poverty. Egyptianisation of commerce and industry would have come eventually, but it would have been gradual, more thoughtful and selective. Instead, in 1957 all remaining British and French citizens were expelled from Egypt, and a third of Egypt's Jews – mostly those of foreign nationality – were driven into exile by police harrassment and economic pressure. The remainder of the foreign community dwindled as all manufacturers and exporters were Egyptianised and Arabic was made compulsory for business transactions. A few foreigners. mostly Greeks, held on, running those small businesses – pensions, tavernas, bookshops, etc. – which escaped these and the later nationalisation measures. The Greek, French and Italian Hospitals of Alexandria were replaced by Egyptian hospitals, as were the schools. And the street names that once spoke of Alexandria's role in the Mediterranean world would now more often reflect parochial concerns.

p.109 † It is surprising how often Forster's description of the city, even in its seemingly ephemeral detail, remains true today. At sunset the sparrows still noisily gather in the trees round St Mark's. But a great sea change has run through the world that once met here at Alexandria.

The Square (now Midan el Tahrir, ie Liberation Square), once embellished with trees and reflecting through the Mixed Tribunals, the Anglican Church of St Mark and the Bourse the interests of the foreign community, is now bare, filled only with the roar and fumes of traffic. The Bourse is gone; the statue of Mohammed Ali and the other buildings Forster mentions here remain, but as mementoes of a past design.

The Mixed Tribunals could in Forster's time be taken as a symbol of reform and limited Egyptian sovereignty. In the 16th century the Ottoman Sultan exempted non-Moslems who had established themselves within the Empire for purposes of trade from taxation and gave them the right to be tried in their own consular courts. With the decline of Ottoman power, the foreign community in Egypt took full advantage of these Capitulations until, by the mid-19th century, it was virtually above the law.

But in 1875 foreigners became subject to the Mixed Tribunals, ie to Egyptian jurisdiction, in all but criminal cases, which continued to be heard in the consular courts. This continued immunity from Egyptian criminal law helps explain why hashish dens (Forster describes his visit to one in *Pharos and Pharillon*) and bordellos flourished in Alexandria: most were run by foreigners.

The consular courts themselves fell under the jurisdiction of the Mixed Tribunals in 1937 in consequence of the Anglo-Egyptian Treaty of 1936, and were abolished in 1948 when the Mixed Tribunals became what are now the Law Courts. From 1937 onwards therefore, and long before the 1952 revolution, the days of the foreign community as a privileged caste were numbered.

Though ordinary Egyptians were little affected by the Mixed Tribunals (organised along French lines and sometimes with European and American judges), these courts became a training ground for

Egyptian lawyers of high calibre who eventually became the country's political elite and helped shape the national movement.

The French Gardens (now Midan Orabi, variant spelling of Arabi, the colonel whose rebellion in 1882 occasioned the British bombardment of the city – see p.99) have been stripped of their foliage to serve as a bus and tram depot.

The *Anglican Church of St Mark* slumbers unobtrusively behind its screen of trees, harbouring still the relics of British victories against Arabi. The funny little bust of General Earle, however, has suffered for its impertinence – demonstrating Egyptians made off with it, perhaps during the Suez crisis (the present archdeacon is benignly hazy about the details).

The Bourse has disappeared: a vacant plot marks the site and there is a dim intention to raise a hotel. The Cotton and Stock Exchanges were made redundant by the sweeping nationalisation measures of 1961. The building was burnt and gutted during the food riots of January 1977 and for five years its arcaded facade served as an impromptu latrine. In 1982 it was demolished.

Rue Chérif Pacha still bristles with flag staffs, and there are some smart vintage shop-fronts, especially of Armenian jewellers, but the silver sold is plate. Here Constantine Cavafy was born in 1863. Here also Messrs Whitehead Morris, the original publishers of this book, were located. As Forster wrote in his Introduction to the 1961 edition, there were many delays and some differences of opinion before the first edition was eventually published in 1922. The manuscript was only agreed early that year when Forster revisited Egypt on his way home to England from India. In a letter dated 15 March 1921 Forster told Cavafy he had given up on the project: "As for my book on Alexandria, I have lost all interest in it. The MS remains in Chérif Pacha Street and for ever will remain there as far as I can see ... What is the use of map and plans in a state of proof? What is the use of any MS? And what, above all, is the use of Chérif Pacha Street? I would wish, next time you walk down it, you would ask, in those tones of yours, that question."

In the street is the National Bank of Egypt, the former *Banco di Roma*; you can still see the wolf. Round the corner at *1 Rue Toussoum Pacha* Lawrence Durrell worked at the British Information Office during the Second World War. "I am in charge of a goodish-sized office of war-propaganda here, trying to usher in the new washboard world which our demented peoples are trying 'to forge in blood and iron.' It's tiring work. However, it's an office full of beautiful girls, and Alexandria is, after Hollywood, fuller of beautiful women than any place else. Incomparably more beautiful than Athens or Paris; the mixture Coptic, Jewish, Syrian, Egyptian, Moroccan, Spanish gives you slant dark eyes, olive freckled skin, hawk lips and noses, and a temperament like a bomb" (letter to Henry Miller, 23 May 1944).

p.111 † *Rue Rosette* has had its name changed yet again, to Sharia Horreya. At its western end, at No. 1, stands what was the *Mohammed Ali Club*, smart and cosmopolitan, with gaming tables at which there was high play. Forster was a member. It is now the Palace of Culture.

Rue Nebi Daniel remains familiar as Sharia Nebi Danyal. The *Mosque of the Prophet Daniel* is more than "a few yards" from the crossroads; you must walk about 200 metres towards the railway station square; the mosque is on the east side of the street and set back from it – the entrance is at the end of a narrow passage. Alexander's body was preserved and Suetonius tells a good story of Octavian's (later Augustus) visit to it 300 years later: "When Alexander's sarcophagus was brought from its shrine, Augustus gazed at the body, then laid a crown of gold on its case and scattered some flowers to pay his respects. When they asked if he would like to see Ptolemy too, 'I wished to see a king', he replied 'I did not wish to see corpses.'" The Emperor Caracalla (AD 188-217) is thought to have been the last visitor to see the body; it was probably destroyed in the city riots of the late 3rd century. But memories were stirred in the late 1970s when during a wedding procession near here the ground opened beneath the bride. Alexandria must be riddled with cisterns, catacombs and chambers; over the centuries they have been filled and covered with sand and debris which seeping underground water can suddenly suck away – the Catacombs of Kom es Chogafa (see p.163) were discovered when a grazing donkey was swallowed by the same process. The bride was never seen again, and if Alexander still lies beneath his city she may lie there with him. For all the commonplace surface of the modern town, Alexandria is haunted by the past.

Without alerting the reader that the intersection of Fuad Premier (the former Rue Rosette, now Sharia Horreya) and Nebi Daniel mark the conjectured site of the Soma, Durrell enjoys a private joke in placing a barbershop here: "Mnemjian's Babylonian barber's shop was on the corner of Fuad I and Nebi Daniel and here every morning Pombal lay down beside me in the mirrors. We were lifted simultaneously and swung smoothly down into the ground wrapped like dead Pharaohs, only to reappear at the same instant on the ceiling, spread out like specimens" (*Justine*, p.35; see also *Balthazar*, p.218).

The *Tombs of the Khedivial Family* were removed in 1954 to the Rifa'i Mosque in Cairo.

Outside another mosque across the street, however, the four antique columns used as gate posts, which may have been part of the *Mouseion*, remain. This is the typical way you encounter the past, if you encounter it tangibly at all, in Alexandria – a dwindling number of remnants used in building after successive building, their original purpose only to be guessed at.

But it is likely that a great deal of Alexandria's past could be uncovered, as suggested by the Polish Centre of Mediterranean Archaeology's excavations, begun in 1959, at *Kom-el-Dik*. First the fortress Forster mentions was removed and the *kom* (the Egyptian word for those great mounds of debris covering ancient sites) explored. Layers of *Moslem tombs* were found, dating from the 9th to the 11th century, and a large complex of 3rd century *Roman baths*. The spur to further and intensive excavation came in 1964 with the unearthing of a small *Roman odeon*, a covered theatre for musical performances, with seating for 700 to 800. Inscriptions suggest it was used also for wrestling contests. It is pretty, the area round it landscaped, which is all very well, but it possesses none of the excitement of an excavation in progress.

That is provided by the deep broad trenches still being dug to the northeast of the odeon. The dusty walls of the trenches are layered with extraordinary amounts of potsherds, and as you peer down several metres from the surface of the kom you can see substantial stone walls and the remains of brick houses. Best of all is to climb down. You walk along a *Ptolemaic street* lined with shop-fronts. If Cleopatra ever went shopping, then here you can say to yourself is where Cleopatra walked. It is a sensation of immediacy rare in Alexandria.

We return with Forster to the Rue Rosette.

In the vicinity of the *Church and Convent of St Saba* (rebuilt in 1975), the seat of the Greek Orthodox Patriarch, is a street now called Sharia Sharm el Sheikh to commemorate the town at the mouth of the Gulf of Aqaba lost to Israel in the Six-Day War of 1967, but previously known as *Rue Lepsius* (named for the German Egyptologist Karl Richard Lepsius, 1810–1884). Forster knew it well; here the literary apotheosis of Alexandria began: at No. 10 (now No. 4), on the second floor, lived Constantine Cavafy for the last 25 years of his life (late 1907 to early 1933) – the period of his poetic maturity. There is a commemorative plaque, put there in 1948. You can go upstairs – his flat is now occupied by the Pension Amir – and stand on his balcony:

An echo from my days of indulgence,
an echo from those days came back to me,
something from the fire of the young life we shared:
I picked up a letter again,
read it over and over till the light faded.
Then, sad, I went out on to the balcony,
went out to change my thoughts at least by seeing something
    of this city I love,
a little movement in the streets, in the shops.

('In the Evening')

Then returning inside, as Cavafy once returned to the room of a lover:

This room, how familiar it is.
The couch was here, near the door,
a Turkish carpet in front of it.
Close by, the shelf with two yellow vases.
On the right – no, opposite – a wardrobe with a mirror.
In the middle the table where he wrote,
and the three big wicker chairs.
Beside the window the bed
where we made love so many times.
They must still be around somewhere, these old things.

('The Afternoon Sun')

Cavafy's apartment has been recreated as a museum on the top floor of the Greek Consulate, 63 Sharia Iskandar el Akhbar.

Forster first met Cavafy in 1917: "It never occurred to him that I might like his work or even understand it ... and I remember the delight to us both, one dusky evening in his flat, when it appeared that I was 'following'. When he was pleased he'd jump and light a candle, and then another candle and he would cut cigarettes in half and light them and bring offerings of mastica with little bits of bread and cheese, and his talk would sway over the Mediterranean world and over much of the world within' (quoted in Pinchin's *Alexandria Still*, p.106). From then on, Forster did all he could to promote Cavafy's work; the inclusion of 'The God Abandons Antony' in this book was the first Cavafy poem to be published in English. Years later Forster remarked, "I did a little to spread his fame. It was about the best thing I did."

On the ground floor of 10 Rue Lepsius was a brothel. "Poor

259

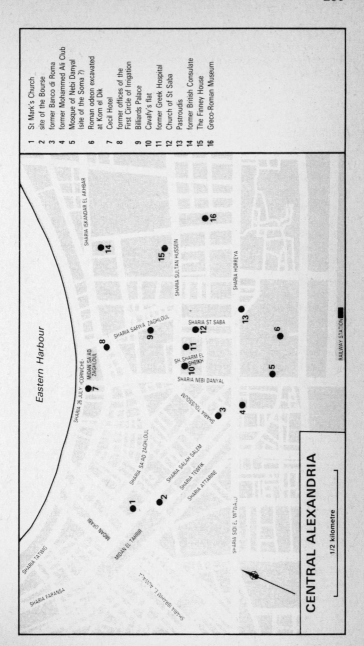

CENTRAL ALEXANDRIA

1/2 kilometre

1 St Mark's Church
2 site of the Bourse
3 former Banco di Roma
4 former Mohammed Ali Club
5 Mosque of Nebi Danyal (site of the Soma ?)
6 Roman odeon excavated at Kom el Dik
7 Cecil Hotel
8 former offices of the First Circle of Irrigation
9 Billiards Palace
10 Cavafy's flat
11 former Greek Hospital
12 Church of St Saba
13 Pastroudis
14 former British Consulate
15 The Finney House
16 Greco-Roman Museum

Eastern Harbour

RAILWAY STATION

things!" Cavafy said to a friend who had accompanied him to his door one night. "One must be sorry for them. They receive some disgusting people, some monsters, but" – and here his voice took on a deep, ardent tone – "they receive some angels, some angels!" His English friends called the street the 'Rue Clapsius', though indeed the entire quarter was ill-famed. Cavafy satisfied his homosexuality by picking up boys in the cafés along the Rue Missala (his favourite haunt, the *Billiards Palace* on the west side of that street, survives still though it is now boarded up – rumour speaks of it becoming a Lloyds Bank). With the Greek Hospital opposite and the patriarchal church round the corner, Cavafy was fond of saying, "Where could I live better? Below, the brothel caters for the flesh. And there is the church which forgives sin. And there is the hospital where we die." He did die in that hospital, his funeral service took place at St Saba, and his body was buried in the Greek Cemetery in Chatby.

"Radiating out like the arms of a starfish from the axis of the founder's tomb" (*Clea*, p.700), the streets of this part of the city housed most of Durrell's characters. Darley and Pombal shared a flat in the Rue Nebi Daniel; Clea's flat was in the Rue Fuad, her studio just off it by St Saba; Justine and Nessim lived in a town house set back from the Rue Fuad – and Balthazar lived in the Rue Lepsius, in "the worm-eaten room with the cane chair which creaked all night, and where once the old poet of the city had recited 'The Barbarians'" (*Clea*, p.702). The Cervoni's house, where at the carnival ball Narouz drove a hat pin through Toto de Brunel's skull, thinking he was killing Justine, was not far from the Greek Patriarchate; both Cohen and Melissa died in the Greek Hospital; and you can still visit *Pastroudis* on Sharia Horreya, a block east from Sharia Nebi Danyal – this was one of the old Greek tea rooms, and Darley and Nessim, and Balthazar for an arak, would gather here.

For a glimpse behind Durrell's fictional Clea, see *La Peinture Moderne en Egypte* by Aimé Azar, Les Editions Nouvelles, Cairo 1961 – containing works by Clea Badaro: though reproduced only in black and white they have strength. She was born in Egypt in 1913 of Armenian parentage, studied in Switzerland and returned to Egypt in 1936. Until recently she had (and may still have) her studio in the Rue St Saba.

The famous parties at the *Finney House*, 3 Rue Docteur Ahmed Abdel Salam, just off Sharia Sultan Hussein, probably provided Durrell with the setting for the Cervonis' carnival ball. The Finneys

epitomise the sudden and brief gilded age of Alexandria. Oswald
Finney made his fortune on the cotton market in the 1920s and
accounted his luck to Josa, an unsophisticated girl of 16 whom he
met in Trieste and soon made his wife. When Finney bought the
house it was a block of flats, and today from the outside it seems
hardly more imposing than that. But inside it was rebuilt like a
Venetian palazzo which Josa with her vivacity and charm made
the centre of Alexandrian society in the 1930s. Oswald died during
the Second World War; just before her own death in 1983 Josa
sold the house (which had been sequestrated by Nasser but returned
to her by Sadat) to the Bank of Commerce and Development which
accepted her condition that nothing should be altered. And so on
the ground floor the manager's office is in the huge cloakroom by
the front door and the staff work at desks set upon a marble floor
laid over the still intact sunken swimming pool and hot baths.
Upstairs the living rooms, bedrooms, library, billiards room, card
room and on the fourth floor the ballroom stand vacant, and on
the roof the miniature Greek theatre silently surveys a spectacular
panorama of Mareotis, the city and the sea. It is home now only
to Mohammed, the Finneys' original housekeeper, who has seen
it through its birth and life and, with sadness, to this final embalming.

"Alexandria, princess and whore. The royal city and the *anus
mundi*. She would never change so long as the races continued to
seethe here like must in a vat; so long as the streets and squares
still gushed and spouted with the fermentation of these diverse passions and spites, rages and sudden calms. A fecund desert of human
loves littered with the whitening bones of its exiles" (*Clea*, p.700).

Today the exiles, those Greeks and other Europeans who did not
leave their bones in the city, have gone back to their homelands
– most of them, anyway. Mariana, the Greek mistress of the Pension
Miramar, speaks for those who stayed behind:

"'Monsieur Amer, I don't know how you can say there's no place
like Alexandria. It's all changed. The streets nowadays are infested
with *canaille*.'

"'My dear, it had to be claimed by its people.' I try to comfort
her and she retorts sharply.

"'But *we* created it'" (*Miramar*, p.6).

p.115 † Forster's tour through the Greco-Roman Museum serves
well enough today. There has been some rearrangement of exhibits,
and a few new ones added; not everything is labelled, though usually
the most important exhibits are. If an exhibit is not where Forster

says it is, it will usually be nearby. The one substantial change to the plan is the addition of Rooms 16A and 18A off Rooms 16 and 18. The terracotta figurines of women which Forster enjoyed so much have been moved from Room 18 to Room 18A. They are indeed worth spending time over; in them can be read the sensibility of the past.

(After publication of *Howards End* in 1910, Forster entered a period of creative sterility and frustration; he did write *Maurice*, his homosexual novel, though knew it could not be published "until my death or England's". He took the outbreak of war as a sign that he must give up all hope of creating, and obtained a post as cataloguer and occasional night fire-watcher at the National Gallery. The more valuable paintings were being put in store: if he were killed by bombs, he told his friends, he would die, appropriately, among second-rate masterpieces. In a letter dated 1923, D H Lawrence said of *Alexandria*, "But what a funny task to set yourself – though I always remember the thrill you got out of the National Gallery catalogue.")

p.134 † In Forster's time, the entire length of the Eastern Harbour was undeveloped for a block inland. So the tram (as he says in his outline of the route at the top of the page) ran within sight of the New Quays. In the early 1930s, the land between the tramline and the harbour was built up, so the tram now finds itself running along what has become Sharia Tatwig, parallel to and between the old Rue de France and the Corniche.

Tatwig Street is frequently mentioned by Durrell; behind it is the 'native quarter', the 'lower town' – it is the entrance to a primordial world. "We doubled back and entered the huddled slums which lie behind Tatwig Street, our blond headlights picking out ant-hill cafés and crowded squares with an unaccustomed radiance; from somewhere behind the immediate skyline of smashed and unlimbered houses came the piercing shrieks and ululations of a burial procession" – among its brothels Justine searched for her kidnapped daughter (*Justine*, p.41f).

Intoxicated, for once intemperate, fleeing from measure and compromise, seeking revelation, Mountolive immersed himself in the quarter and was mauled by frenzied child prostitutes (*Mountolive*, p.623f).

The first scene is reminiscent of Demeter searching for Persephone, but in this case failing to find her; the second, of Dionysos being torn apart by the Maenads, but who also fail to fulfill their mythological role.

It is not all nightmare: replete with inversions and comical associations, it is a world made home by Scobie – septuagenarian ex-sailor, part-time policeman, occasional transvestite – who can walk its streets in an aura of local respect and affection, can kill his neighbours with bathtub whiskey, and after his own death be celebrated as a Moslem saint (*Balthazar*, p.224f; *Clea*, p.714f).

"Scobie by the way is Tiresias" (letter from Lawrence Durrell to Richard Aldington, late January 1959) – there are many associations between *The Alexandria Quartet* and 'The Waste Land', where Eliot provides this note: "Just as the one-eyed merchant, seller of currants, melts into the Phoenician Sailor, and the latter is not wholly distinct from Ferdinand Prince of Naples, so all the women are one woman, and the two sexes meet in Tiresias" – while Liddell writes in 'Studies in Genius: Cavafy' (*The Mind and Art of C P Cavafy*, p.28): "Perhaps of all Eliot characters, Cavafy is most like Tiresias, the seer of 'The Waste Land' . . . In this little, old, sexually abnormal Alexandrian poet, looking without fear, and without very much compassion, on the futility and anarchy which is contemporary history, Hecuba, Cratesiclea, Anna Comnena, Pompey, Antony and John Cantacuzene melt into each other, and are not wholly distinct from the equivocal characters that haunt the dark, hot streets of Alexandria in our own century."

> *"Old Tiresias*
> *No-one half so breezy as,*
> *Half so free and easy as*
> *Old Tiresias"*

(*Balthazar*, pp.233 and 353).

The walk along the *Rue de France* remains for the most part as Forster describes it as is the pleasure of wandering aimlessly at evening about the lower town. (The *Terbana Mosque* is now yellow- and red-striped; the *Mosque of Abou el Abbas Moursi* was rebuilt in modern style in 1943.) Durrell's chiaroscuro over-emphasises the darkness for effect, as might a visitor out of timidity. Wherever Alexandria's mind or heart or memories may have gone, this is the Arab soul of the city.

p.140 † At *Ras el Tin Palace* at 6pm on 26 July 1952, King Farouk, last of the dynasty founded by Mohammed Ali, abdicated and sailed away to Italy, his private yacht loaded with 200 trunks hurriedly filled with personal possessions. His last words (to General Mohammed Neguib) were, "Your task will be difficult. It isn't easy, you know, to govern Egypt."

The palace is closed to visitors and this western headland is off-limits owing to the barracks here. The *Yacht Club* is now on the Fort Kait Bey (eastern) headland.

p.150 † The castle has been rebuilt.

p.151 † The ancient fragments Forster saw lying on the beach have almost all been cleared away: I have seen one grey granite column drum lapped by the sea. There are numerous column drums in the facade of the castle, however. It is difficult to peer too closely at some parts of the building (eg the castle foundations along the passage to the right), as the fort has anti-aircraft emplacements and barracks and the armed soldiers will have little comprehension of your antiquarian curiosity.

p.152 † This view is less instructive than it was: the Fort at Kom-el-Dik has been cleared away by the excavations revealing the Roman odeon, etc., and the buildings along the Corniche have obscured many of the old landmarks of the Alexandria skyline.

p.156 † There was an old oriental-style house in the *Rue Attarine*, long since pulled down, where the *boab* (the Alexandrian concierge) collected boys and girls for prostitution. Cavafy kept a room here towards the end of the last century, and would sometimes sleep with Greek boys: "The room was cheap and sordid,/hidden above the suspect taverna./***/ And there on that ordinary, plain bed/I had love's body . . ." ('One Night').

About the poet (and the city), a one-time friend of Cavafy's, Timon Malanos, has written: "At one time one could live in the neighbourhood of certain isolated quarters of Alexandria, without one's own part of the town, the 'good quarter' we may say, knowing anything about one's way of life. The reason was that between them stretched *terrains vagues* that have since been filled up with houses, giving the city a unity which it formerly lacked. So in one of those isolated quarters, slave to his temptations, he passed his nights. Nevertheless in the morning, realising how low he had fallen at night, he repented, and wrote in large letters on a piece of paper: 'I swear I won't do it again.' And yet, when night came again he went back to his 'fatal joy', disregarding his oath" (quoted in Liddell's *Cavafy*, p.67). The reference is to Cavafy's poem 'He Swears'.

Born in the Rue Chérif Pacha, later living in the Rue Tewfik Pacha, in the Boulevard Ramleh and then in the Rue Rosette, Cavafy moved in 1907 to the Rue Lepsius in the ill-famed Missala quarter: he no longer had to rove so far, nor by then was he so concerned about hiding his homosexuality: he began writing erotic homosexual poems in 1903 and 'publishing' them (ie distributing them amongst his friends) from 1912.

The note for p.111 shows that Balthazar of *The Alexandria Quartet* lived in the apartment in the Rue Lepsius that had once been Cavafy's. To a degree, Durrell's character is based on Cavafy. There is the same wide-ranging conversation that Forster described in his early meeting with the poet: "Balthazar talked discursively (half asleep) of the Vineyard of Ammon, the Kings of the Harpoon Kingdom and their battles, or of the Mareotic wine to which, not history, but the gossiping Horace once attributed Cleopatra's distempers of mind" (*Clea*, p.846). And homosexual affairs, similarly shabby and demeaning: "To look like a god, to have a charm like a shower of silver arrows – and yet to be simply a small-spirited, dirty, venal and empty personage: that was Panagiotis! I knew it. It seemed to make no difference whatsoever. I saw in him the personage of Seleucia on whom Cavafy based his poem. I cursed myself in the mirror. But I was powerless to behave otherwise" (*Clea*, p. 704) – the poem referred to is 'One of Their Gods'.

But Balthazar was also a cabalist, for which there is another source: "I have unearthed some facts about a cabalistic group, direct descendants of the Orphics, who throughout European history have been quietly at work on a morphology of experience which is pure Pythagoras. There are about six or seven in the Mediterranean area. They teach nothing; they assert nothing; they do not even correspond; they are pre-Christian adepts. I am going along to see Mr Baltazian one of these days to find out all about the circle and the square. He is a small banker here" (letter from Lawrence Durrell to Henry Miller, spring 1945).

p.160 † See note for p.26.

p.168 † Not far from here, at *1 Rue du Mamoun* (now Sharia el Mamoun) lived Lawrence Durrell. Interviewed by the BBC for the television programme *Spirit of Place*, he said: "It's certainly the weirdest feeling to find myself after nearly forty years in this strange garden belonging to an old Italian architect; and in this garden and in the little tower that I fixed up on the roof of the house I wrote *Prospero's Cell* and some rather good poems for *Personal Landscape* and lived out two and one half years of great, extravagant and colourful life in wartime Alexandria. It was a good writing period in a sense, though of course the war was an exhausting moment to think about writing because there was no future attached to anything one did. But perhaps it was a good thing in a way because it compressed up life and forced one to do what one should always do, namely not think about tomorrow, live entirely for today." The little tower is illustrated on the cover of the 1986 printing of *The Alexandria Quartet*.

The route Forster described east along the Mahmoudieh Canal now passes through an industrial quarter; it would be a long and not pleasant walk from Kom es Chogafa (see note for p.204). To reach Durrell's place you could instead start at the main railway station square (Midan Mahattat Misr) and head southeast down Sharia Moharrem Bey (there is a tram). About 1½ kilometres along, turn left (north) into Sharia el Rassafa and in about 300 metres this will cross Sharia el Mamoun. You could also come into the north end of Sharia el Rassafa by leaving the Rond Point (see p.172) along the old Rue Menasce which runs southwest.

p.170 † "Mrs Stitch gazed over the balcony into the gardens.

" 'Forster says they ought to be "thoroughly explored",' she said. 'Something for another day.' To Guy, 'You've got his *Guide*?'

" 'I've always wanted a copy. It's very scarce.'

" 'Just been reprinted. Here, take mine. I can always get another.' "She produced from her basket a copy of E.M. Forster's *Alexandria*.

" 'I didn't know. In that case I can get one for myself. Thanks awfully, though.'

" 'Take it, fool,' she said.

" 'Well, thanks awfully. I know his *Pharos and Pharillon*, of course.'

" 'Of course; the *Guide* is topping too' " (Evelyn Waugh's *Officers and Gentlemen*, pp.126-7 in the Penguin edition).

p.172 † It was at the *Nouzha Gardens* that Forster had his first rendez-vous with Mohammed el Adl, the tram conductor (see note for p.177). Forster brought a gift of sticky cakes. "I do not care for cakes. What did you pay for them? How many centuries ago did you buy them?" (He later told Forster he thought they might be drugged.) They then took a tram to the Egyptian's home, and Mohammed amused himself by handing the cakes round among the passengers.

p.174 † Cavafy's first 'published' poem ('Walls', 1896) was written while he lived with his family in the *Boulevard Ramleh* (from 1887 to 1904): "With no consideration, no pity, no shame,/they've built walls around me, thick and high./And now I sit here feeling hopeless." A sense of entrapment and tedium permeates his poetry until 'The City' at Rue Lepsius in 1910: "There's no ship for you, there's no road" – which has the ring of a challenge accepted, and is followed in 1911 by 'The God Abandons Antony' and 'Ithaka' in which courage and understanding arise from loss and disappointment.

In the *Rue Debbane* was the Grammata bookshop, a favourite haunt of literary Alexandria. Its owner, Stephen Pargas (Alias Nikos Zelitas), was publisher of *Ta Grammata*, in whose pages many of Cavafy's poems were first seen. Cavafy might come here late at night with a poem he had just finished: "I brought it to you now, Niko, so that I can go to sleep in peace." And on another occasion: "Take it, Niko, it's burning my fingers."

The *Cathedral of the Coptic Orthodox Patriarchate* has been rebuilt.

Just before the Boulevard reaches the tram terminus, on the left is the Metropole Hotel, converted from apartments and offices in 1934. The salons on the first floor at the eastern end immediately over the Grand Trianon patisserie are decorated in a style intermediate between Art Nouveau and Art Deco and are worth looking at – also because here were the *offices of the Third Circle of Irrigation* where Cavafy worked from 1889 to 1922. Ibrahim el Kayar, who worked under Cavafy, recalled: "Cavafy was very cunning. He covered his desk with folders, opened them and scattered them about to give the impression that he was overwhelmed with work ... 'I am very busy,' he constantly replied on the telephone ... Sometimes my colleague and I looked through the keyhole. We saw him lift up his hands like an actor, and put on a strange expression as if in ecstasy, then he would bend down to write something. It was the moment of inspiration. Naturally we found it funny and we giggled" (quoted in Liddell's *Cavafy*, p. 128).

The *Grand Trianon*, which in Cavafy's day was called Athenaios, was another of his favourite cafés (there is now an Athenaios diagonally opposite, on the north side of the tram terminus). Beautifully decorated in the Art Nouveau style, the Grand Trianon has just been gutted (1986):

"What did you do with the panels, the decorations?"

"Threw them out!"

"You didn't sell them?"

"No. Rubbish, only rubbish. In three months it will be all new: metal, plastic – modern!"

In this vicinity one might have met, as Forster describes in *Pharos and Pharillon* (p.91), Constantine Cavafy: "They turn and see a Greek gentleman in a straw hat, standing absolutely motionless at a slight angle to the universe ... Yes, it is Mr Cavafy, and he is going either from his flat to the office, or from his office to the flat. If the former, he vanishes when seen, with a slight gesture of despair. If the latter, he may be prevailed upon to begin a sentence – an immense complicated yet shapely sentence, full of parentheses that never get mixed and of reservations that really do reserve; a sentence that moves with logic to its foreseen end, yet to an end that is always more vivid and thrilling than one foresaw ... It is the sentence of a poet."

p.175 † This "featureless spot" is now the *Midan Sa'ad Zaghloul* which is as much (if not more so) the centre of the city as the old Place Mohammed Ali (Midan el Tahrir).

The *Cecil Hotel*, built in 1930, stands on the west side of Midan Sa'ad Zaghloul, overlooking the harbour. As Durrell says in his Introduction, it is here that he initially stayed when he first came to Alexandria, and where he returned on his recent visit.

"Outside the Cecil long lines of transport-trucks had overflowed the taxi-ranks ... At the Consulate ... a very fat man who sat like a king prawn at his desk ... addressed me with familiarity. 'My task may seem invidious' he fluted, 'yet it is necessary. We are trying to grab anyone who has a special aptitude before the Army gets them. I have been sent your name by the Ambassador who had designated you for the censorship department which we have just opened, and which is grotesquely understaffed ... I suppose you might need a week to find yourself lodgings here before you settle in' ... I walked slowly along the Corniche towards the Cecil, where I purposed to take a room, have a bath and shave" (*Clea*, pp.676-7).

Thus Darley's return from an Aegean island to Alexandria. The moment corresponds to Durrell's first arrival: at the beginning of the war he had been teaching English at Kalamata and Athens, but in April 1941 fled to Egypt via Crete as the Germans overran Greece.

"The Alexandria I now saw, the first vision of it from the sea, was something I could not have imagined ... A faint and terrible moaning came out across the water towards us, pulsing like the wing-beats of some fearful prehistoric bird – sirens which howled as the damned must howl in limbo ... The harbour suddenly outlined itself with complete clarity upon the dark panels of heaven, while long white fingers of powder-white light began to stalk about the

The Cecil Hotel in the 1930s.

sky in ungainly fashion ... Then at last we saw what they were bracketing: six tiny silver moths moving down the skylanes with what seemed unbearable slowness. The sky had gone mad around them yet they still moved with this fatal langour; and languidly too curled the curving strings of hot diamonds which spouted up from the ships, or the rank lacklustre sniffs of cloudy shrapnel which marked their progress" (*Clea*, pp.667-8).

Wavell had driven Graziani out of Egypt at the end of 1940, but the Germans reinforced the Italians and the Axis forces re-entered Egypt in April 1941. Although Cairo suffered no serious air-raids – almost certainly because of Churchill's warning that if either Cairo or Athens were attacked Britain would "begin the systematic bombing of Rome" – enemy bombings of Alexandria increased and 650 civilians were killed during the summer (see note for p.103).

"'Clea, you should shelter.'

"... I shook her softly, and she whispered: 'I am too fastidious to die with a lot of people like an old rats' nest. Let us go to bed together and ignore the loutish reality of the world.'

"So it was that love-making itself became a kind of challenge to the whirlwind outside which beat and pounded like a thunder-storm of guns and sirens, igniting the pale skies of the city with the magnificence of its lightning-flashes, and kisses themselves became charged with the deliberate affirmation which can come only from the foreknowledge and presence of death. It would have been good to die at any moment then, for love and death had some-where joined hands. It was an expression of her pride, too, to sleep there in the crook of my arm like a wild bird exhausted by its struggles with a limed twig, for all the world as if it were an ordinary summer night of peace" (*Clea*, p.727).

That is at Clea's flat in the nearby Rue Rosette; the Cecil is asso-ciated with Justine: "I see her sitting alone by the sea, reading a newspaper and eating an apple; or in the vestibule of the Cecil Hotel, among the dusty palms ..." (*Justine*, p.23); "They met, where I had first seen her, in the gaunt vestibule of the Cecil, in a mirror" (*Justine*, p.58); "In the gaunt lounge of the Cecil Hotel she would perhaps be waiting, gloved hands folded on her handbag, staring out through the windows upon which the sea crawled and sprawled, climbing and subsiding, across the screen of palms in the little muni-cipal square which flapped and creaked like loose sails" (*Mountolive*, p.550); etc. The dusty palms were there until recently – instead of dusting them, the palms themselves have been taken away. Other-wise so it remains: the gaunt lounge, the mirrors, the wind and the sea.

But at the Cecil you wait for Justine in vain. She was once here, in Alexandria: "... A strange, smashing, dark-eyed woman I found here last year, with every response right, every gesture, and the interior style of a real person, but completely at sea here in this morass of venality and money. The only person I have been able to talk to really; we share a kind of refugee life. She sits for hours on the bed and tells me all about the sex life of Arabs, perversions, circumcision, hashish, sweetmeats, removal of the clitoris, cruelty, murder. As a barefoot child of Tunisian Jewish parents (mother Greek from Smyrna, father Jew from Carthage) she has seen the inside of Egypt to the last rotten dung-blown flap of obscenity. She is *Tropic of Capricorn* walking. And like all people with the Tibetan sensibility she felt that she was going mad – because nobody knew what she was talking about. It has been fun re-articulating her experience for her, and curing her panics, and finding her books to show her how great a part of the world of sense and creation is nonsense to Alexandria.

"I think if I could get to some Greek island and live in real poverty with somebody like her, I could work like a fiend. I have really grown up now and have plenty to say. I wonder how soon I can get free from the world of sub-men to say it" (letter from Lawrence Durrell to Henry Miller, spring 1944).

This prototype for Justine was Eve Cohen who became Durrell's second wife. *Justine* is dedicated "To Eve, these memorials of her native city." (See second note for p.177.)

It is the sea, and the prevailing northern breeze driving the sea against the rocks along the Corniche, that remind you of Alexandria's past and possibilities. And at the very worst, the sea, for Europeans, is an avenue of escape. But for an Egyptian it can seem to lead nowhere: "From my balcony at the Cecil I cannot see the Corniche unless I lean out over the railing. It's like being on a ship. The sea sprawls right below me. A great blue mass, heaving, locked in as far as the fort of Sultan Qaitbay by the Corniche wall and the giant stone jetty-arm thrusting into the sea. Frustrated, caged. These waves slopping dully landwards have a sullen blue-black look that continually promises fury. The sea. Its guts churn with flotsam and secret death" (*Miramar*, p.38). It is interesting to compare this with Amr's views of seafaring, pp.60-61.

p.177 † Though already in his mid-30s when he arrived in Alexandria, there is no evidence that Forster had ever enjoyed more than an unreciprocated love for another man. In the winter of 1916-17, however, riding the tram to and from his lodgings in Ramleh, he became attracted to a young Egyptian conductor, Mohammed el Adl. The relationship developed out of courtesies on both sides; soon Mohammed was refusing to accept Forster's fare, saying he never expected so much courtesy from an Englishman.

Before long, Forster was spending night after night at the tram stop, waiting for the desired tram, the desired conductor; Mohammed saved him further loitering by telling him his hours, and now they met frequently and chatted. Forster pressed for a more intimate meeting, and their first rendezvous was at the Nouzha Gardens (see note for p.172).

This was the beginning of the deep love and first sexual relationship underlying the *joie de vivre* that Durrell in his Introduction detects in every affectionate line of *Alexandria*. "The practical difficulties – there is a big racial and social gulf – are great; but when you are offered affection, honesty and intelligence with all that you can possibly want in externals thrown in (including a delightful sense of humour), you surely have to take it or die spiritually" (letter from Forster, 1 June 1917, to Florence Barger).

It is noteworthy that of Alexandria's major literary celebrants, only Forster formed an important relationship with an Egyptian – of either sex. Though it is Alexandria's involvement in the Mediterranean world that is the subject of Forster's History, he hints at a broader expanse: Alexandria as "a maritime gate-way to India and the remoter east" (p.10); and "Perhaps, on the quays of Alexandria, Plotinus talked with Hindu merchants who came to the town. At all events his system can be paralleled in the religious writings of India. He comes nearer than any other Greek philosopher to the thought of the East" (p.72). Alexandria was Forster's bridge to his beloved India, not only geographically, culturally or spiritually, but personally – breaking through the barriers of class, race and sex to acquire that intimacy with the psychology and aspirations of Britain's imperial subjects that permitted him to write, after the war, *A Passage to India*.

Mohammed died in May 1922. Forster was struggling with *A Passage to India* ("I had a great deal of difficulty with the novel, and thought I would never finish it"). He had corrected the proofs of *Alexandria* and it was to be published in December, but the 'letter' he wrote to Mohammed in November that year reads eerily like a private counterpart to his reconstruction of "an immense ghost city", a secret dedication of the book which he had begun around the time of those first encounters on the Ramleh tram: "Mohammed I try to keep this real, but my own words get in the way, and you are decayed to terrible things by this time – dead six months. I do not mind that, but I fear you becoming unreal, so that all our talks and the occasional nights we have slept in one bed will seem to belong to other people ... Dear boy, I want those memories to be of you, not stained by me. I do not want to prate of perfect love, only to write to you as if you are real. So I try to think of your putrescence in your grave sometimes. It is real, and contemporary with me, it leads me back to the real you."

Justine, p.57: "Rue Bab-el-Mandeb, Rue Abou-el-Dardar, Minet-el-Bassal (streets slippery with discarded fluff from the cotton marts), Nouzha (the rose-garden, some remembered kisses) or bus stops with haunted names like Saba Pacha, Mazloum, Zizinia Bacos, Schutz, Gianaclis. A city becomes a world when one loves one of its inhabitants."

Forster lovingly wrote of Alexandria's past and present reality, its pageant of failures and losses, from which, as when Antony is abandoned by the god, at least integrity and dignity can be salvaged. As in his 'letter' to Mohammed, so in the final lines of *A Passage to India* there are resonances of Cavafy's poem.

"'If it's fifty-five hundred years we shall get rid of you, yes, we shall drive every blasted Englishman into the sea, and then' – he rode against him furiously – 'and then,' he concluded, half kissing him, 'you and I shall be friends.'

"'Why can't we be friends now?' said the other, holding him affectionately. "It's what I want. It's what you want'.

"But the horses didn't want it – they swerved apart; the earth didn't want it, sending up rocks through which riders must pass single file; the temples, the tank, the jail, the palace, the birds, the carrion, the Guest House, that came into view as they issued from the gap and saw Mau beneath: they didn't want it, they said in their hundred voices, 'No, not yet,' and the sky said, 'No, not there.'"

p.177 ‡ This *Ancient Theatre* is not the Roman odeon uncovered at Kom-el-Dik in the 1960s (see note for p.111). Instead, as Forster suggests, it stood nearer the sea. The excavations at Kom-el-Dik, however, including the Ptolemaic street level recently exposed, do offer a bit more than grit and gravel to build one's imaginings on.

The old *British Consulate* moulders in unkempt grounds behind the gate on Sharia Iskandar el Akhbar emblazoned with the lion and the unicorn. It proved too appealing a target for Egyptian rioters:

the new Consulate has moved in with the old Residence, at 3 Sharia Mina, in the Roushdi quarter of Ramleh, a residential area long favoured by the upper echelons of the foreign community. David Mountolive, Durrell's fictional Ambassador, lived here during those blistering summer months in Cairo when the King would come to Alexandria and the diplomatic corps would follow. "The new Summer Residence was delightful and set in a cool garden full of pines above Roushdi" (*Mountolive*, p.507).

Durrell never volunteers dates for the period covered by *The Alexandria Quartet*, and though, as he says in his note preceding *Mountolive*, "I have exercised a novelist's right in taking a few necessary liberties with modern Middle Eastern history and the staff-structure of the Diplomatic Service," one can fairly accurately pin it down.

In *Mountolive*, when the Palestinian conspiracy has been discovered, the old King is dying and Nessim is able to buy time by donating Korans larded with money to Memlik's library. Fuad I died on 28 April 1936 and was succeeded by his son Farouk.

Mountolive, however, who passed the evidence for the conspiracy over to the Egyptian Government, had arrived in the country as Ambassador. In fact, until the signing of the Anglo-Egyptian Treaty on 26 August 1936, Britain had a High Commissioner in Egypt, who only then, at least nominally, ceased being *primus inter pares* among foreign diplomatic representatives and assumed the title of Ambassador. This was Sir Miles Lampton (later Lord Killearn), High Commissioner and then Ambassador from 1933 to 1946.

So apart from the scenes of Mountolive's youth in Egypt, the main action of the first three volumes (*Justine, Balthazar* and *Mountolive*) of the *Quartet* takes place from about 1935-6 to 1937-8, "with the news from Europe becoming worse every day" (*Balthazar*, p.384). Darley then spends "two or three winters" (*Balthazar*, p.211) on a Greek island, writing *Justine* and raising Nessim's daughter by Melissa.

These island years correspond to the period in Durrell's own life on Cyprus when from 1952 to 1956 he was a teacher, press officer to the British Governor during the Enosis emergency and for a time single-handedly raising his daughter by Eve Cohen, the prototypal Justine. In order to write he had to rise every morning at 4am. It was a difficult and depressing time, but in summer 1956 he wrote to Henry Miller: "I have just finished a book about Alexandria called *Justine* ... I had fallen into a bad patch of distress and apathy after Eve left for England in the middle of August with the child, which I miss, and by a stroke of luck a lovely young Alexandrian tumbled into my arms and gave me enough spark to settle down and demolish the book. She is French, Claude, a writer with something oddly her own. Night after night we've been working on our books, typewriters at each end of the dining-room table, sitting up over a scale map of Alexandria before a log fire tracing and retracing the streets with our fingers, recapturing much that I had lost, the brothels and the parks, the dawns over Lake Mareotis, etc." Durrell also had before him Forster's *Alexandria*.

Darley returns to Alexandria in the spring of 1941 – the date of Durrell's first arrival in the city (see second note for p.175). *Clea* spans the period of Durrell's actual stay in Egypt: "with the ending of the war Europe was slowly becoming accessible once more – a new horizon opening beyond the battle-lines" (*Clea*, p.841). Durrell left Alexandria for Rhodes in June 1945.

p.178 † Hence Forster's *Pharos and Pharillon*.

In Mahfouz' *Miramar*, the pension (a "massive old building") overlooks the *promontory of Silsileh* and stands on or very near the site of the vanished Ptolemaic palaces. A note to p.1 of the novel puts the area in its present context: "The actual approximate site of the author's imagined building, with the fictional Pension Miramar on its fourth floor and a fictional Café Miramar on the ground floor, is occupied at present by a busy place of entertainment that specialises in the diversions traditionally enjoyed by visiting seamen and bears (no doubt by coincidence) the same name as the novel."

p.181 † In the *Bacos* quarter of Alexandria, a quiet lower middle class area, Gamal Abdul Nasser was born on 15 January 1918 (see note for p. 103).

p.182 † The *Corniche* was subsequently extended from Silsileh all the way to Montazah.

p.185 † Just west of here is Clea's island, off which she and Darley would swim and dive, and where, to save her from drowning after she had been nailed to a wreck by Narouz' old harpoon, Darley had to cut off her hand (see *Clea*, p.828f).

It is not Marabout Island as Forster describes it (p.185), for "when the sea ran high it would be covered" and it is "unmarked on the Admiralty charts".

Clea liked to think of it as *Timonium* where Antony lived as a recluse after Actium, and which Forster places somewhere in the

Western Harbour (see p.29) – though as can be seen on Forster's hand-drawn map of ancient Alexandria, he thought it might have been in the Eastern (Great) Harbour. "And when there was nothing for them to do but wait for the certain death which would follow upon Octavian's arrival – why he built himself a cell on an islet. It was named after a famous recluse and misanthrope – perhaps a philosopher? – called Timon. And here he must have spent his leisure – *here*, Darley, going over the whole thing again and again in his mind. That woman with the extraordinary spells she was able to cast. His life in ruins! And then the passing of the God, and all that, bidding him to say good-bye to her, to Alexandria – a whole world!" (*Clea*, p.831).

p.186 † Such paintings on housefronts, to show that the owner has been on the hajj, are still common throughout Egypt. The Kaaba, the sacred black cube at Mecca, is a frequent motif, as is the means of travel, eg a boat, or fancifully a single-engined propeller plane with open cockpit, or more likely a wide-bodied chartered jet.

p.188 † The *Selamlik* is now a hotel, one of the most pleasant places to stay in Alexandria, though the view is impaired by the new Palestine Hotel, the most vulgar in Egypt.

p.188 ‡ Forster did much of his 'searching' at *Montazah*, helped arrange entertainments, gave lectures on ancient Alexandria, and himself convalesced from jaundice here, coming to love the place and often returning for weekends.

p.199 † Though it is possible to get this far by train, the journey is slow and the conditions unpleasant: better to hire a car or taxi.

Nevertheless, once at Rosetta, the best way to follow Forster is to start from the train station and walk south: there are several grand houses along this main narrow street, or to the left and right on parallel streets, and then it becomes a colourful market covered with awnings. By carrying straight on you reach the *Mosque of Zagloul*, but now the eastern part (mosque of El Diouai) has been rebuilt and painted white round a glaring arcaded courtyard, while the western part (the sanctuary of the Mosque of Zagloul proper) is under several feet of water and crumbling, the columns rising like a forest of banyans.

You should also follow the Nile to its mouth, walking or sailing: delightful, as Forster says.

Underlining Forster's remark that Rosetta can have no sea-harbour because the coast here is mere delta: A couple of miles north of the town there is a spit of land, the river washing mud up on one side, the sea washing sand up on the other. And at the very point there is a small yellow mosque, the sea and the river rising up through its foundations, curling the paint off its walls, the whole thing disintegrating and tipping towards that line where the blue steady Nile is pounded by the light green waves of the Mediterranean. A soldier came up to me as I was taking pictures. "Have you come to save the land from the sea?" It seems that since the building of the Aswan High Dam the river has stopped laying down silt, has stopped pushing the Delta out into the Mediterranean. Ecologists come, I suppose, and watch the waves nibbling away at Egypt at the rate of several feet a year. The mosque will soon tumble and be drowned. The soldier was like some pathetic Canute, stationed at the northern limit of his country to guard its retreat.

p.204 † There is no longer access by railway to the *Wady Natrun*: either go by car or taxi or take the Alexandria-Cairo bus along the Desert Road. Though there is a railway line from Alexandria westwards along the coast to Mersa Matruh, journeys to *Abousir* and *St Menes* should be made by car or taxi.

p.204 ‡ This village is best reached after visiting Pompey's Pillar and the Catacombs of Kom es Chogafa. Return to Sharia Amud el Sawari, the street running along the east side of the enclosure round Pompey's Pillar and the Temple of Serapis (see map on pp.158–9), and walk south. It becomes Sharia Karmus and leads to a bridge over the Mahmoudieh Canal. The canal was the artery by which Mohammed Ali brought Alexandria back to life; today it is stagnant, stinking and blocked by islands of vegetation and hulks of rusting barges. Its function has been taken over by roads and the railway to Cairo.

Cross this small steel bridge and immediately turn right, following the bank of the canal perhaps 200 metres until, on your right, you notice a cable ferry (you can return to town this way: on the other side catch the yellow No. 2 tram). At the point where you see the ferry, but on your left, is a low narrow tunnel through which you must stoop to cross under the railway line. Emerging, turn left, then right past the cotton factory. This is a place where old clothes are reduced to cotton fibre and baled. All round is a wasteland of dirt and mud and industrial refuse and stench.

Off to your left you will see the raised road leading from Alexandria's Western Harbour to Cairo. Cross this road – and Lake Mareotis (Mariout) lies before you, blue and vast against the flat horizon, broken by islands of reeds. And running off to the right, squeezed now between the lake and the road, a long line of huts, and flat-bottomed boats pulled up along the shore, and it does look perfectly Japanese.

Justine (p.168f) climaxes with Nessim's duck shoot on Mareotis: Darley, who had feared for his own life, is told of Capodistria's death and Justine's disappearance.

p.206 † Though there is still a train from Alexandria to Bahig, it goes more slowly now and is unpleasant. Instead, by car follow the 'new' coastal road westwards; it runs between the sands and the coastal ridge (see map on p.208). After visiting the temple, lighthouse and ruined causeway at Taposiris, you can follow another road down to Modern Bahig (Burg el Arab). Just south of here the road swings eastwards towards Bahig Village and continues to the Cairo-Alexandria Desert Road. Before Bahig Village there is a turning right to Bahig Station: you follow it over the railway line where it continues southwards as a dirt track to St Menes (see p.120).

Durrell adds a piece of information about *Taposiris*, that near here the vine was discovered (*Clea*, p.660).

The Summer Palace Nessim built for Justine was at *Abousir* (eg *Justine*, p.131f): "Long ago, in the course of a ride to Benghazi along the lonely shoreline, he had come upon a fold in the desert, less than a mile from the sea, where a fresh spring suddenly burst through the thick sand pelt ... Nessim's eye had dwelt with wonder upon the distant view of the old Arab fort, and the long-drawn white scar of the empty beach where the waves pounded night and day ... He had not spoken of it to anyone, but in the back of his mind had lurked the idea of building a summer pleasure house for Justine." The Summer Palace is also described (*Justine*, p.33) as being "near *Bourg El Arab*" – p.209. At Burg el Arab Anwar Sadat laid his plans in great secrecy for the 1973 Egyptian attack against Israeli positions in Sinai.

Sixty kilometres west of Abousir is *El Alamein* (see note for p.103). There is a museum here, with tanks, heavy artillery and other debris left behind after the battle, while to the east of the town is the starkly beautiful British Cemetery, and to the west the cenotaphs to the Greek, Italian and German war dead.

p.210 † For directions to *St Menes* via Abousir (Taposiris) and Burg el Arab, see note for p.206. Also St Menes is clearly signposted in English and Arabic from the Cairo-Alexandria Desert Road.

p.216 † Access to *Wady Natrun* is no longer by railway, nor is there the company through which to make arrangements. Instead, you approach along the Alexandria-Cairo Desert Road, built in 1917; there is a Rest House equidistant from the two cities (about 95 kilometres from either) where buses stop several times a day. A taxi can be hired to take you round the monasteries. By car, a brief visit to Wady Natrun can be accomplished in half a day. Until recently, permission to visit the monasteries had to be obtained from the Coptic Patriarchate, St Mark's Cathedral, 222 Sharia Ramses, Cairo. Now it is possible just to turn up and knock, though it might be wise to double-check with the Patriarchate first. Women are not permitted within Deir es Suriani.

The instructions Forster gives for reaching each of the four monasteries no longer apply. Instead, from the Rest House you drive into the valley, passing through a village, and come to a sign indicating Deir Abou Bishoi and Deir es Suriani. The road is paved all the way to Bishoi, and Suriani is only a short distance over the sands. Of the four monasteries, Suriani is the most interesting. From Bishoi the road continues to Deir Abou Makar at the southern extremity of the wady. The northernmost monastery, Deir el Baramus, is now the most difficult to reach and keeps its distance from the world across a long trek of sand.

CHANGES IN STREET
AND PLACE NAMES

The following is a partial list of street and place names mentioned in the text or notes. To help the reader find his way, their modern equivalents have been supplied. Though a name may have been officially changed, it may still be known popularly by its old one – and indeed streets may be marked by signs bearing either the old or new names. Often the only change has been for *rue* to be replaced by *sharia* (street), or for a name to be Arabised while remaining recognisable. Street signs are usually both in Arabic and Latin letters.

Avenue Alexandre le Grand	Sharia Iskandar el Akhbar
Rue Attarine	Sharia Orabi
Rue de l'Ancienne Bourse	Sharia Borsa el Qadima
Canopic Way	Sharia Horreya (formerly Rue Rosette, then Rue Fouad Premier)
Rue Chérif Pacha	Sharia Salah Salem
Corniche	Sharia 26 July along the Eastern Harbour – this is *the* Corniche, which Forster knew as the New Quays. A corniche road extends eastwards to Montazah and is called Sharia el Geish. In fact, Sharia 26 July is always called the Corniche.
Rue Fouad Premier	Sharia Horreya (see Canopic Way and Rue Rosette)

Rue de France	Sharia Faransa
French Gardens	Midan Orabi
Rue de la Gare de Ramleh (also known as Boulevard Ramleh	Sharia Sa'ad Zaghloul
Rue Ibrahim Premier	Sharia Ibrahim el Auwal (see Rue des Soeurs)
Rue Lepsius	Sharia Sharm el Sheikh
Mareotis	(see Mariout)
Mariout	The ancients called the lake Mareotis; the Arab name is Mariout. The foreign community kept the old name alive and either Mareotis or Mariout would have been used in Forster and Durrell's time. Today Egyptians call it Mariout.
Rue Misalla (Misalla means obelisk: see *Cleopatra's Needles*, p.175)	Sharia Safiya Zaghloul
Place Mohammed Ali (also known as The Square)	Midan el Tahrir (Liberation Square)
Municipal Gardens	Shallalat Gardens
Rue Nebi Daniel	Sharia Nebi Danyal (anciently the Street of the Soma)
New Quays	(see the Corniche)
Boulevard Ramleh (properly Rue de la Gare de Ramleh)	Sharia Sa'ad Zaghloul
Ramleh tram terminus	adjoining Midan Sa'ad Zaghloul on the east and officially sharing in that name
Rue Rosette	Sharia Horreya (see Canopic Way and Rue Fouad Premier)
Rue des Soeurs	The upper end of Sharia Ibrahim el Auwal
Street of the Soma	Sharia Nebi Danyal (see Rue Nebi Daniel)
The Square (Place Mohammed Ali)	Midan el Tahrir (Liberation Square)

INDEX